ONE SAILOR'S LOG AND MANUALS
FOR SOLO-SAILING AND SOLO-MEDICINE

the Floating Harpsichord

PETER H. STRYKERS, M.D.

TEN SPEED PRESS

1🄰

TEN SPEED PRESS
P. O. Box 7123
Berkeley, California 94707

Book and cover design by Real World Design Group
Illustrations by Eartha Newsong
Front cover calligraphy by Toby Salk
Typesetting by *turnaround*, Berkeley

Library of Congress Cataloging-in-Publication Data

Strykers, Peter H.
   The floating harpsichord.

   Includes indexes.
   1. Strykers, Peter H.   2. Alistelle (Sailing ship)
3. Sailing, Single-handed—Pacific Ocean.   I. Title.
G480.S8   1987   910′.09164   86-28505
ISBN 0-89815-190-2

Printed in the United States of America

1 2 3 4 5 — 90 89 88 87

To: Gondica, Julia and Tom, Peter, Vincent, Estelle, little Lucas, to my mother, and to my patients.

"O si tacuisses, Philosophus mansisses"
Boethius, A.d. 480—524

Contents

Acknowledgements

The nucleus for this book came out of a small minitape recorder in which I daily dictated my thoughts during the single-handed solo sailing trip to Hawaii. The daybook part of this book is pretty much as it was transcribed by Christine Klampe who was able to make sense out of my Dutch accent and put my dictated words on paper. Because I have difficulty deciphering my own handwriting and am a rather poor typist, I could not have put so many words together without my word processor. Marty Costain then proceeded on the computer and was kind enough to make the necessary corrections.

Patti Breitman, executive editor of Ten Speed Press, and Malka Weitman are to be commended for doing the tedious task of editing my English as a second language.

For the Equipment and Supplies chapter, I owe thanks to the Racing Committee and members of the Single-handed Sailing Society whose instruction and lectures were so essential for my safe passage. I got great help from Linda Rettie, who let me share her knowledge and experience gained from her two Trans-Pacific solo crossings. She was also nice enough to deliver my boat back in excellent condition. My competitors in the race were always helpful and were willing to listen and answer my questions before and during the race.

The musical musings could not have come about without the wise instruction from my former harpsichord teacher and dear friend, Laurette Goldberg. Also responsible are Katie and Rosario Mazzeo, who, during our long friendship continue to encourage my musical development and let me perform in their beautiful house overlooking the Pacific near Carmel.

My parents are responsible not only for my musical genes but also for providing me with the finest teachers and musical instruments.

My medical colleagues were generous with their time, giving suggestions and corrections in the different fields of medicine. I especially want to thank Richard Levine M.D. (Gastroenterology) for his help, encouragement and enthusiasm about the book.

Risa Kagan M.D. (Gynecology) and Karin Hughes R.N. were of great help in getting the section on medicine for the female solo sailor off the ground. Edward Becker M.D. (Dermatology) was a tremendous help in my rewriting the section on diseases of the skin and suggesting two dermatological preparations which will take care of 95% of the skin afflictions the solo sailor may encounter.

Among the other colleagues who were instrumental in the medicine part, I would like to mention Khosrow Afsari M.D. (Infectious Diseases), Russel Schulze M.D. and Francois Antounian M.D. (Orthopedics), Richard Stern M.D. (Cardiology), and Henry Renteln M.D. (Public Health).

Drs. John and Vincent Ford DDS were kind enough to give most of the information on dental care.

Without the help and research of Brookside Hospital's librarian, Barbara Dorham, many of the medical "pearls" would not have been part of the book. She also gave me many grammatical suggestions and made a multitude of spelling corrections.

I am also grateful to Dr. David K. Rea of the Department of Oceanic Sciences at the University of Michigan for correcting my thoughts on the Musicians Seamounts.

Eartha Newsong who made the pen and ink drawings has to be congratulated for her patience with my wandering mind.

The title of the book was conceived by Frederick Frank while I was enjoying his hospitality during my visit to his gallery and atelier at his "Pacem in terris" in Warwick, New York.

Even though my wife Gondica was worried and consequently not too thrilled about this particular solo sailing trip, she continued to be supportive and was of great help especially in supplying the boat.

There are other people whose efforts were instrumental and whom I would like to mention here. For practical reasons this is impossible. I trust they will understand.

Foreword

This book is primarily about solo voyaging and focuses on the 1984 Transpacific solo-sailing race from San Francisco to Kauai, Hawaii, in which I was a participant. As a result of my experiences during this race, I wish to encourage others to give solo sailing a try. Today, with the availability of modern electronic equipment, one can solo sail in great comfort and safety—certainly no heroics are required! At the same time, it is a challenge to find out, alone at sea, how capable and self-sufficient we really are. I think most solo racers would agree that winning is secondary to the accomplishment of finishing a solo race.

Anyone who has sailed on a weekend on the San Francisco Bay (or any other heavily trafficked waterway) with winds of variable strength and direction, shallow areas, rocks, and other navigational obstacles, should be able to sail from California to Hawaii by himself. With just a breeze, the wind and current will bring even the not too proficient sailor to his destination. There are only two prerequisites: the boat must not leak and the sailor must never give in to the temptation, no matter how appealing, to swim in the warm and inviting Pacific Ocean.

I must mention, especially to my "salty" readers, that this book is not only about sailing. While sailing is certainly one of my hobbies, music, especially baroque music, is my avocation, and musings on this subject are interspersed throughout the Daybook.

For the sake of convenience, I have used masculine pronouns in referring to sailors (and physicians). I hope my female readers will not take offense, as none was intended.

Having been a physician in family practice for twenty-five years and an "expedition doc" in many remote areas of the world, I decided to put together a section to address the medical problems the solo sailor and, in a broader sense, the solo voyager may encounter. My wish is that this book will be enjoyable and informative and will also encourage others to try the delights and rigors of solo sailing. I would be especially interested in feedback! Contact me c/o Ten Speed Press, P.O. Box 7123, Berkeley, CA 94707.

Early Sailing Experiences and Boat Purchases

My sailing experience goes back to sailing on the Frisian Lakes in my native Holland in the 1940s. Shortly after moving to California I bought my first boat, an Islander 29, and sailed it mostly on the San Francisco Bay. Before long, my boat partner and I "moved up" to an Islander 37. It was on this boat that I *really* began to enjoy sailing. I made several trips to Baja California with friends, and it was on those voyages that my interest in self-steering devices began to develop.

In 1975, two friends accompanied me on my first long ocean sail to Baja California—my brother-in-law, Reinoud Berger, and Jack Costain. Reinoud had had some lake sailing experience in Holland and Jack, a true novice, received sailing instructions on the way!

On our third day out, we ran into some rough weather. By this time, I was nearing exhaustion. Because my two mates were even less experienced sailors than I, it had been necessary for me to be at the wheel most of the time, and I had not been able to get enough sleep. I decided, somewhat reluctantly, to get some rest and leave my friends in charge of the boat for the first time. Not long after retiring I awoke to terrible noises and found out that we had unintentionally jibed twice. Jibing happens when, while going before the wind, the sails go from one side of the boat to the other side. Jack had been hit by the block on the main sheet, which had come off the traveler. He was bleeding and out of commission from the blow received. Everything was in disarray. The wind was blowing about forty knots and all the sails were up. The mainsail came down fairly easily, but it took Reinoud, secured to the boat by a life harness, about an hour to get the jib down. By now Reinoud would not consider taking the wheel because he felt so incompetent in this rough weather and he was also rather frightened.

There we were, going "bare poles." This means that all the sails were down and the boat was moving at a good speed with the force of the wind on the hull and rigging alone. Reinoud tried to keep me awake by constantly talking to me. I began hallucinating. The wind was moving both the clouds and the boat south at the same speed. And so it appeared to me that the stars were moving north in the opposite direction, and that we and the clouds were stationary.

I flashed back to the air raids in Holland during World War II, and became convinced that the stars were planes flying north and that World War III had started. ("Why then, do they have their lights on?" I reasoned.) My mind drifted in and out of a hallucinatory state. ("But so many planes!".) I was also convinced —completely mistrusting my compass—that every cloud bank on the horizon was the coast.

By daybreak we decided to turn east towards the coast. The sun was out and we were feeling much better about our predicament. By now our dead reckoning was in shambles and we were very curious to find out how far south we had been pushed by the wind. The answer came from a young man in a canoe fifty yards off the beach, who informed us that we were at Pismo Beach.

It was on this trip that I decided to sail with a more experienced crew next time, and to take along people more knowledgeable than I—or even better, to get the boat set up for self-steering. In 1974, I sailed the boat to Hawaii and had my first experience with an early-prototype self-steering vane.

After the Islander 37 returned to the mainland, I did more coastal sailing. During this period, Jim Gelhaus became co-owner of the Islander 37 with me, and together we started looking for a bigger boat.

The new boat would have to have plenty of headroom, as we were both over six feet tall. For easier handling, we wanted two masts so that we could have more, and consequently smaller, sails. For a single-hander it is an advantage if the sails are not too big so that it is easier to change them in a hurry. We were not particularly interested in a light racing boat.

The boat would have to have large water and fuel tanks for long ocean crossings. We wanted a moderately long keel for directional stability, but not so long as to become unresponsive to the rudder. The cockpit had to be self-bailing, large, and not too exposed, in order to keep the sailor dry. Handling of sails would have to be done as much as possible from the cockpit, so that going forward on the boat in rough weather would be kept to a minimum.

We looked at many boats, but always came back to the Explorer 45, a double-headed ketch, designed by S. C. Huntingford and built in Taiwan. It was outfitted with American rigging by C. & L. Marine Corporation. There were two Explorer 45s available in the San Francisco area, one new and one used. I usually prefer to buy a used, proven boat, and sailors who have gone through the agony of getting the bugs out of a new boat will agree with this preference, but in our case it was financially advantageous to buy the new one.

A word of warning to the new boat owner! Give your boat a simple, easily understood name! This will become clear when you try to phonetically spell the boat's name to some tired and/or seemingly deaf marine operator, or worse, in an emergency, to the Coast Guard over a radio filled with static. We named our boat Alistelle after our daughters' names, Alison and Estelle. Our unusual name caused us some difficulty. In every communication with the marine radio operator we had to spell in phonetic alphabet the name of our vessel over and over again—even if it was the same operator. It seems to me that the radio call letters should be sufficient to identify a boat. But this is not so.

After we bought the boat we had some scary moments about the title. Boat buyer beware! It took forever to get the pink slip.

I think the broker had to sell one more boat to pay off ours. It would be advisable to have some form of title insurance similar to the type used when buying a house.

Then came the usual leaks and other frustrations of a new boat. After some trial runs on the Bay, we thought the Alistelle was ready for a trip south along the coast to Baja California. The broker sent us a registered letter to let us know he would not be responsible for the consequences of taking the boat out on the ocean "so soon"!

There were actually no major problems until, on the way back, the engine quit in the middle of Monterey harbor. We spent three days looking for a diesel mechanic in Monterey during that long Fourth of July weekend. It turned out that we had been within twenty feet of this man, whose boat was docked right next to ours. By the time we found him, less experienced mechanics had made matters worse, and a few more days were needed to fix things. A rented car brought us back to the Bay Area.

A few evenings later I flew to Monterey to bring the Alistelle back. I left the harbor at midnight and sailed the boat single-handedly back to the San Francisco Bay Area. At that time she had only an automatic pilot, and was not yet equipped with a self-steering vane.

I remember that night vividly. I left Monterey harbor Wednesday at midnight and arrived Friday morning to resume the practice of medicine! I was elated and had no difficulty sleeping that Friday night (off call!). I was very tired, but excited because for the first time for a long distance (120 miles) I had had the opportunity to single-handle the boat.

When buying a new boat I have found that usually the boat and equipment are in good shape, but it is the commissioning that leads to difficulties. It seems that today real craftsmen are hard to find. Each boat owner has his horror stories about boatyard experiences.

The Alistelle was once in a boatyard because of a leak around the engine shaft. After this problem was supposedly fixed, the boat was put back into the water. However, she was still leaking and I was advised that there was also a leak around the rudder shaft, which could be repaired for another $2,000, if you please! After spending some time looking at the problem myself it turned out that there was no grease around the rudder shaft. A grease gun corrected this problem in a few minutes. Since that time the boat has gone to Mexico and Hawaii without trouble. And I spent the $2,000 on something else. It seems that a correct diagnosis is as essential in a boatyard as it is in a hospital! Everything always seems dandy during the negotiations at the boatyard. But once the boat is high and dry out of the water, the situation changes. The unlucky boat owner is now at the mercy of the yard. Even after the boat is back in the water, the boatyard holds title to the boat until the owner has come up with the "gold."

On my last trip to Hawaii, I was lucky enough to land in the hands of a boatyard where, for the first time, I got an estimate that was adhered to. Not only was the work done excellently, but added repairs were made. And the final price was below the original estimate.

The fact that the boat workers were looking at me more as a Transpacific solo racer and were forgetting I was a doctor may have had some influence on the better service I enjoyed. Later, back in the Bay Area, a young woman who takes care of the varnish on boats even gave me a discount ("I always give Transpacers a discount.")! The financial discrimination against doctors was replaced by the camaraderie of sailors.

The Alistelle is a double-headed ketch, weighing approximately 30,000 pounds. She is forty-five feet long and has a beam of thirteen feet. There is plenty of head room. Her ballast is approximately 10,000 pounds, so that she can right herself after a knockdown. There are two heads with showers. The cockpit is amidship and a good-sized dodger protects the sailor from the elements. The aft cabin gives the owner privacy in the most comfortable area of the boat and it has its own head and shower. She has a capacity for 198 gallons of water and 175 gallons of fuel. The diesel engine will cruise the boat at six knots and will use about one gallon per hour, which gives the boat a range of about one thousand miles on engine. We added an Orinda automatic pilot, keeping the proximity of the manufacturer (ten miles away) in mind. However, a few months after we purchased the boat, the manufacturer moved to Florida! A Raytheon twenty-four-mile radar with a radar alarm was also installed. In addition to the VHF radio, we installed a Combi unit. This electronic marvel is able to tell at a glance wind speed, wind direction, and boat speed. It also indicates depth in feet, fathoms, or meters and it has an alarm that will warn the sailor if the depth reaches any preset minimum level.

A self-furling system was installed on the forestay. In the event of a sudden increase in wind strength, this self-furling sail can be wrapped around the forestay from the cockpit. A small line on a drum around the forestay can be used to turn it and wind the sail neatly around the stay. This way there is no need to bring the sail down and store it when not in use. The sail can also be adjusted to any size according to the strength of the wind. There is no need to go forward on the boat to take the sail down. The self-furling system is great *when it works!* In the Daybook you will find out what happens when this system fails.

Soon after we bought the boat, my co-owner Jim Gelhaus moved to England with his British bride. I now was the sole owner.

L.O.A.	45'3"
L.W.L.	34'0"
BEAM	13'0"
DRAFT	6'8"
HULL	FIBERGLASS
SPARS	ALUMINUM
BALLAST	10,430 lbs.
DISPLACEMENT	30,000 lbs.
SAIL AREA—CUTTER	861 sq. ft.
SAIL AREA—KETCH	920 sq. ft.
HEADROOM	6'3"
BERTHS	7–9
WATER (S.S. TANK)	198 Gal.
FUEL (BLACK IRON'	175 Gal.

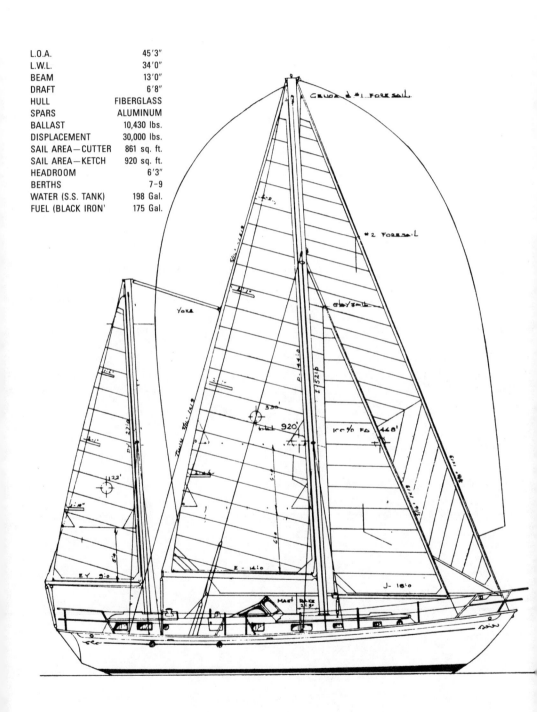

The Race

For a year, thoughts about going to Hawaii single-handedly had been on my mind. After finding out that 1984 was a year in which the Single-handed Transpacific Sailing Race would take place, I joined the Single-handed Sailing Society (S.S.S.). Soon afterwards I made a down payment to secure my entry in the race.

I had never considered racing before. During the Islander 37 days I had joined a few races, but never very seriously. This time I had some misgivings. The race would restrict my freedom to a certain degree. The date of departure was set. I would not be allowed to use the engine except for charging the batteries. If caught in the Pacific High without any wind, I would have to wait for the wind to return; if I used the engine, I would be automatically disqualified.

In the final analysis, I opted to join the race for several sound reasons. The Pacific is the ideal ocean for a cruise because of its relatively stable and warm weather. I would be reassured by the fact that other sailors would be nearby. And a racing committee was working very hard to make this a safe race. There would be lectures about weather, radio communication, pre-race inspections, life raft survival, etc. I would enjoy instruction from people who had participated in this race before. Above all, there would be the camaraderie and the challenge of the race itself.

Every single-handed ocean crosser has his own particular goals. Sir Chichester wanted to break the records of the clipper ships. Some wanted to prove that it could be done in smaller ships. Hassler tried to design the perfect boat and self-steering vane. A seascape painter wanted to be closer to his subject.

My aim was much more prosaic. I just wanted to have a good time with as much luxury as possible. This would include watching the beautiful Pacific sunsets with a gourmet dinner and good wine accompanied by my favorite music on a state-of-the-art music system, followed by reading a good book, or making music on my harpsichord. And I would enjoy all this without the interruption of a telephone.

This was still a gentleman's race without sponsors and high financing and advertising. There would be only minimal publicity, in contrast to the OSTAR, the Observer's Single-handed Transatlantic Race, which was taking place at the same time. This Transatlantic race sometimes attracts over a hundred entrants. Most racers are sponsored by boat manufacturers, newspapers, etc. The boats are often of the latest design and built especially for the race. Many of the boats are the multi-hulled trimarans and catamarans. All boats carry the ARGOS satellite transmitter, which enables the race committee to know each boat's position at all times. This is a tremendous safety factor; however, the units are very expensive.

Most of the contestants in the 1984 Transpacific Race were very competitive racers. It is a tribute to my competitors that I, such a novice sailor, always felt at ease. It was obvious that I was almost *hors concours*, and I do not think there was much doubt who would come in last.

And now a date had been set for the Transpacific Race—June 16. Required equipment had to be installed and the life raft had to be recertified. The boat had to be measured and inspected, and a qualifying 400-mile offshore single-handed ocean trip had to be made. And there was still my medical practice to see to.

There were lectures about solo sailing to be attended, and lectures about solo medicine to be given. I had to refresh my celestial navigation knowledge, decide on what radio, satnav, or Loran to buy, what sails to take along, and determine how to climb the mast without anybody helping. Food and other supplies had to be secured. My racing number had to be exhibited and had to be large and clearly visible. I had entered the race early enough so that I could choose my own number. I chose the number "7"—not for obscure numerological reasons but for more mundane and practical reasons. It can be applied with tape in straight lines without the difficult curves of the other numbers!

My main concern was safety and comfort. Winning the race was secondary. That does not mean that I did not get the racing bug, but by the time the race was to begin I had run out of money and time, and my sails inventory had only been expanded by a storm jib and a used, too small foresail.

Racing Strategy

Ocean sailing not only requires preparations such as selecting food and outfitting the boat; one of the most essential preparations is planning the passage. This planning entails the study of the prevailing winds, the frequency of hurricanes, and the strength of currents. The shipping lanes and their particular traffic patterns have to be reckoned with. The careful sailor is aware of obvious navigational hazards, such as small islands, navigational markers, and shoals.

One advantage of sailing from the West Coast to Hawaii is that there are no little islands in between. These islands might be helpful in case of emergency, but there would be the worry about having made a navigational error and being awakened by the sound of the surf (at best) of some out-of-the-way island. The sailor, knowing that there is a chance of hitting some small island, will worry about that possibility. As a matter of fact, there are few ocean masses as large as the one between North America and the Hawaiian island chain that do not have small islands somewhere.

Through the years the National Ocean Survey has been gathering data from all over the world and has been able to plot the prevailing winds, currents, frequency of hurricanes, ocean water temperatures and amount of rainfall for most oceans at monthly intervals. Pilot charts are available with all this information updated for every month of the year.

Some understanding of the general circulation of the winds on this planet is helpful. The prevailing winds are basically caused by the rotation of the earth, and to a greater extent by the difference in temperature in the different parts of the world. The highest temperatures are found near the Equator, where the hot air rises, causing a relatively low pressure area with very little wind called the doldrums.

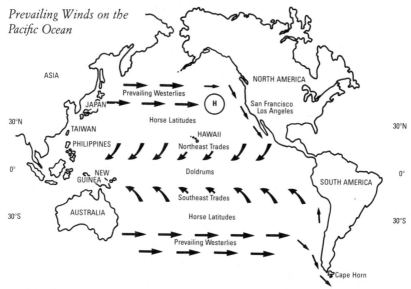

Prevailing Winds on the Pacific Ocean

Further north and up to 30° north latitude (that is, the latitude of New Orleans) the winds are usually clockwise or northeasterly. In the southern hemisphere, down to latitude 30° south, the winds blow out of the southeast. These are called the northeast and southeast trade winds respectively. From now on, we will disregard the southern hemisphere. The air from the Equator finally sinks into the belt of high pressure at the 30° latitude, producing variable light winds that either become the northeast trade winds south of the 30° latitude or the prevailing westerlies, as the winds north of the 30° latitude are called (winds are always named after the direction they come from). These areas of light, variable winds at 30° are called the horse latitudes. The name derives from the term "dead horse." A dead horse was a note against (usually) one month's wages, given to sailors on British square riggers when they signed on to a crew. It usually took about one month for the ships to clear these latitudes. For a long time it was the custom to throw the paper dead horse overboard when the sailors were celebrating having paid the "loan."

Along the coast of California the wind usually blows from the north to northwest. For the commercial sailing ships headed for California, after rounding Cape Horn it was impossible to sail against the northerly winds. They would therefore sail with the southeast winds and later further north with the northeast trades, often all the way to the Philippines, and then sail to California with the westerlies and further south with the northeast trades.

Even the modern yacht, which is able to sail further into the wind than the old square riggers, has a hard time sailing up the coast. The sailor who has been on a cruise along the California coast knows how much longer it takes to "beat" back up the coast. Many tacks have to be made and, with the adverse current, progress, if any, will be slow. Most of us succumb and turn the engine on. No wonder that our forefathers sometimes had to go to the Philippines first.

About 1,000 nautical miles off the coast of California at the latitude of San Francisco (38° north) there is, under normal circumstances, an area of high pressure called the Pacific High. The pressure in that area may be over 1030 millibars. Because of the high pressure there is little or no wind in this neighborhood.

This area of high pressure may move up or down, north or south, in a matter of days. Away from the High the pressure falls off rapidly down to below 1020 millibars. The winds blow clockwise around the High. For the sailor, and even more so for the racing sailor on his way from San Francisco to Hawaii, it is essential to have some idea where the High is situated; the Hawaii-bound sailor likes to use these winds south of the Pacific High. For that purpose the National Bureau of Standards weather broadcast service transmitted, besides its usual weather forecast and storm warning transmissions, the location of the Pacific High and the 1020 millibar isobar, as a special favor for the racing sailors.

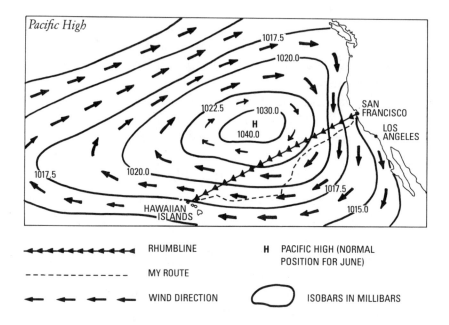

Pacific High

RHUMBLINE

MY ROUTE

WIND DIRECTION

H   PACIFIC HIGH (NORMAL
    POSITION FOR JUNE)

ISOBARS IN MILLIBARS

An isobar is a line connecting the points of a given area that have the same barometric pressure. Isobars appear on the specific weather chart as lines. They change for the different seasons. The isobars and the location of the Pacific High for other months in previous years are also available. This allows the sailor to roughly predict the isobars for the time he plans to sail these waters.

The Pacific sailor, going west, should try to stay eight millibars south of the Pacific High. Since the Pacific High is often 1028 millibars, this means staying at 1020 millibars. Below the 1020 isobar he is likely to find the good trade winds. If the sailor, through the weather forecast, is able to verify the barometric pressure of the High he should follow the navigator's rule of thumb: Keep eight millibars between you and the High. This has been confirmed by other sailors during other crossings.

It will become obvious how the Transpacific sailor not only is watchful to take the shortest route (the Great Circle Route), but is also, as most of the Transpacific racers were, willing to veer south of that shortest route to try to get the better winds. If the High stays relatively north, the Great Circle Route might be the preferred one, but rarely is there such luck.

When we look at the chart, the most obvious and shortest route between San Francisco and Hawaii would be the straight, or rhumb, line. However, most charts are made in the Mercator projection, which tries to make an image of part of the round earth on a flat piece of paper. The shortest route is therefore not a straight line on the chart, but a line curved slightly to the north. Depending on what part of the round earth we are trying to project, the curve will be closer or further away from the straight rhumb line. As a matter of fact, in this case the Great Circle Route on the chart is in reality only less than thirty nautical miles shorter than the straight rhumb line. That is, for practical purposes, a little over one percent. The total distance from San Francisco to Kauai is slightly more than 2,100 nautical miles. The racing sailor will therefore have to decide how much further south, if any, he is willing to go and consequently enlarge the distance to be sailed.

Having been sucked into the Pacific High before, and still remembering the days spent in the hot sun on a mirror-like ocean on my first trip, I decided not to again risk going too far north with my heavy boat. Therefore, I anticipated going further south than my colleagues were planning.

The magnetic compass heading to sail from San Francisco to Hawaii was, as I had been told and had figured out from looking at the charts, roughly 230 degrees. My plan was to try to follow the 230-degree heading on the magnetic compass as much as feasible, while taking into consideration the direction of the wind and the barometric pressure. At the beginning of the race, because of the direction of the wind, I had a difficult time preventing the boat from going south of the magic 230 degrees.

The compass had been adjusted the previous year and no new equipment had been installed.

Metal material close to the compass can change the magnetic field. There used to be a saying that the presence of the captain's wife was a bad omen on ocean voyages. Often the ship would go off course with all the risks of running aground, or worse, hitting rocks ashore. There is usually an explanation for these mishaps, as in the case of the legendary disasters in the Bermuda Triangle. In the case of the captains' wives in the olden days it was the magnetic interference of the metal bars in the ladies' corsets which would throw the compass off when they stood watch with their hubbies.

I do not have a pacemaker or artificial metal hips yet, or any other metal medical niceties. (You would not believe what kinds of hardware modern man can have installed in his body nowadays!) I felt therefore that I could trust my compass. From previous experiences I realized how important it is to have complete confidence in the compass. For that reason, during prior trips when the position was known, bearings were taken to check out my compass by comparing it with the local chart.

To determine our magnetic course we have to take into consideration the Great Circle Route, the current, the prevailing wind, and most of all, in the case of the Transpacific race, the presence of the Pacific High. The golden rule in that race was to stay at or below the 1020 millibar. If the barometer indicated a higher pressure, the sailor probably should change his course in a more southerly direction. The barometric pressure was therefore one of the most important guides to follow.

My barometer had never been checked. My colleague Linda Rettie gave me a tip on how to roughly calibrate the instrument. Airplane pilots use barometric pressure to determine their altitude. It is very important for them to know the barometric pressure at a certain airport so that they can adjust their altimeter before landing. The airports regularly broadcast the pressure for that purpose. By listening at different times to the nearest airport radio station, it is possible to get multiple readouts. These readouts are compared with the readout of the barometer aboard. The barometer can then be adjusted accordingly.

Equipment and Supplies
INTRODUCTION

There are several items of essential equipment for the single-hander. It is important that the solo sailor have all the gear necessary to simplify the handling of chores on the boat, such as navigation, sail-changing, and steering, so that he has time to read, cook, relax, and sleep. The equipment mentioned will also make life a lot more enjoyable on a boat with a crew but is less critical in that case.

With a crewed boat there is usually a watch established. The sleeping solo sailor needs to take precautions to prevent a collision.

The automatic pilot and self-steering vane will enable the solo sailor to sail day and night.

Celestial navigation takes time that the single-hander can use for other chores. On the crewed boat there is often one person who can spend all day taking sights. A Loran or satellite navigator are thus not essential on a crewed boat, but are still very helpful.

Climbing the mast without help from crew members requires a special technique and appropriate equipment.

The safety factor also requires extra gear. If the solo sailor falls overboard his chances of being picked up are minimal, while on the crewed boat there is the chance that he will be rescued by his companions.

COLLISION PREVENTION

The main worry the layman seems to have about solo sailing is the risk of collision at sea. Sailing near the coast in heavily trafficked areas can be very dangerous if the sailor is sleeping. I certainly would not like to single-hand my boat for a considerable time in the North Sea. On the Pacific Ocean, over a hundred miles off the coast and away from the shipping lanes, I feel very safe.

Fishing boats usually are not that far off the coast. The shipping lanes can be predicted by outlining the Great Circle Routes on the chart of the Pacific Ocean between the major ports on the West Coast and Japan or Hawaii. Farther south and west, the shipping lanes from the Panama Canal to Hawaii and Japan have to be plotted. Because of the high price of oil and the accuracy of modern navigation methods, one is very unlikely to encounter any major shipping outside of these rather narrow lanes on the big ocean.

Navy ships and submarines often travel outside the shipping lanes and the alleged encounters with them will remain a mystery. For example, there are some fishermen who suspect that the mysterious disappearances of some fishing boats may have been caused by collisions with navy ships, friendly or foreign. In one case, fishermen in Vallejo, California complained that their nets disappeared and later were seen hanging from submarines returning to the harbor.

During my trips to Hawaii, once I was away from the coast I saw an average of three ships each trip. I never saw a large ship outside the shipping lanes, nor did I see a smaller-type fishing boat more than 200 miles offshore. The large ships were often surprisingly close by. Perhaps out of curiosity they had changed course to see what my little boat was doing so far from shore.

The possibility of collision is obviously greater at night, and some solo sailors make it a habit to sleep during the day for that reason. Lights can be very helpful, but strong lights are an impossibility for the small sailing boat without a big generator on board. Often the lights are obscured by the sails. A problem with red and green lights is the danger that the approaching ship, seeing the green starboard light, will take the right-of-way while our single sailor is snoring in the cabin! Some single sailors use only one white light, even though it is illegal. Some like to use a strobe light, which is highly visible and uses little electricity. It is, however, supposed to be used only as a distress signal and it may attract unusual attention from passing boats, which often is a hazard in itself. I used the legal red and green lights and a white stern light.

Some sailors advise one to use two red lights, one above the other, on the mast during sleeping hours. This indicates to the approaching vessel that the boat is "unmaneuverable." Sir Chichester used these in heavily trafficked areas.

If the solo sailor notices an approaching vessel at night he had better light everything up, including spreader lights, cabin lights, etc. When the boat lights up like a Christmas tree there is more chance of getting the attention of the sleepy (not sleeping, we hope) crew on that big ship.

Far offshore, the large ships often have watches which, because of lack of personnel, may be careless. The possibility of picking up the minuscule radar image of a small sailboat is remote. One night, during my qualifying sail before the race, as I lay sleeping off the coast near Point Reyes, the radar alarm woke me up and I saw a large vessel coming towards me at great speed. I put more lights on, grabbed the VHF microphone, and tried to call the approaching vessel. That sounds easier than it really is. How do you get a ship's attention without knowing its name in a shipping lane where there are many other ships nearby who are also listening to your panicked call? How do you quickly reach the particular ship that is coming towards your boat? Yelling "Hey you there, get out of my way!" may evoke some mixed attention. You can give your own position and hope that the other skipper is also correct in determining his position. But by this time your boat may be already at the bottom of the ocean.

From previous similar encounters I have learned a way to get the vessel's attention, presuming that the captain is monitoring the VHF radio, has a minimal I.Q., and understands some English. (By the way, it is amazing how many captains of foreign ships barely speak English. Like the airplane pilots on international routes, captains of large ships in international waters should be able to speak some English.) Here is my personal "pearl." Maybe others have already been using this system, but I have never been told about it. I announce over the radio that I am using the low power option. This lowers the range of the transmission so that the listener is aware of being within a few hundred yards of the transmitter. This way the other ships at greater distance are excluded. In this instance, I was lucky again. The British captain spoke much better English than I did. He was awake and had already spotted me on his radar screen. He was looking forward to disembarking in San Francisco in a few hours. When I told him what woke me up, he admitted that the radar alarm is not yet in use on most commercial ships. That is quite surprising to me, but it probably has something to do with the conservative approach of commercial shipping.

The cost of a radar alarm versus the cost of the radar itself is very small. I would sleep better if I knew that the other ships also had an alarm that would go off when my little blip appeared on *their* radar screens. Officially, the watch has to be alert at all times on commercial ships, but I suspect that looking at a radar screen for long hours becomes quite hypnotic, and even commercial ships could profit from an inexpensive radar alarm system just in case the man on watch dozes off, heaven forbid. This may be difficult for captains to admit, and it may be the reason that the radar alarm is not commonly used in commercial shipping.

Radar will detect metal surfaces better than any other substance. The aluminum mast is often enough to give a good target on the radar screen. For the boat with a wooden mast, and for extra protection for any ship, a radar reflector is necessary for safety on a long trip. This reflector is made up of several metal plates in different planes interconnected so as to make a ball of about a foot in diameter. It should be hung from the rigging as high as possible, preferably in the "rain catch" position. Follow the directions from the manufacturer. Radar reflectors are also used on navigational beacons to give a signal on the radar screen. They are mandatory in ocean races, but are only of use if the approaching vessel is using radar.

So far only methods to *be* seen have been discussed. Because the sailor must sleep, he is for periods of time unable to scan the horizon with his binoculars.

Methods *to see* are equally important. It may take some individuals up to thirty minutes to adjust to night vision when they return to the cockpit after having been in the lighted cabin to look at the chart or make some coffee. At least one red light should be available in the cabin. I like to wear red goggles while using the regular white lights in the cabin.

Occasionally in smooth weather, the sailor may smell diesel oil or hear the sound of diesel engines. Sometimes there may be an unexplained forewarning. This happened to me once during a trip when I woke up for no apparent reason at all and saw, much to my surprise, a large ship nearby.

There are now available radar warning systems, which work on the same principles as radar alarms sold for picking up automobile radar traps. These radar warning systems are relatively inexpensive and many sailors used them during the race.

Again, this warning system functions only if the other ship has and is using radar.

The ultimate protection requires the sailboat to have its own radar set. Added to the radar set is an alarm system which will go off when an image reaches a preset circle on the radar screen. The boat itself is always in the center of the circle on the radar screen. I have used it constantly at night or when asleep during the day. I was awakened in the shipping lanes several times when a boat was nearby. Later, when there was no traffic, there were many false alarms because my radar had picked up dense rain storms coming my way. I think that this radar alarm, along with the self-steering vane and auto pilot, were crucial in making my trip so delightful and comfortable.

There are different estimates about what the statistical chances are that the solo sailor will get run down by a ship. John Letcher calculated that the chance for a collision on the 2500-mile trip from Alaska to Hawaii was 1:20,000. In his book, *Self-steering for Sailing Craft*, he vividly describes his night-time encounter with a large ship off the California coast near Point Conception. He saw the ship coming, but it never saw him. It approached him head-on, even though John had his lights on and was aiming his searchlight towards the approaching ship. John thinks that the bow wave washed his sailboat away from the hull of the big ship so that there was no contact between the hulls. This is reassuring and makes sense, even though one should not count on it too much! The bow waves of these large ships at high speed are big enough to push a small sailboat away from the hull. Thus, no real ship-to-ship contact is made. John's rigging was damaged when the wave rolled his boat and his mast hit the side of the big ship. John was towed to Santa Barbara and refitted there.

SELF-STEERING VANE and AUTO PILOT

Anybody who has been at the wheel of a boat on a cold ocean night will understand the advantage of a self-steering device. The invention and perfection of the self-steering vane, rather than highly technical electronic advances, has been the main reason for the growing popularity of solo sailing.

When I sailed to Hawaii in 1974, the self-steering vane was just beginning to be commonly used. For his circumnavigation, Sir Chichester had a type that was developed in England by Hassler. Mine was a prototype of Chichester's with the serial number "two" on it. The modern vane has been considerably improved since those days.

Before the availability of the self-steering vane, the solo sailor had to attend to the wheel at all times. Under advantageous circumstances, if he balanced the sails very carefully, he might be able to let the boat run on her own. During the night he usually had to lower the sails and put the boat in irons, or heave to, in order to be able to sleep.

A boat is put in irons when either on purpose or by negligence she is allowed to come up into the wind and lose her headway in the water. Without some action from the skipper, she usually will stay that way, as a wind vane turns with the wind. However, wave action may push the boat away from the wind, which could become dangerous, as the boat would be parallel to the waves. To prevent this situation, the heave-to procedure is used.

When a boat is heaved-to or hove-to she will also stay into the wind, but because of the helm being locked one way and the foresail being backed (on the wrong side), she is more likely to stay in this position. The locked rudder will counteract the backed foresail.

If the boat wants to fall off one way, the rudder will turn the

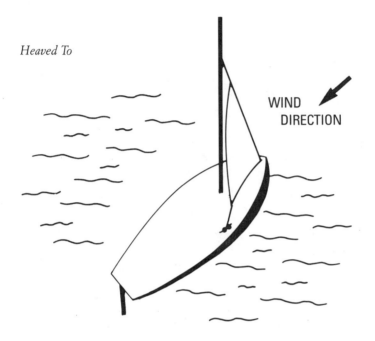

Heaved To

WIND
DIRECTION

boat back, and if she falls off the other way, the wind will push the "backed" foresail and, consequently, the bow of the boat, back into the wind. This method is not only used to give the sailor some rest, since the boat will barely move, but it is also a way to ride out a storm or hurricane. All one needs is a small strong storm foresail "aback" and the rudder turned and locked one way. Big ocean liners ride out a storm by pointing into the wind while using a little engine power to keep enough headway to be able to steer the boat and keep her pointing into the wind.

The principle of the self-steering vane is to install a wind vane and connect it to the steering mechanism. First the boat is made to sail on the ideal angle to the wind. Then the sails are balanced and the rudder is placed so that the boat keeps going steadily in the same direction as much as possible. After all this is accomplished, the rudder is connected to the wind vane and the vane is placed pointing into the wind. When the boat changes position relative to the wind, the wind will turn the vane. The vane in turn will move the tiller, or the steering wheel.

Points of Sail

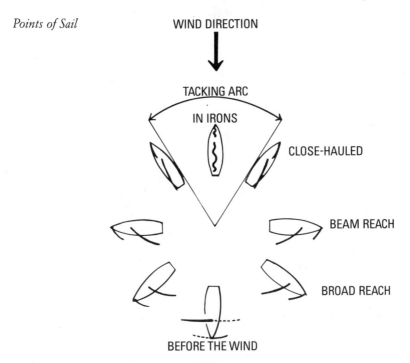

WIND DIRECTION

TACKING ARC

IN IRONS

CLOSE-HAULED

BEAM REACH

BROAD REACH

BEFORE THE WIND

This system was used even in the early days of solo sailing. The problem is that it only works under ideal circumstances and with a perfectly balanced boat. Under most conditions the force of the wind on the vane is not strong enough to move the rudder. What was needed was a power steering mechanism. The major contribution to this power steering was made by H. G. Hassler, who began designing different systems as early as 1953. The two systems now in use are the pendulum system and the trim tab system.

With the pendulum system, the vane is connected to a small auxiliary rudder. This rudder is turned on its vertical axis by the wind vane. The rudder, or pendulum, can also turn around the horizontal fore-aft axis. The pressure of the water while the boat is underway will try to bring the pendulum back into the center line of the boat, parallel to the keel. This power is sufficient to turn the rudder. When the boat is going faster, more pressure is exerted on the pendulum, giving the extra power needed to turn the wheel at higher boat speed.

Pendulum System

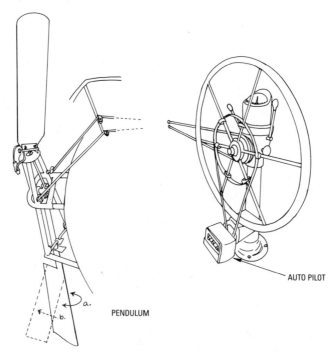

PENDULUM

AUTO PILOT

The other system uses the principle of the trim tab. In this case, the wind vane turns a small trim tab attached to the trailing end of the rudder, not unlike the trim tab on the wing of an airplane. While the boat is underway, the pressure of the water on the trim tab is great enough to make the rest of the rudder swing and correct the course. This trim tab can be attached to the main rudder or, more commonly, to an extra rudder.

Trim Tab System

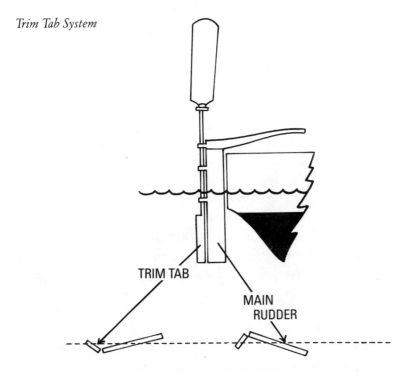

TRIM TAB

MAIN
RUDDER

The advantage of the last trim tab system is that the second rudder can be used as an emergency backup for the main rudder. Another benefit of the trim tab system is that there is no need for the lines required by the pendulum system. These lines are necessary to connect the pendulum to the steering wheel or tiller, but they often clutter the main cockpit. The trim tab system is therefore completely independent from the existent steering mechanism, though the balance of the boat is still regulated with the main rudder and the sails.

My boat used a pendulum system made locally in Sausalito

(the Monitor Vane). Because of the constant and very strong forces exerted on these self-steering devices, the strength of material used and the manner of installation are important. Breakdowns on extended trips are common.

The self-steering vane will keep the boat at a certain angle to the wind. The advantage is that the sails will not get fouled when the wind changes direction. On long, offshore trips the winds are usually steady out of the same quarter except maybe for some local rain squalls. These squalls are not such a major problem far offshore. Along a coastline, they could be dangerous for the sleeping solo sailor, whose boat could be run aground as the wind changes direction. For this purpose an off-course alarm is available. It uses a compass. The sailor can feed the degrees of deviation and the amount of time he allows the boat to veer off course into the alarm.

When the boat is well balanced and the wind not too light, the self-steering vane is a better helmsman than most skippers. It reacts quicker and seemingly never tires! One of the great delights of solo sailing is watching the self-steering vane turn the wheel as if it were anticipating the waves and wind changes. It is almost like having a live person on board. One learns to trust it, talk to it, love it, and get furious at it. No wonder that most solo sailors have a special name for it and have long conversations with it, praising or cursing it.

The automatic pilot uses an electric motor to turn the wheel or tiller. The course is determined by a compass that is preset at a certain magnetic heading. When the boat veers off course more than a desired number of degrees, the motor turns the rudder accordingly.

The auto pilot has been available for many years, but until recently, it was not used by many sailors. The main disadvantage for the sailor, in contrast to the power boat captain and airplane pilot, was its need for an abundant use of electricity.

With the advance in electronics, the new auto pilots have

become much more efficient. Some of the latest models use less electricity than an ordinary light bulb. The amount of electricity used is, of course, dependent on the size of the boat, the relative balance of the boat, and the smoothness of the water. Another disadvantage for the sailor, in contrast to the power boat captain, is that when the wind changes, the boat on auto pilot will continue to steer on the compass heading, possibly interfering with the setting of the sails. This problem has been alleviated in some models by connecting the auto pilot to a vane. These units can get their signals either from the wind direction or from the compass heading at the discretion of the operator.

The latest, and smaller, auto pilots have two separate boxes connected by wire. One contains the compass with a sensor. The other contains the actual motor to drive the wheel by belt or chain. Two adjustments can be made on the auto pilot. One serves to adjust the deadband and controls the amount of deviation allowed from the preset course before the wheel will turn. In case of a smooth sea, small changes in direction activate the auto pilot to turn the wheel. In heavy seas we only want major changes in direction to activate the auto pilot. In this case we widen the deadband. The other adjustment is for the amount of rudder-turning the auto pilot will cause. In smooth seas only small adjustments to the wheel should be made, while in rough seas larger turns are required to keep the boat on course. The faster the speed of the boat, the less correction is necessary to make the boat turn. The more waves, the more deadband; i.e., more leeway is needed before the wheel will turn. Some units are portable and connect directly by chain or belt to the wheel or tiller. Other units are built in. The auto pilot engine is often connected directly to the rudder and, in that case, the auto pilot can be used as an auxiliary system in case the regular steering mechanism fails (i.e., broken cables or hydraulic failure, etc.).

Because the auto pilot and self-steering vane are so important to the single-hander, I recommend having two independent systems. This not only gives an extra margin of safety, but if one system breaks down, it will be possible to repair the other while the boat is steered by the working unit. Also, depending on wind direction and strength, the auto pilot may be preferred above the self-steering vane. When going before the wind, especially when the wind is light, the auto pilot works much better than the self-steering vane because the boat is going in the same direction as the wind and there is consequently very little wind force to move the vane.

When "beating," which is going almost against the wind, the self-steering vane is preferred.

Peter Bird, one of my fellow race contestants, can confirm the need for two separate self-steering systems. He lost his one self-steering mechanism during the race and came in several days after the race was officially closed. Peter is generally not in too much of a hurry, though. He is the person who solo-rowed from San Francisco to Australia a few years ago!

ELECTRONIC NAVIGATION

Every long distance sailor should be proficient in celestial navigation. A minimum of two sextants was required for the Hawaii race. Charts of the Pacific and the Hawaiian islands also had to be aboard. Celestial navigation takes time, however, which the solo sailor can better use to do other chores. Electronic equipment often breaks down on a ship and the mariner should be able to navigate without it. In the Daybook we will go through an exercise in simple celestial navigation (day 17).

The oldest and the least expensive electronic navigation equipment is the radio direction finder. With the help of an aerial in the form of a loop turning on its axis, a bearing of a radio station can be taken and plotted on the chart. There are special radio stations for the use of the coastal navigator so that he can take several bearings at one time. The position will be at the point on the chart where the plotted bearings meet. In an emergency a small portable AM radio can be used for "homing in" on a known commercial radio station. By turning the radio, one should find the angle at which the station comes through the loudest. The course to the radio station is then at a 90° angle from the axis of the radio's antenna. The compass should be able to tell the sailor whether he is coming or going.

There are three other commonly used systems of electronic navigation help available. The first is Loran (long range navigation), which as a rule is less expensive than the second system, satnav (satellite navigation).

The third system, Omega, used by the bigger ships, requires few stations and is more efficient than Loran, but is much more expensive. It may give worldwide coverage before Loran.

Loran has come a long way. When sailing to Hawaii for the first time in 1974 we used Loran A. It was a bulky unit that gave a rough estimate of position. With the advent of Loran C and the progress in electronics, the new Loran C has become standard on any boat that cruises not too far from the coast. Loran uses pulse transmissions from master and slave stations on the coast. Measurement of the time difference in arrival of the transmissions at the ship makes it possible to plot a line on a chart. By simultaneously measuring the transmissions from another slave station, another line is obtained. Where these two lines cross is the ship's position.

Most navigation charts show different colored lines for each master and slave station. The latest Loran units have these lines computed and read the position off directly into latitude and longitude. The advantages of Loran are multiple. It is relatively inexpensive; some units now sell for around $1,000. In an area with good Loran coverage, the readings are extremely reliable and accurate to within several feet. Because of this accuracy, Loran can be used as an anchor alarm. If the anchor is dragging and the boat is moving twenty to thirty feet, an alarm may go off at a preset distance. Loran requires very little in terms of an antenna, and it constantly keeps the position up to date, in contrast to the satnav where updated positions are made only every few hours, when the satellite is overhead. Many of the newer Loran units have several waypoints. These are imaginary positions on the computer in latitude and longitude. The user can, for example, find out how far away a waypoint is, how long it is going to take to get there at the present speed and with the present current, and what heading the boat has to go to arrive there. To top all that, Loran can interface with the automatic pilot. Theoretically, one does not have to attend to the boat at all. The captain can put the boat on automatic pilot, interface the pilot with Loran, and decide where he will have to make turns. Those will be his waypoints. He instructs the computer to steer the boat from waypoint to waypoint! In the future, we will be able to do this with cars too, as long as the radar allows the cars to circumvent each other.

The major disadvantage of Loran is the small area of the world it covers. It does not seem likely that this area is going to be greatly increased.

On my trip to Hawaii I was able to use Loran only for the first few days. Close to Hawaii, other racers were able to use the East Pacific chain of Loran stations. By using skywave reflections from the ionosphere it is possible to use Loran to a limited degree outside the Loran-covered areas.

More expensive than Loran and not quite as accurate is the satnav (satellite navigation). About cigar-box size (similar in size to a Loran unit), the satnav has the tremendous advantage of having no geographical limitations and it is therefore ideal for the ocean crosser or the circumnavigator. It gives a direct readout in latitude and longitude, as some of the newer Loran units do. Its drawback is that it only gives an update of the position when a (working) satellite is overhead. This usually happens every few hours. Also, the satellite has to be in a favorable orbit to give a reliable readout; that is, not too high and not too low.

Most modern satnavs have the capability of maintaining the position as long as the estimated speed, drift, and heading are fed into the computer. Many satnavs also have the waypoint capability as mentioned in the description of Loran.

For the slow sailor the updates every few hours are quite satisfactory, but for the airplane pilot the dead reckoning (updating) between satellite readouts by the computer is essential. For the occasional coastal sailor in a Loran-covered area I would recommend Loran. For the ocean crosser who has to make a choice, I definitely recommend satnav.

New developments in the electronic and satellite world will make our present satellite navigation outdated. The Global Positioning System (GPS), under development by the Department of Defense, will make it possible for the user to fix his position (latitude, longitude and altitude) at any time, anyplace with an accuracy of ten meters. Civilian navigators will also have access to GPS but only to a signal code providing less accuracy than the military code. With the addition of more satellites, full use is expected to be possible by 1989. The price of one unit, now costing at least $20,000, is expected to decline in the future.

RADIO COMMUNICATIONS

Being able to converse with people ashore or on the ocean is not only convenient, it is also one of the most important safety factors. Close to shore it is relatively easy to communicate by way of very high frequency (VHF) radio. This unit is relatively inexpensive (a few hundred dollars). It is easy to install and requires only a small antenna. Battery drain is only minimal and the reception is very clear. The major disadvantage is the limited reach of these radio waves (line of sight). For the average sailboat on lakes or close to shore, VHF is ideal, except that sometimes on weekends, it is used so extensively that the channels in metropolitan areas become crowded and simple conversations become difficult. VHF remains the popular way to contact the Coast Guard in an emergency, and it is a great medium by which to talk to other ships and people ashore (via Marine Telephone Radio). Often, when the need for using the VHF in an emergency is the greatest, there may be damage to the rigging; for example, a broken mast. This may make the antenna which is often installed on the top of the mast inoperable. Thus, it is advisable to have an emergency VHF antenna aboard. I got this tip from the Racing Committee when they were inspecting my boat before the race.

The VHF radio is of limited value for the offshore sailor. He may be lucky enough in an emergency to have another ship close by and monitoring the VHF radio, and able to help the disabled vessel or to transfer a message to the coastal radio telephone via single-sideband (SSB). The offshore sailor uses the VHF radio to contact vessels in the neighborhood. On the single-handed Transpacific race the VHF was used between the contestants and served sometimes as an outlet for the lonely sailor. Messages could also be transferred from one vessel to another. The second contact could then communicate with a third boat, which was out of range for the first boat. In this way, messages could be transferred longer distances. The boat with the long distance radio (either ham radio, or SSB) could in turn transfer messages to the shore. During the Hawaii race we monitored Channel 69 on VHF at 09:00 hours every day to find out whether a racer was in the vicinity. Normally, VHF contact is rarely made between lonely yachtsmen offshore.

The offshore yachtsman has two choices if he desires to communicate with people on land: ham radio or single-sideband (SSB). A ham radio requires a license to operate, which involves taking an exam. Among other things, the operator must know Morse code. There are no official radio telephones available on these channels. The ham operator has to talk to one of his buddies ashore and ask him to forward messages. The advantage of a ham radio is mostly that it is relatively inexpensive to use. The ham radio has many times filled a need in emergency situations. In the disastrous Mexico City earthquake of 1985, when all normal communications were down, it was a ham operator who was able to intercept the Mexican people's call for help and relay the information to the world outside the quake area.

The SSB units are very expensive to buy, and the official SSB radio telephone stations are very expensive to use. Almost as much money as the purchase price can be spent on grounding the boat and on the antenna, which must be high and long. I chose SSB mostly because of lack of time to take the ham exam. I have heard many disappointing comments about non-functioning SSB units. I was rather lucky that, except for some minor problems, I was able to communicate with the shore at all times, and could contact any radio station in the world. Of all my equipment, including the radar, it was the most expensive item I installed. However, having SSB, along with the radar, the self-steering vane, and the automatic pilot, contributed significantly to the feeling of safety during my trip. In retrospect, I could have done without it (that goes also for the radar and even for the satnav), but I would not have had the same peace of mind. Of all the participants in this race, I was the only one to have SSB, and because of the different frequencies allowed, I was unable to communicate with the few solo sailors who had ham radio. The only way to talk directly to the other sailors was via VHF, which everybody had to have, but which was helpful only at small distances.

The radio can also be useful in getting medical advice. If close to shore, the VHF can be used to contact the U.S. Coast Guard. For the offshore sailor with a high seas radio transmitter, medical advice can be obtained quickly and efficiently through the DH MEDICO program twenty-four hours daily. The frequency used is 500 kHz. For those vessels equipped with radiotelephone, use 2182 kHz (SSB) or 156.8 MHz (channel 16 on VHF). This service is available throughout the world. To prevent confusion caused by language difficulties when requesting medical help from a foreign country, a medical section in the International Code of Signals is in use worldwide. This can be obtained from the U.S. Goverment Printing Office, Washington, D.C. 20402.

The weather chart recorder or weather facsimile chart is an electronic instrument that produces charts of different weather conditions received from over fifty transmitters via paper print-out. To obtain the desired information a button is pushed for the station in the geographic area of interest to the mariner. These "weather pictures" are of great value for safety as well as for comfort and fuel savings. Knowledge of wave conditions and wind and ocean currents will help the sailor plan a more efficient trip. Both existing and forecast positions of barometric highs and lows, temperatures, and speed and direction of wind and current are shown on the charts. These instruments are priced from $3,000.

The updating of the weather charts is done by the National Oceanic Atmospheric Administration via single-sideband radio.

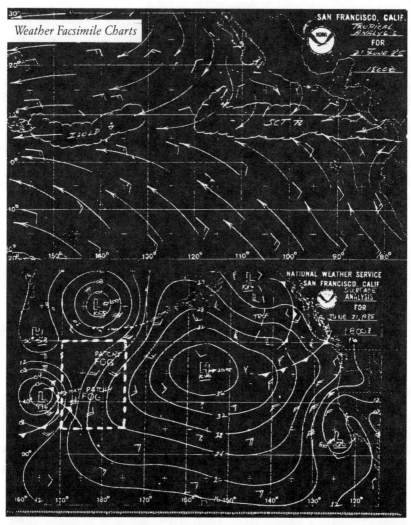

The ultimate safety system for long distance single-handed sailing is the ARGOS system. With this system the yacht has a transmitter which gives the position of the boat at all times, via satellite, to the receiving station ashore. (In a race, the Racing Committee would know the position of all boats at all times.) The captain can turn the transmitter to the emergency mode, indicating that he is in danger.

Jacques de Roux, on the third leg of the 1982 single-handed race around the world (from Sydney to Rio de Janeiro), was holed and dismasted and unable to communicate by radio, and he put his ARGOS on emergency mode. Richard Broadhead, another solo racer who was only 300 nautical miles away from de Roux and whose radio was working on this leg (his radio did not work on the other three legs), heard about the predicament from a New Zealand ham operator. With the help of French racing headquarters and the National Oceanographic Center in Monterey, California, and the ham operator in New Zealand, Richard Broadhead was given the exact location of de Roux, taking into consideration drift and currents. Broadhead, comparing his own satnav position with the ARGOS positions of his boat and de Roux's, was able to find de Roux. De Roux's boat sank several hours later in the cold and desolate waters of the southerly roaring forties.

The ARGOS transmitter system was not available on the single-handed Transpacific race, but it is used on the OSTAR, the single-handed Transatlantic race. It is the ultimate safety device for locating the disabled solo sailor, especially when his radio is not working, which is such a common occurrence.

In the 1986 single-handed sailing around the world competition, Jacques de Roux was a participant. At press time it was reported that his boat was spotted off the Australian coast, sailing erratically without its skipper and its sail halfway up the mast. He is believed to have fallen or been washed overboard and he presumably drowned.

RADAR

When a radar unit was installed with the purchase of my boat, I thought its main use would be in the fog off the California coast, which is so common during the summer. I did not realize how many other reasons there would be for the use of radar. It was never clear to me why even in daylight the big ships had their radar antennas turning. I had not realized the other advantages of radar. It not only "sees" from the highest point of the ship, but it also gives immediate bearings, i.e., angles of any point, whether of a beacon or a point ashore. It also marks the distance to this object so that with the help of only one point of reference, a position can be determined. Its field of vision is 360 degrees, so that we can look forward and backward at the same time. The radar screen covers the 360-degree circle while the boat is in the center of this circle. The circle can be adjusted to cover from one-half mile up to twenty-four miles. In the small harbor, one uses the small half-mile scale, while on the ocean the twenty-four mile scale is used. The radar units come in different sizes. The maximum range of my unit, twenty-four miles, is more than adequate for a slow-going sailboat. It is another story for an airplane flying at twice the speed of sound. Once, about a hundred miles off the coast of Great Britain, the captain of a British supersonic Concorde let me look at his radar screen, which showed the outline of all the British isles. All of a sudden I felt like a little boy!

On my Hawaii trip these advantages were of little help. The major contribution of radar for me was in the use of the radar watch. This is another small unit connected to the main radar that uses an audio-visual alarm to alert the sailor when the image of a foreign object crosses the circle on the radar screen. The object could be another ship, a navigational beacon, the coast, or a thick rain squall. The circle can be preset to encompass from one-half mile up to twenty-four miles at the discretion of the operator.

This unit is not dependent on the use of radar by the other vessel. This is in contrast to the previously mentioned units, which pick up radar signals from the approaching boat (similar to anti-radar trap units for automobiles).

CLIMBING THE MAST ALONE

Circumstances may make it mandatory to climb the mast while underway to retrieve or untangle fouled halyards or to do other repairs. To climb the mast with the help of others is relatively easy, but when there is no second person to "winch" the sailor up the mast, a special technique is required.

The solo sailor must be able to climb the mast without help. This has a special significance for me, having had difficulties in the past getting my mainsail down. This can be disastrous in a storm when sometimes the sailor has to go up the mast to be able to lower the sail. For instance, in my case the sail slides sometimes stuck in the sail track on the mast.

Most sailors use the block and tackle technique to hoist themselves up the mast. I am very leery about this method, especially when the mast is about forty-five feet in length, and the 2/1 or 3/1 block becomes very long and cumbersome. It is the only piece of equipment that prevents the sailor from falling down except for the times when he can rest his feet on the spreader or on other parts of the rigging. The stories about people falling down or hanging suspended in the air for hours, attached to the boat by a line from the heeling mast, are not rare. Having had some experience in mountain climbing, I abandoned the idea of block and tackle. For probably less money than complete block and tackle gear would cost, one can buy two or three ascending devices, a few carabiners, and one line of climbing rope, which should be the length of the mast.

No mountain climber or river rafter wants to be without a carabiner, but just try to find one on a ship. They are great tools and serve many purposes on the sailing yacht. The same applies to the ascenders as a means to go aloft to the top of the mast.

It is true that one can use a special knot (stopper knot or rolling hitch) which can be moved up and down the rope and which will freeze as soon as vertical pressure is applied. That is very nautical, but I prefer the mountain climber's ascenders, and I use the rolling hitch as another safety measure. The ascender will carry up to one thousand pounds of vertical pressure. When the weight is removed it can slide up the rope without difficulty. In descending, a small spring is manually pulled and the climber can move the foot or bosun chair down. As soon as the spring is released, the weight will again lock the ascender in the rope.

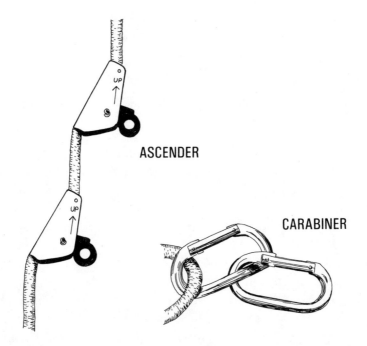

ASCENDER

CARABINER

Each foot is in a sling connected to the carabiner, which in turn is connected to the ascender. The ascender's teeth will grab the climbing rope any time weight is applied. For extra safety I use the bosun chair again connected to a third ascender. For ultimate safety I use a fourth ascender or the self-locking knot on the climbing rope connected to the life harness.

*Climbing
the Mast Alone*

It is important to buy mountain climbing rope because the ascender will not lock firmly on most marine-type halyard lines. I tie the climbing rope to the halyard to be used, raise the halyard, and cleat the bottom of the rope to the mast. The mountain climbing rope should be stretched to its maximum because these mountaineering lines are very elastic.

Use one ascender for each foot, use one for the bosun chair, and as I do, use the special knot to tie your harness to the climbing rope. Going up may be slow because every step has to be done separately, but climbing in this fashion, the sailor cannot fall. If he has the climbing rope stretched and tightly fastened to a cleat at the bottom of the mast, he will not swing away from the mast if the boat starts heeling. The climber has four means to stay aloft at all times: two feet, the bosum chair, and the life harness. The chair and harness will keep him aloft, even if he has lost consciousness. He can free his hands at any time and nothing will happen. The only time he will need to use his hands will be to move one of the ascenders up or down. What a difference from the block and tackle, when one moment of forgetting to hold the tackle taut may land you back on deck rather quickly! I tried the ascenders out under smooth circumstances and I am convinced that if it is really necessary to go aloft alone, this is the way to go.

The local mountaineering shop will be glad to be of help. The most commonly used ascenders are the Gibbs ascender, which I use, and the Jumar. The staff will be able to advise and probably will express their thoughts about the sailor's block and tackle! Old sailors' sagas die hard.

ELECTRICITY

Most sailors, and certainly racing sailors, are unwilling to add unnecessary weight to their boats in order to have the luxury of full use of modern electrical gadgets. Not I! My purpose was comfort and luxury first; winning the race came second. I was willing to add the extra weight of large batteries, and I also added a more powerful alternator to my diesel engine.

For a comfortable evening and night I calculated the need for the following numbers of amperage hours. My system uses twelve volts, direct current.

Radar + radar watch		
8 amps × 8 hours	=	64 amp hours
Running lights		
3 lights @ 5 amps × 6 hours	=	90 amp hours
Interior lights		
4 lights @ 2.5 amps × 4 hours	=	40 amp hours
Hi-fi		
4 amps × 4 hours	=	16 amp hours
Refrigerator		
2 amps × 12 hours	=	24 amp hours
Total		× 234 amp hours

To spend a quiet evening without the interruption of noisy generators, I needed 234 amp hours of battery power. For this purpose, two large "house" batteries were installed, each consisting of two, six-volt batteries in line (deep cycle). For slow discharge these two six-volt batteries in line are apparently preferred above the regular twelve-volt battery. For starting the engine a separate twelve-volt, regular 180-amp hour battery was installed. The two house batteries were each rated 200 amp hours. Indeed, I could usually use all the electrical amenities on one night on just one battery.

To charge the batteries, the existing thirty-amp alternator was replaced with a larger, ninety-amp alternator. All batteries and the alternator were provided with both amp and volt meters. I may be a gauge freak (I cannot stand cars without tachometers and volt and temperature gauges), but it is very helpful to see what amperage a certain electrical appliance is drawing and how fast the batteries are being recharged. Recharging the one battery used during the night took slightly over two hours the next morning.

I noticed that when the battery was low the alternator would charge eighty amps, but as soon as the battery was partially recharged, the amp meter would show a charge of less than forty amps. I decided that it was probably more efficient to charge the batteries more often and not up to full capacity. Electrical engineers would probably have liked to comment on this simplification, but there was no one nearby to ask.

In case of failure of the engine or alternator, I had two small Honda gasoline generators stacked away.

In this day of energy conservation I should mention the options available for having electricity on board that is not produced by fossil fuel (i.e., diesel oil in my case). One way to produce electricity is to use the forward movement of the boat. Some people use the propeller to turn a small generator, and some use the windmill principle. These two methods, I am sorry to say, may slow the racer's boat down, even more than the extra weight of the fuel and the small generator. It would take an energy expert to figure out what would be best for the racer.

Solar panels are the ideal source of electricity. These panels will not slow the boat and they add very little weight. Some of the Hawaii race contestants used this method as their principal electric energy source. They were the purists. To satisfy *my* need for electricity most of the boat would have had to be covered with solar panels. There are, however, some large sailboats with all-electric gear, including winches, that are completely solar-powered. The French are great experimenters in this respect. In the next few years a lot of progress is expected in making these units more efficient and durable.

SAILS INVENTORY

Only two sails were added to my sails inventory for the race. The main reason was that I had run out of time and money to have more sails custom-made.

One of my regular sails was a 150 Genoa (550 square feet) on the self-furling jib which could be replaced by a much smaller and heavier yankee. The 150 Genoa, or jennie, was the largest sail aboard. Behind the foresail and still in front of the main mast was the staysail (about 160 square feet). Behind the mast and flying from the mast was the mainsail (330 square feet), and flying from the smaller mizzen mast (the mast in front of the

Sails Inventory
Small Head Sails

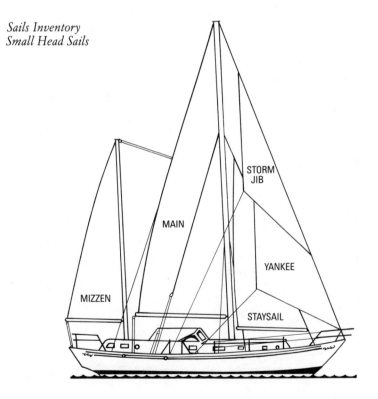

rudder and behind the main mast) was the mizzen sail (122 square feet). Added to this inventory was a small very heavy storm jib. This sail was to be used in winds above fifty miles as the only sail to keep the boat moving. It was to be flown high from the forestay.

Addressing the more informed reader, I would like to mention one more sail. Because it was available for a very low price, I bought a very light Olson 30 drifter sail, which I hoped to use as a mizzen staysail. It would be flown free from the top of the mizzen when going before the wind.

This is certainly not a very sophisticated sails inventory for a solo Transpacific race. But, as mentioned before, getting there was the priority; getting there first was another matter.

Sails Inventory
Large Head Sail

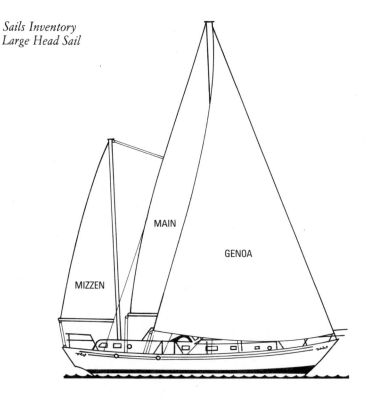

LIFE RAFT and SURVIVAL SUIT

One of the requirements for offshore racing is the life raft. I have used a Zodiac life raft for several years. It is supposed to inflate automatically with a sudden pull on a line which opens a CO_2 cylinder. The life raft must be recertified every two years. Only a few companies are licensed to do this. They inflate the boat to check it out, inspect its contents, and replenish it with the required items. This procedure, besides being rather costly ($180), is also frustrating. I brought my life raft to the inspection personally in order to watch it inflate automatically. That was a mistake. It was in perfect working condition and inflated rapidly, but there was no assurance that the raft was going to work the next time, when I might really need it! One thing I learned when the life raft unfolded was that the survival instructions inside were written in French, even though the raft had been purchased in the United States! I advised the crew who would be taking my boat back from Hawaii to take some French lessons right away!

A half-gallon of drinking water was placed in the raft as a bonus. I had hoped that, for the price, they could at least have put in some Perrier, as a pleasant surprise for the shipwrecked.

Another requirement is an emergency bag with extra water, extra flares, a small sextant and hand compass, and a mirror and knife, etc., available close by the life raft, just in case.

I was able to borrow one mandatory and important item, the EPIRB. This is a relatively small, battery-operated radio transmitter that, when activated or submerged in water, sends out an emergency signal by radio which, hopefully, will be picked up by commercial airlines. The information is then transferred to the Coast Guard. They in turn can use the signal as a homing device to locate the lonely sailor in his life raft.

Some of this equipment is rather expensive, and the actual

use of it is relatively rare. I asked the Yacht Club if it would not be possible for the Club to buy some of this equipment and rent it out. Apparently, the legal liability makes this prohibitive. There have been some legal suits claiming deficiencies, even in certified life rafts.

The survival suit can be worn in case of emergency and will improve the average survival time in water of 50° Fahrenheit from three to six hours to three to six days. A survival suit is especially indicated in cold water sailing. In cold climates a survival suit, in addition to a life raft, would be ideal. The recently developed survival suits cost between $200 and $700, and are considerably less expensive than an adequate life raft.

Survival suits sold between 1975 and 1980 by Imperial Manufacturing Company (Aquanautics subsidiary) may have a defective flexible hose in Model 1409. (The flexible hose is used to inflate a collar on the suit.) Aquanautics will send a free repair kit to the owner of the suits which it can identify. Suits sold after March, 1980 have an improved inflator hose.

FALLING OVERBOARD

For the offshore solo sailor falling overboard will usually prove to be fatal. On the crewed boat, if this accident is noticed soon after the fact, a man overboard pole will be immediately launched in the water. This is a floating pole that carries, high on the top of it, a flag and a light. The pole should be higher than the waves so that it is visible from far away. It is surprising how quickly one loses sight of a person in the water, especially when the waves are high or in the fog and darkness. "Man overboard" drills on crewed sailing ships are therefore a must. If the loss of the overboard sailor is noticed much later the rescue will of course become much more difficult. On my first trip to Hawaii I insisted that the man on watch not only wear a life vest with reflector tape but also have a waterproof strobelight, a whistle, a dye marker (colored powder to spread on the water for aerial rescue) and waterproof flares. Nowadays I might add a EPIRB (battery operated emergency radio beacon, see under EPIRB) if the situation warrants it and I definitely would add a balloon on a long string. The balloon, high in the sky, can be seen from far away and dramatically increases the chances for a successful rescue. They are now made for that particular purpose and are commercially available with metal strips for easy radar detection.

For the offshore solo sailor these items are of little help because nobody will be aware of his predicament. He may have made previous arrangements for a potential rescue in case he does not transmit over the radio at a certain time. However, the use of radios on small sailing vessels is so unreliable that it probably would lead to many unnecessary rescues. If indeed the rescue proved necessary, in all likelihood it would be unsuccessful anyway. The sailor almost certainly would have drowned even before the rescue had started. If he was wearing the survival suit when falling overboard he might have a chance to be saved.

In the future there may become available an EPIRB small enough for the solo sailor to carry at all times and use to transmit an emergency signal if he finds himself alone in the water. But for the time being, the solo sailor had better make sure he does not fall overboard.

The boat should be set up in such a way that the times that he must come out of the relative safety of the cockpit and go forward to change the sails are kept to a minimum. Self-furling sails are helpful that way. When walking on deck, the knees should be bent to keep the center of gravity as low as possible. I prefer to walk on the windward (high) side if possible so that, when falling or slipping, there is more chance to end up in the boat rather than overboard. The lifelines should be double, strong, high, and should be all around the boat. Some people add netting which makes it impossible to slip through the two lifelines. This netting also prevents smaller items from going overboard but it has many disadvantages in that it makes it more difficult to handle sails and lines and to climb aboard if hanging overboard on the safety harness.

Theoretically, whenever the sailor is outside the cabin, even in the cockpit, the safety harness should be worn and connected to a strong part of the boat. In rough weather this should definitely be the case. After the boat makes a 360-degree roll a sailor might be shaken up but he would still be *in* the boat.

In order to be able to walk back and forth on the deck without having to clip my safety harness on and off too often, I installed a line from the bow of the boat to the stern on both starboard and port. The clip of the safety harness could then glide along the line when walking back and forth on deck. Preferably, there should be two lines from the harness to the safety line, each with its own clip, so that when changing to another line, the sailor is never disconnected from the boat. To be maneuverable, the line connecting the safety harness to the safety line on the boat has to be fairly long. This may make it rather difficult for the sailor to climb back on board after he has fallen off the boat and is hanging on his safety harness. The sailor should therefore, preferably when nobody is looking, try to hang on his safety harness in a quiet spot in the harbor and reboard the boat from that position. He may be in for some surprises.

The safety harness in itself can be hazardous to your health. It is easy to trip over it or get all tangled up in it. I know that many solo sailors "sin" by not using it when the weather is good and the chance of going overboard is relatively small!

Some solo sailors drag a long line in the water behind the boat. When they fall into the water, they try to swim to the line and pull themselves aboard. When the boat is sailing at a speed above three or four knots this becomes quite a challenge because of the drag of the person in the water at that relatively high speed. For that purpose these solo sailors install a trip line connected to the self steering vane and trailing behind the boat. By "tripping" the line, they disconnect the vane, causing the boat to turn into the wind and consequently loose speed.

If the boat is so well balanced that she keeps sailing on her own at a steady pace without the help of the vane or autopilot, the sailor will soon become tired of holding onto the line. In that case the boat will continue to sail like Wagner's *The Flying Dutchman* and may arrive at the harbor like the horse which arrives at the stable without its rider.

HOLE IN THE HULL

The chance of running into a log or other foreign object is increased for the solo sailor because of the impossibility of having a constant lookout. When this happens, quick action has to be taken. One person cannot man the manual pump to discharge the water and fill the hole at the same time. A good electric bilge pump and good batteries are essential.

If the engine is in working condition, the salt water intake can be removed from the through-hull fitting. The bilge water will then serve as an engine cooler and will be discharged by the engine. My electric bilge pump extracted about seventy-five liters (approximately twenty gallons) per minute and the engine cooling pump extracted about the same amount. I had one extra emergency electric bilge pump, providing altogether the capability of 225 (3 × 75) liters per minute.

Water will enter at about 300 liters (eighty gallons) per minute through a hole the size of a silver dollar, if it is just below the waterline. If the hole is four feet below the waterline, this amount will double. A silver dollar is a relatively small hole, and the pumps will not delay the sinking for very long.

The solo sailor should not use the manual pump, but should concentrate on filling the hole. This can be done by stuffing the hole with cushions and inflated life jackets, etc. Externally, a sail can be used by passing it under the bow and holding it with ropes over the hole in the hull. The pressure of the ocean water will usually hold the sail in place. Internally, the opening in the hull can then be closed with fiberglass or cement. There is also underwater epoxy available. It can be mixed in a bucket of salt water and applied under water.

There is umbrella-type damage control gear available. The umbrella is guided, closed through the hole and opened once outside. The water pressure will press the canvas of the umbrellas against the hull.

If the hole is close to the waterline, the boat should go on a favorable tack to make her heel as much as possible to get the hole out of the water. Shifting weight inside the boat will increase the heel.

Small, cone-shaped plugs made out of softwood in different sizes can be pushed into the hole with a hammer or can be used to plug deficient through-hull fittings. For more information about through-hull fittings the reader is referred to day 10 of the Daybook.

JURY RIGGING

Before departure, the prudent off-shore yachtsman will try to be prepared for a possible breakdown of some part of the rigging during the voyage. On a windy day a broken mast or boom is not an uncommon sight in a sailing area. With the necessary tools on board, the sailor, with some ingenuity should be able to jury-rig a temporary mast and arrive safely in port, albeit less glamorously and a little late.

Broken cables (shrouds, stays, and steering cables) can be temporarily repaired with cable clamps. Extra wire and rope should be available for repairs.

When sailing offshore, a good hand saw and a hand drill with different bit sizes should complement the toolkit. A sheet of marine plywood might come in handy for all kinds of emergency repairs.

One not so uncommon emergency is losing the rudder. In the Hawaii race, it was a requirement for the racer to be able to jury-rig an emergency rudder. I sawed a rudder out of marine plywood which could be used with the help of the self-steering vane. I was lucky not to have to prove its effectiveness under emergency circumstances.

STOVES and HEATERS

Marine stoves should be hung in gimbals and have a rail to attach clamps in order to immobilize the pots and pans.

Especially in colder climates the coal stove can serve not only to heat the food, but also to keep the boat's interior warm and dry. However, few modern boat owners want to put up with the inherent difficulties of keeping a coal fire going and the cleaning problems afterwards.

One of the most commonly used and relatively inexpensive stoves is the alcohol stove. That does not mean that they are very popular. Most owners hate them with a passion. These stoves are very touchy and the owner who has not had an alcohol fire while using one is in the minority. They take a long time to get started, and once they are going there is often too much alcohol, and another alcohol fire starts in an inappropriate place. They are relatively inexpensive to buy, but the price of alcohol makes them expensive to use.

Kerosene stoves are inexpensive to buy and use. They are hotter than alcohol stoves and relatively safe. The use of an oven is not practical in this case.

Bottled gas stoves (propane, butane, etc.) are the most practical in my opinion, as long as the user takes precautions to prevent the heavier-than-air gas from escaping and filling up the bilge. To prevent this occurrence, the tank should be outside in a vapor-proof locker with approved fittings and lines. At the stove in the galley there should be a switch with a warning light. The switch activates a solenoid which opens or closes the tank. When the stove is not in use, the switch will prevent any possible gas from leaking away from the tank.

The danger with this system is that when the battery is drained or the battery switch is turned off, the electric solenoid will close the valve and stop the fire in the burner. If later on, the battery is charged or the switch turned on and the stove is left on, the gas will escape without initially being ignited at the stove.

Once I had three stove burners on to heat the cabin. I was working on the boat and turned the battery off for a minute, not thinking about the stove. After I turned the battery on again, I began, luckily, to smell gas escaping from the stove.

If properly used, the solenoid switch will prevent propane leakage, but it obviously creates other risks. Recognizing its dangers, I still prefer the propane stove. It is easy to use and clean, and one moderate size tank lasts for weeks with many people aboard. Propane can now also be used to heat the cabin. There are very efficient propane cabin heaters available which can be used with a thermostat. They certainly are cleaner and easier to use than the diesel heater that I had removed from my boat.

The Galley

FOOD and WATER

One advantage for the solo sailor is the fact that he alone will be eating or drinking the food! There will not be any tension as a result of comments like, "Who ate the last of the pudding?" Believe it or not, this kind of tension can ruin the camaraderie of long ocean voyages. For the solo sailor there is often plenty of storage space available for food and water.

For normal ocean voyages one-half to one gallon of drinking water daily per person is sufficient. The problem is that nobody can predict the length of the voyage, especially on a sailboat so dependent on the variable winds. Another problem is that tanks can leak, water can go bad, and other misfortunes can happen to interfere with the water supply. It is recommended that the sailor have several different ways to store the water and not to be dependent on one storage capability.

In emergency situations, rain or condensation water may be collected from the sail via the dripping boom. A small plastic solar still should be stocked in the life raft. Fairly simple and relatively inexpensive desalinization units that make drinking water out of sea water are available now. They may have some use for the boat with a large crew or when sailing in areas where drinking water is hard to come by.

Most solo sailors will have to do without ice. Even if there is a refrigerator aboard, there is always the possibility of it breaking down or the chance of electrical power problems.

Fresh meat is one of the few items that the iceless sailor will have to do without. Fresh bread will usually last only a few days, depending on the ambient temperature. Putting bread in plastic bags with a desiccant will prolong its life. Crackers may have to take the place of bread. For the more culinary-minded sailor there is the possibility of storing flour and yeast so that he can bake his own bread. On my first trip to Hawaii the crew members baked very acceptable bread.

Plenty of fresh fruit should be part of the sailor's food supply, i.e., oranges, apples, grapefruit, lemons, and limes. Limes were the standard food for the British sailors as an anti-scurvy treatment, giving them the name of "limeys." These fruits keep longer if they are individually packed in bags so that if one starts rotting, the other ones are not affected. This applies also to vegetables such as celery, carrots, potatoes, onions, and garlic. They can stay fresh a long time with these precautions.

Rice, macaroni, or other pastas and beans may become the mainstay of the evening meal, sprinkled with onions, along with dried or canned meat. Cereals with either canned or dried milk may start the morning, after the eggs are gone. Crackers with margarine and jam will enliven the lunch. Dried fruits such as figs, raisins, apricots, and prunes can be used as snacks. Dried or canned soups are always wonderful, especially in cold climates, and they are made quickly and easily consumed on a bouncing boat. Watch the boiling water and use thermostable cups.

In these days of multivitamin preparations, the chance of getting scurvy or other vitamin deficiencies is remote. The prudent sailor will take some vitamin tablets along, especially when he has to board the life raft.

Recently, Yurika has made pre-packaged meals available which compare favorably with frozen meals. They do not have to be refrigerated. The sealed, plastic bag is dropped into hot water and heated through. Then the bag is opened and there is your meal with meat, vegetables, and potato! These packages often served as the main course for my evening meal.

There is no reason for great concern about damage to the wine on the boat as long as the old Bordeaux stays home. The Portuguese noticed that their sherry tasted better in the colonies than in their homeland. It turned out not to be a psychological phenomenon. The movement of the ocean improved the taste of the sherry to such a degree that the more expensive sherry was put on ships going to the colonies and then brought back for consumption in Portugal!

FISHING

I have never caught a single fish on any of my ocean voyages. This must have something to do with their intelligence. At my home I have a collection of Japanese koi fish in a pond. When I feed them in the morning they hear me coming, recognize my red morning robe, and are waiting for me. There they eat out of my hand like I was St. Francis of Assisi in person. Out on the ocean I can have my fishing bait out for days, but the fish refuse to bite. Maybe I do not want them to bite? This could be because I have difficulty seeing and handling injured animals. Injured people are another matter—I've gotten used to them, being a physician. And so I have given up on fishing. I did not even try to fish during my solo sail to Hawaii.

However, the reader should not be discouraged as there *are* people who live off the fish in the ocean. But, he will have to consult other "experts" on this subject. Ken Neumeyer's book, *The Sailing Farm*, describes not only how to make a living from fishing on a sailboat, but also how to gather and prepare edible seaweeds.

Transpacific Single-Handed
Sailing Race
San Francisco–Kauai, Hawaii
June–July 1984

DAY 1

June 16, 11:00 hours. Testing 1, 3, 5, 7. O.K. My little mini tape recorder works. Well, here we are. My first dictation. I am about two miles out of the Golden Gate. It is quite foggy and when there is fog there is usually little wind. Today is no exception and the wind is now only about eight knots. I have almost all the sails up. The big Genoa is completely out on the self-furling, the staysail is behind it and the main is, of course, raised. The mizzen is furled because it does not help very much when sailing against the wind.

The start was somewhat confused for me, mainly because my senses were and still are clouded from lack of sleep the last few days. I saw everybody else pass along what I thought was the wrong starting buoy. I decided, however, to follow the pack, presuming they were much better informed than I.

This is the time to test the radar alarm. I can make a circle on the radar screen. The circle represents a ring around my boat of between a half of a mile to twenty-four miles, depending on my setting. Any hazard reaching that circle will set off an alarm. This could be the coast or another boat or a navigational marker. Now is the time to check it out because there are many boats around, while in a few hours I'll be alone on the ocean.

The alarm keeps going off. It will give me peace of mind in the next few days to know that it is working and this will undoubtedly help me sleep more soundly.

There were a lot of well wishers on other boats at the starting line off the Golden Gate Yacht Club. Some boats had photographers aboard and one powerboat had a television crew. I was unable to recognize any of my friends, although I knew they were around on some of those boats.

At the moment there is a powerboat with a film crew coming towards me. A helicopter is flying overhead and the transcriber of this tape will probably hear it. Somebody will be taping the evening news on television tonight so I will be able to see the start after my return.

Some of my competitors are around. There is Ken Roper, Number 17 in the Harrier, a Finn Flyer 30 sloop, and I saw Peter Hogg in the only multi-hull Newick 40. Everybody seems to be a little faster than I, but that is to be expected in these light winds when the smaller, lighter boats have a relative advantage.

14:00 hours. Since my first dictation I have gotten a little further away from Hawaii! While the wind died down even more, the flood tide was increasing in strength and gradually pushed me back to the Golden Gate while I was frantically trying to tack against the wind. I was considering dropping my anchor when I was getting close to the rocks, waiting out the flood tide and resuming my trip with ebb tide. Luckily, there was a spot close to the shore where the current was only slight, and by quick and frequent tacking I was able to minimize my retreat. Now I am recuperating and exhausted, but I think I am over the hump. There is more wind and the flood tide is diminishing.*

It is a lot of work to bring the large Genoa around when alone, and I am already looking forward to getting on that big ocean where frequent tacking will be a thing of the past. Things are looking up. The sun is coming out, the wind is increasing and the tide is diminishing. I am still not making much progress, but at least with this wind I am keeping up with some of the other sailors who apparently are having the same problems.

17:00 hours. Doing much better. Wind speed twelve knots. My speed around six knots. I can only see two other boats and

---

*After the race was over I learned that one sailor was pushed back under the Golden Gate Bridge and decided to have a drink at a bar and try again with the next outgoing tide.

I seem now to be slightly faster. The self-steering vane is working magnificently, giving me a chance to do some household chores. The batteries are being charged. Last night there was no shore power in the harbor while the refrigerator was on. Tonight in the shipping lanes I would definitely like to use my radar and radar watch. My batteries should therefore be up to snuff. The compass heading is about 180 degrees south (magnetic). Ideally, I should be going 230 degrees, but that is too much into the wind.

I had my first whiskey, and artichokes with crackers, and I am looking forward to a good night's rest.

DAY 2

June 17, 12:45 hours. Latitude 36°51′ N., longitude 124°28′ W.
I had a good sleep indeed since I decided to sleep in the most
comfortable aft room. The stern is the most comfortable place
in a boat with the least amount of movement. Even if it takes
longer to get to the wheel from there, the added comfort makes
it worthwhile, now that everything is so well under control.

The radar alarm woke me up and alerted me to the presence
of some fishermen. I also had to reef the Genoa on the self-furling forestay because the wind had increased. It is now blowing
between twenty and twenty-five knots with gusts up to thirty!
Great! Once in a while my speedometer reads ten knots.

Combi Unit
With Wind Speed (25 Knots),
Boat Speed (10 Knots)
and Wind Direction

I do worry somehow about my competitors. Some of them have pretty small boats and they must have a hard time with these strong winds and high seas. Every morning at 9:00 hours we are supposed to listen in and report our position on channel 68 of the VHF radio. I had a hard time making sense of the conversation because of static, but obviously some contestants are nearby and I will try again tomorrow.

I also tried to listen to the weather forecast on the single-sideband radio (KMI) at the specified time, but nobody came on the line. I could hear the special weather broadcast for the race on station WWV, but again there was too much static to understand what was said. Tomorrow I'll tape it on my little cassette and play it back a few times. Maybe that way I'll be able to decipher some of it.

My heading is now 220 degrees, which should bring me to Hawaii, south of the Great Circle Route. The barometer shows a pressure of 1027 millibars. As mentioned earlier, I would like to stay out of the Pacific High where there is very little wind. In order to stay south of the High it is advisable to stay south of the 1020 millibar. This means that I should go farther south. However, since I have good winds and am going where I want to go at present, I will leave well enough alone. I had a good breakfast with eggs this morning.

DAY 3

June 18, 10:00 hours PDT. Latitude 35°16′ N. longitude 126°38′ W. Speed remains between seven to nine knots. The wind yesterday kept increasing in the afternoon so I reefed the main to the first reefing points, which made the boat go much smoother without loosing speed. The mizzen is now also up and reefed. The big Genoa is well furled in. The wind is about twenty knots. If this weather continues to Hawaii, I might set a record and win the race!

The Monitor vane is working like a charm and I spend most of my time below deck. What a great invention this self-steering vane is. When single-handling, our forefathers had to put the boat in irons during the night to sleep. Or they would bring all the sails down. Rarely could they sail day and night. Maybe that is the reason that so few of them undertook long solo ocean voyages, except for some brave souls like Joshua Slocum.

During the night the radar reflector fell from the spreaders with a big bang. The line had chafed through.

I had my first real dinner last night with wine and steak. For my dessert I had an old can of peaches. Those, however, came back up pretty soon afterwards. I don't know whether it was the age of the can or *mal de mer* that was the cause.

Only twice did I vomit and each time it came "out of the blue," because I really have not felt bad at all. It must be that I still have some resistance left over from my qualifier sail. Just to be on the safe side, however, I applied my second anti-seasickness scopolamine patch today.

During the night the radar alarm woke me up and I saw that a large vessel was coming at me from the port side on a collision course. I tried to contact the captain several times over the VHF radio. Finally—either my radio had not been working or he was not standing by—he acknowledged me. It was a Japanese freighter en route from Long Beach to Okinawa. The next shipping lane I will encounter is the one from the Panama Canal to Japan.

Officially, every ship with a radio aboard is supposed to monitor the emergency channel at all times. I doubt that my Japanese friend was monitoring the VHF radio until he saw me. I have to admit that I myself am often guilty of this omission. Sometimes one gets into difficulties by not obeying this rule. Once, while sailing back from Baja California, I got caught. We were about thirty miles off the coast near Santa Barbara. It was a beautiful sunny day and my oldest daughter Julia and her friends were sunbathing in bikinis on the foredeck. We were watching a four-engine navy plane that was circling the area. We were slightly concerned because one of the four engines had quit. Originally, when the pilot started passing over us at rather low altitude, I thought that the bikinis on the foredeck had something to do with it, but when he returned at even lower altitude, I became convinced that he was planning to ditch in the water near us so we would be able to pick up the survivors.

I picked up the microphone and started transmitting on the VHF radio: "Calling Coast Guard station, calling Coast Guard station. This is the sailing yacht Alistelle; Whiskey, Romeo, Julia, five three five three. We have a navy plane overhead that seems to be in trouble and seems to be planning to ditch in the immediate vicinity. Please advise!" Answer: "Calling the Alistelle, calling the Alistelle. This *is* the navy plane, this *is* the navy plane. Thank you for your concern but we are *not*, repeat *not*, in danger. You are in danger, you are in a *missile testing zone*. Proceed immediately 320 degrees magnetic." This we did rather quickly. The pilot had been trying to reach us on the VHF— which we were not monitoring!

June 18, 14:00 hours PDT. Course 220 degrees. Still have twenty-knot winds and making fabulous progress. Major debacle today. I was doing my routine maintenance checking the water level of batteries and cleaning the bilge pump which became plugged with sawdust from battery boxes installed at the last minute. I was charging the batteries when, all of a sudden, smoke began coming out of the engine department. I thought I had a fire. The engine was overheated and one of the hoses had already disintegrated. This had happened on the qualifying sail so it was not new for me, but I realized that from now on, I will be unable to use the engine for battery charging. To prevent this from happening and to warn me ahead of time, I had had an alarm installed which was supposed to ring if the engine temperature became high or the oil pressure low. Either I had not heard it or it had not been functioning.

For this eventuality I had brought along two Honda gasoline generators. My alternator, connected to the engine, was able to produce eighty amperes per hour, while the small Honda generators together are only able to raise ten amperes per hour.

With my hi-fi, refrigerator, cabin lights, running lights, radar, radar watch and electronic navigation equipment, I figure I will use at least twenty amperes per hour. That means after one night alone I need a 140-amp ($7 \times 20 = 140$) charge. That will take my regular generator about two hours, but it will take both Honda generators fourteen hours of running time.

First of all, there are only about four gallons of gasoline aboard. Also, I don't want to think about the damage the noise of two generators for fourteen hours daily will do to my psyche. I might go for a swim which very likely would separate me from my boat! There goes my dream. No more refrigeration. No more ice in my whisky soda! No more radar, so I had better sleep on deck and have an alarm clock go off every hour so I can check the horizon when in a trafficked area. No more hi-fi music in the evening, and no more reading in bed.

One possible and partial solution is to start the engine a few times a day for a few minutes until the engine temperature starts rising. I will continue my trip, however uncomfortable it may turn out to be. I have turned off the refrigeration already and will have to eat a lot of steaks and eggs in the next few days! I have done about one-eighth of the trip. It would therefore be possible to turn around, but the winds are good and I will have to learn to live with less luxury.

I got caught in irons for the first time today when the wind shifted.

June 18, 20:00 hours PDT. Hallelujah, life is great again. It turned out that my overheated engine was caused by the accidental closure of the salt water engine cooling intake valve. This must have happened when I was adding water to the batteries. My foot must have pushed on the valve. Anyway, I replaced the melted hose and opened the intake valve. I prayed that the water impeller had not disintegrated because of the high temperature and started the engine. Did I watch that temperature gauge intensely! The engine remained cool! Refrigeration is on again.

This morning I tried for the first time to make radio contact with the mainland. I did not get through initially and I finally made a radio check with the Coast Guard on channel 2182. They could hear me. It was rather disappointing that my expensive single-sideband was not working. I even tried Fort Lauderdale in Florida. With the single-sideband it is better under certain atmospheric conditions to use a station that is further away. I finally got through to KMI in Point Reyes, California. There are about fifty different frequencies one can use and it sometimes takes a long time to find out which one is best to use.

I finally talked to my answering service and related my coordinates (latitude and longitude) to them. In the hospital doctors' lounge there is a chart of the Pacific so that my position can be plotted whenever they hear from me.

My anchor is semi-permanently attached to the bow of the boat. Every time the bow gets in the water, the anchor gives quite a loud jerk. I was thinking about bringing it inside. I will not be able to use it for the next few weeks and it might be safer and quieter. I have some idiosyncrasies with anchors. They never seem to hold for me and I appear to use them as if they are disposable.

A few years ago I was anchored in the sloughs near Sacramento. The rivers there are quite narrow and the current is very swift. We were anchored near the shore with two anchors. The place was crowded with small powerboats. Because of the size of my boat and the presence of that status symbol, the self steering vane, I automatically became the traffic coordinator. Everybody was mighty impressed with my seamanship when I was giving orders left and right. There were no protests, but there was an atmosphere of subdued gratefulness.

By the time I was ready to leave, everybody was eager to learn how I would get out. The current was very fast and after I had raised one anchor, the boat started to swing around the other anchor and was going to crush the nice little powerboats. There was no time to bring up the second anchor, but I was able to cut the line quickly with my sharp knife without being seen by my eager sailor pupils. I did not want to fall short of their expectations. There was great admiration about how I left that anchorage so easily—minus one anchor, but they did not know that! That was anchor number one!

The next day I went sailing to Half Moon Bay. I had bought a brand new anchor. With me was a German graduate engineering student from Berkeley. He was an excellent sailor with the good German quality of being very meticulous. If the war had lasted any longer, he probably would have been U-boat captain! He had several suggestions on how to improve some aspects of the boat. Beware of suggestions from other sailors. There are usually good reasons why something is done a certain way if the boat has been used for a considerable amount of time.

I remember Reinoud, my brother-in-law, had suggested putting the winch handles in the dinghy which was tied on top of the cabin. It seemed it to be an excellent idea and I asked myself, "Why did I not think of that before?" The next big wave gave the answer. The dinghy filled with water and I had a miserable time fishing the handles out of that cold water with bare hands.

One of the improvements that Peter Hoch, my German engineering friend, suggested was to untie the anchor from the line when bringing it forward. The rather heavy anchor was stored aft with the heavy line attached, making it necessary to bring both the anchor and line from the end of the boat forward when they had to be used. The improvement would enable us to bring the anchor forward first and the long anchor rope afterwards. No need to carry all that weight at one time! "Excellent idea," I confirmed. Peter Hoch was quite ceremonial when he was dropping the new anchor (with the price tag still on it) into the water. "May I have the honor of dropping this new anchor for the first time in this beautiful bay?" he asked. I told him to go right ahead. His facial expression suddenly turned gray. He realized that he had forgotten to tie the anchor back to the rope! Afterwards he dove for hours in vain. For several years he has written me once a year, and he still blushes when the incident is mentioned! That is why I decided today to leave the anchor where it was.

DAY 4

June 19, 20:25 hours. PDT. Latitude 33° N., longitude 130° W.
While checking the sails, I noticed a ship overtaking me on starboard. I made contact easily on the VHF radio. It was the Spring Delight, a British ship whose captain spoke with a British accent. We talked for quite a while and exchanged jokes. We were careful enough to go on the short range power output so as not to get caught with some risque jokes which might impel Federal Radio Communications to revoke our licenses. He confirmed that he had spotted me easily on the radar, so I will not worry too much about my radar reflector being stored below deck.

I am still having difficulties making up my mind whether to go further south. The barometer still reads 1030 millibars, but I am making speed and this seems to be the way the boat likes to go. Maybe I will be punished later when I get sucked into the Pacific High.

The pulley of one of the lines of the self-steering vane came off and the line is chafing quite a bit. I used the automatic pilot for that reason and it works remarkably well.

I had a great evening yesterday. The weather is getting warmer and the sunset was beautiful. On top of that I prepared a wonderful dinner. (There is nobody else to evaluate my culinary abilities.) The wine was excellent and after dinner, rounded off with cognac and coffee, I listened to some Beethoven violin sonatas, one of which I had never heard. During the day I am pretty busy with routine maintenance and fixing little things, but at cocktail hour I start enjoying life.

My brand new running lights are already giving me trouble. It seems impossible to manufacture lights that remain in operation after being sprayed for a few days and nights by the salty seawater. That is another job for tomorrow. Tonight I will use an emergency stern light only, without the green and red running lights. I know that some of my competitors don't use any lights as soon as they are out of the shipping lanes. I will use the radar alarm. This will help me sleep better.

DAY 5

June 20. Latitude 32°4′ N., longitude 132° W. This morning I did not hear anybody on the VHF, so all the other sailors must be far away. I am going pretty much before the wind which makes steering much more difficult and I spent most of the morning trying to balance the sails with the poled-out jib.

The fiberglass repair job on the pulley for the self-steering vane lasted only a few hours. I will just let it chafe and move the line up every once in a while. My running lights were already completely corroded by the saltwater, but I was able to fix them.

The refrigerator is not working well and I am unable to repair it. I think it needs a new thermostat. It comes on once in a while, but no more ice! I have become so Americanized that for me it is a disappointment not to have ice in my whiskey. The British consider this one of our barbaric habits, but I like what has become such an American institution. To cool my beverages I will have to use a netted bag, trailing it in the water behind the boat.

I spent a long time trying to get the sails balanced. The self-steering vane has difficulties keeping the boat on course when going before the wind because the boat is going in the same direction as the wind. That leaves very little momentum to move the vane. The little automatic pilot works remarkably well under these conditions.

A bird has been following me for several days. She (of course!) disappears for several hours and then returns for her bread. She is rather shy, and though invited, has not been willing to land on deck.

Last night was again one of these evenings where I felt that the enjoyment of that one evening alone made the whole trip worthwhile. The sunset was spectacular and it was enchanting to listen to the peaceful sounds of the water slapping at the boat and the wind rustling the sails. I listened to a tape of some Bach cantatas performed by "my" Philharmonia Baroque Orchestra. They were led by my good friend and fellow Dutchman, Gustav Leonhardt. The principal singer was Max van Egmond, who had stayed over with me in my house for this concert. At the time I promised to send a copy of the tape to him in Amsterdam, and I will do this when I return.

The sunset was gorgeous, striated and multicolored, changing rather quickly in color and form, somewhat like a kaleidoscope. The sun comes out in several red lines like search lights. I have never seen anything similar elsewhere in the world. I took some photographs.

DAY 6

June 21, 5:00 hours PDT. Latitude 31°10′ N., longitude 134°10′ W. Woke up because it was really blowing. The auto pilot was not able to steer the boat and neither was I. It turned out to be a rain squall. I got soaking wet standing at the wheel and I wished I had not disconnected the monitor vane. I had taken it off to prevent damage by the mizzenboom. It was difficult to steer the boat and I finally put her in irons. After the blade was connected to the vane, the boat went as great as ever.

I made contact with the ladies of the answering service. It is hard to communicate with all the static. A husband of one of the ladies is a ham radio operator. This lady understands that one has to repeat every word a few times to get outside of the static. Instead of using, for example, the word "no," it is better to say the longer word "negative." "Affirmative" or "roger" stand for "yes."

My speedometer decided to quit this morning. This is not ·unusual. It probably means that some material like seaweed has been caught in the little propeller at the bottom of the boat. The propeller is connected to the Combi unit with an electric wire. It is not a terribly essential item, but I wanted to fix it in order to know my speed and to keep my log (distance in miles traveled) up to date. To get the debris out of the propeller one has to quickly remove the propeller from the hull. That leaves a substantial hole in the hull. The water gushing in through this temporary (I hope) hole is under high pressure. To fill the hole there is another plug. Time, of course, is of the essence.

Everything went very well. The sun in that clear blue Pacific water gets all the way underneath the boat. I was fascinated with the blue light in the bottom of the boat for those precious seconds when the water was pouring in! No time, however, to get high on that beautiful sight. It reminded me of doing a surgical procedure where there is no margin for mistakes. No need for malpractice insurance here. It is *my* boat, and if she sinks it is *my* life. My two sons, Peter and Vincent, have already been dividing the inheritance and have the boat earmarked for themselves. They would have to cancel the circumnavigation they are planning soon after my demise. It would be too bad, because I was unable to obtain any insurance for this single-handed trip. This is not necessarily a reflection on my seamanship. *Not one* of the racers was able to obtain insurance for the single-handed Transpacific race! The reasoning behind this is not clear. Statistically, more damage is done to the boats with crews during the much rougher return trip to the mainland against the wind. Neither I nor any other sailor ever has any difficulty obtaining insurance for the trip back, as long as there is a crew. It is the single-handling which seems to be the problem.

The main reason there were only fifteen starters out of twenty-four original contestants may have been this inability to obtain insurance. When the bank has title to the boat, they insist, understandably, that "their" boat be insured. This automatically excludes sailors who have loans on their boats. I hope that for the next race, insurance will be available so that these sailors can also participate. The safety record of the race during the past few years should speak for itself.

19:00 hours. PDT. What a day, what a day! It started out all right. I decided to go a little more south because of the high reading on the barometer. Then, BANG, the whole jenny came down, the self-furling and everything. Luckily, the forestay was still there. The pulley of the self-furling was still hanging on top. The whole Genoa, my largest sail, was hanging in the water. I tried to raise it out of the water, but like a giant water balloon, it refused to give. I was pulling with all my power, but it did not move an inch. I was considering cutting it because if the wind increased suddenly with this tremendous "brake" on portside, it would be impossible to predict what calamities could follow. The boat probably would keep spinning around counter-clockwise.

I am usually pretty good under these circumstances, if I do say so myself. That is because I am such a lousy sailor. I often unwittingly create these calamities and this makes me an expert in rectifying them. This time, by carefully rolling one side of the sail, I was able to get the Genoa aboard in one piece.

I decided to use an extra halyard to bring the Genoa up again, realizing that I would not be able to use the self-furling gear anymore. The Genoa is my largest sail, so I like to use it if I can. It is rather heavy and hard to handle. It will not be easy to bring it down in a hurry. This might create some problems if all of a sudden the wind picks up, especially at night.

Half-an-hour after I had hoisted the Genoa this way, it wrapped around the forestay with a big part of the sail ballooning out. It took hours to get the sail unwrapped. I was also afraid I might have to climb the mast, which would have been dangerous regardless, but especially in this weather. The Genoa is finally up with only a few turns remaining on the top, but at least no more big balloon.

I put the boat on more of a wide beam to diminish the chance of another catastrophe. That is not exactly the right direction, but I feel I deserve a rest. I am too tired to prepare any food. After having a Mai Tai I feel that Neptune is good to me after all, now that the speed is a nice five to six knots.

During all this hassle I almost fell in the water, and if I had not worn my harness, I would probably be getting tired of swimming by now! All my muscles ache from the work I did today. I took a picture of the wrapped Genoa. Good night.

DAY 7

June 22, 15:00 hours PDT. Latitude 30°05′ N., longitude 134°55′ W. This morning's job was to try to further unwind the big Genoa. I had to lie down and look up to the top of the mast with binoculars, trying to diagnose the problem. It came loose without major difficulties. The fact that there is practically no wind also helped. I was very proud when the full Genoa unfolded. The ecstasy did not last very long because, BANG, the whole Genoa came down again a little bit later. The brand new second halyard had chafed through! There is a small possibility that by going up the mast I might be able to rectify the problem, but the risk involved in doing so is, I think, not justified. I still have one more jib halyard left to try out.

There is obviously no chance of winning the race anymore, but I do hope to finish it, which means I have to cross the finish line in Kauai before the July 8 deadline. My distance in twenty-four hours was the smallest ever. Not only was most of the time spent in irons trying to unravel the sail, but there was almost no wind either.

I put the big Genoa through the bow hatch in the forecabin and will not use it for a long time, unless I try once more with the last halyard. My original happiness with the furling, reefing headsail certainly has changed!

During the night I had to get up several times. It reminds me of my days as an intern: half-hour work, half-hour sleep.

The wind vane does not work very well in these light winds and sailing is much more tiresome. The boat occasionally gets in irons with this low speed. In a good strong wind I never have to worry about tending the wheel.

I am below the 30° latitude and it is getting nice and warm. I wear a bathing suit occasionally to protect my previously unexposed parts from too much sudden sunshine. When working on deck I wear a parka as protection against superficial injuries. The barometer is dropping below the 1025 millibar so I still have to go further south, especially now that the wind has died down so much. The small light Olson 30 drifter is flying from the staysail halyard and that is the only sail forward of the main!

DAY 8

June 23, 16:00 hours PDT. Latitude 28°40′ N., longitude 136°40′ W. Where is the wind ? A lot of rattling and noises during the night from booms going back and forth. I can barely get the boat moving. Boy, do I do a lot of fiddling and experimenting with the sails. I can forget about the wind vane in these low winds. The barometer is now down to 1024, but I may be stuck in the Pacific High. According to the radio, the 1030 millibar is at latitude 31°. I hope that it is moving north and not coming down on me even worse.

Last night I talked to a cargo ship, the MS Maui, which was on her way from Los Angeles to Honolulu. She crossed my bow going about twenty knots. The captain wished me a good journey.

This morning I made contact with two other sailors: Jeffrey Hartz in the Baobob and Ken Roper in the Harrier. It is good to talk to other sailors. One gets a little depressed if no progress is being made and the boat just does not move if there is no wind. I guess it is one of these nice(?) human traits that things do not seem so bad if somebody else is in the same predicament. Misery loves company. The way things are going, I barely make sixty to seventy miles a day. Twenty-four of these miles are due to the current of one knot anyway.

Talked to the answering service this morning with pretty good reception. Maybe it will be better to use the higher frequency in the morning (1602).

DAY 9

June 24. Latitude 27°15′ N., longitude 137° W. After some sleep I woke up and found the boat in irons. A sailboat was going far away past my stern. I reached it on the VHF radio. It happened to be Robert Marotta. He was in turn in contact with Ken Roper in the Harrier and Jeff Hartz in the Baobob. He had heard from them that three racers had quit fairly soon after the beginning of the race. One was Randy Waggoner on the Radical. He had to be towed in by the Monterey Coast Guard. Paul Connolly had many troubles and returned to San Francisco. The third one to fall out was Bill Prout in a Pearson 36. It is not clear why he returned. They must be pretty disappointed after having made all the preparations.

Everybody seems to go more west than I do. That is why Bob Marotta passed by my stern. I cannot move this heavy boat with these light winds and have to go further south to pick up the trade winds. The other ones joked that I was going to Tahiti. We will see.

There still has not been time to play the harpsichord. These light winds really keep me hopping.

I have a small alarm clock with two different alarm settings for one day. The main purpose is to remind me of the different times for the weather forecasts, etc. I had forgotten where I put the darned thing. There are over fifty drawers and other storage places on this boat. One advantage is that I do not have to look in my pockets because I have no clothes on. Twice a day the alarm goes off and every time I try to hear where the sound is coming from. Every day I get a little closer and today I finally found it. Like most people I had great intentions of taking an inventory before I left, but I ran out of time and so I have to search now and then.

More often than that! I just spent twenty minutes looking for the next cassette tape for my mini-recorder. These things are so small. I am always surprised how easily I lose things. In the hospital anything that is found usually belongs to Dr. Strykers, unless proven otherwise. I usually get my stuff back before I have missed it and that is disappointing for the finder who wants, of course, to see my happy smile of relief. Ashore I like to blame somebody else for misplacing things. This solo sail is a good testing ground.

It is, by the way, a little confusing to differentiate all the various alarms. There is the regular twice-a-day alarm clock to alert me to the weather broadcast or to awaken me. Then there are the depth alarm, the radar watch alarm, the warning systems for high engine temperature or low oil pressure, an alarm for water in the bilge, and the off course alarm.

Tomorrow I hope to reach the halfway point. I don't know how to celebrate that. Before departure, Linda Rettie gave me a bunch of letters, each one to be opened on a certain date. A sort of solo sailor's Advent calendar, but tailor-made. Linda has sailed single-handedly to Japan and has experienced the moods of solo sailors. Today she tells me that on this, day 9, I will feel down. Wrong, Linda, I feel great! I am very talkative today, maybe because of the new tape in the cassette, but if I continue like this I had better go on half-speed or I'll run out of tape. O.K., half-speed we go.

I will have to vacuum and do some household chores later in the day. I make such a mess with my pipe. Ashes all over the place. I wish I could get rid of it. I already lost one overboard when a sheet knocked it out of my mouth. Thank God I still have my teeth.

Tonight I will tune my harpsichord and finally get to play, I hope. My hands are still a little swollen from handling the sheets and from exposure to the salt water, so my playing is going to be a little rough on the small harpsichord keys.

The music that my transcriber can pick up in the background

is my dear friend and fellow Philharmonia board member, Judith Nelson, singing a Bach cantata with "our" orchestra. It is interesting how differently my friends interpret my priorities. The musicians, of course, are interested in my musical experiences while the sailors, especially Linda and Sue, want me to win and win! I must say I have that competitive spirit, but not enough to raise the Genoa once more tonight with my last foresail halyard. Maybe tomorrow?

Day 10

June 25, 21:00 hours PDT. Latitude 25°20' N., longitude 137°40' W. Today I am late in dictating. Listening to some Boccherini string quartets that I've never heard before. It is always exciting to find out how much great music is relatively unknown.

I talked over the VHF again to the Harrier and the Baobob. They are still going farther westward. In my opinion they are making a mistake, because I now have fairly good winds. They also told me that on day 3 I was probably ahead of everybody! That was the day that I made almost 200 miles in twenty-four hours. Radio station WWV announced that at latitude 25 there are fifteen-knot winds! That's where I am headed.

This morning there was very little wind. I was brave and energetic and decided to raise the big Genoa sail once more with the last jib halyard. I know that this is my last chance. The big sail gave me an extra two knots of speed. The big Genoa is poled out with the large spinnaker pole on starboard and the main with a preventer on port and the mizzen again on starboard. I use the automatic pilot more than the wind vane, now that I am going so much before the wind. Maybe this will be the basic rig until Kauai *if* the jenny holds up.

Still Monday. I just finished dinner with a bottle of Chardonnay Macon Village and am listening to Mozart's *Figaro*. It's amazing how one can feel so exuberant with music. This morning I was all excited in another way, trying to get the big Genoa up once more to get the boat moving. From experience I know how music can change my mood. When I am depressed a little music will lift my spirits; I use music as an anti-depressant. It is very effective and there is an immediate therapeutic result, not like our medical anti-depressants which sometimes take ten days before taking effect. And music causes no bad side effects. I wonder whether the suicide rate among musicians is lower than the average. My musical colleagues must be able to use that same outlet. I wish those Austrians would not use a factory harpsichord for their *Figaro*. That's the only thing that bothers me in this recording, but it is not enough to interfere with the therapeutic effect of Mozart. It's funny how basically oversensitive one becomes to these little details. In a way, in music as in other art forms, familiarity with a little bit better performance makes any other one intolerable.

I find myself caught between Scylla and Charybdis, except in this case I am caught between two joys rather than two evils. Part of me wants to win the race and make it as short as possible, and part of me wants to extend the race and enjoy it as long as possible. Like Odysseus, I'll sail the middle road.

We live in a lucky age. True, we still have poverty, but that is nothing new, and there is the nuclear threat. But I don't think the plague was much fun either, and at least we can blame only ourselves for a nuclear war!

I envy Louis the XIV for the fine harpsichord music he could hear after dinner with François Couperin, *musicien ordinaire du Roi*, playing for him. But Louis can keep his gouty toe for which we now have some medicine. He can also keep his diligence with four horses. I would rather keep my Porsche with 234 horsepower! But Couperin? *Enfin!*

At least for the moment I am having a good time. I have all the advantages of the electronic age like stereo, satellite navigation, and refrigeration. There is no worry about beriberi. At the same time I am using the wind and do not have to steer the boat like our forefathers did. The self-steering vane is interesting in that it was invented in the twentieth century without the use of any more knowledge than was available in the Middle Ages. No electronics, just a few gears.

It is nice to be in these southern latitudes so I can sit outside in the evenings. It is too bad the moon is in its last quarter and that there will be no more full moon on this trip. What a luxury to sit naked watching a beautiful shimmering sea, uninterrupted by any twentieth century noises (one of the advantages of being out of the path of the Great Circle Route which is taken by commercial airlines). I hope that the wind does not pick up too much. I might have to bring down the big jenny in a hurry, which might be quite a challenge.

I was unable to contact any of the other boats. They are apparently that much further north. I am glad I made the decision to go farther south. There are relatively good winds and my barometer is still above the 1020 mark. I am edging around the Pacific High, I hope!

I talked to the answering service today and found out that Sue will be in Kauai July 3, which is great. She can help me with preparations for the return trip.

I have passed longitude 138 and I am about twenty miles north of latitude 25.

One major catastrophe today! This morning, when preparing breakfast, I opened the faucet and no water! I looked in the bilge. All my fresh water, 200 gallons of it minus the few gallons I had used so far, had left the fresh-water tank and found its way into the dirty bilge. There it was, mixed with some oil and other debris! After I had checked to make sure I had the emergency ration of two five-gallon tanks aboard, I drained the bilge. The water was up to the bottom of the engine. The bilge pump emptied the bilge very quickly. Just before I left, I had bought and installed a new fresh-water pump. The pump was too powerful for the hoses receiving the water. One hose had formed an aneurysm that apparently had ruptured. To prevent something like this from happening, I had installed an alarm that was supposed to go off when the water level in the bilge reaches a certain height. It is a small, battery-operated unit that should give an audible and visible sign (blinking light) when there is more than the usual amount of water in the bilge. It apparently was not functioning. Its primary purpose is to notify me when sea water is entering the boat before it reaches catastrophic levels in the bilge. I had not thought about the possibility of filling the bilge with my own drinking water!

Sailors have different worries. My main worry is not so much a hurricane or falling overboard. My concern is the large amount of through-hull fittings on this boat. These are openings in the hull with a valve that can be opened or closed. They are necessary to get rid of waste or to suck sea water for flushing the head or for engine cooling. There are thirteen of these risk factors on my boat. Each of the two heads has four, one for taking in sea water to flush the toilet, one for getting rid of the waste, and a third one for discharging the sink. The last one is connected to the sump pump that discharges the water used in the shower. There is one for the galley sink discharge. The engine uses one for sea water cooling of the diesel engine. Then there are three for the self-bailing cockpit. There are two more, but under normal circumstances these are above the water line and serve as engine exhaust and discharge for the bilge pump.

These valves are connected to rubber hoses with hose clamps like the hose connected to the radiator of a car. The difference is that when the radiator hose gives out, the engine will soon start heating up. On the boat, when this clamp or the hose itself gives out, the ship will very quickly sink unless the through-hull fitting is closed immediately. That is the price one pays for all these luxuries. To diminish this risk of sudden flooding, I used only one head and closed the four valves of the second head. That still leaves me with nine potential problem through-hulls. The little, battery-operated bilge flood alarm would have been a good precaution *if* it had worked.

Joshua Slocum, the first solo circumnavigator, did not have these problems. He had no through-hulls on his thirty-five foot Spray. He had no "head" aboard, but used the "poop" deck.

No shower, no sink—only buckets. He had other problems and needed other gear, such as thumbtacks to discourage the bare-footed natives from jumping on board.

For fresh water I figure a gallon a day for one person. So I have enough drinking water, but the hot fresh-water showers are over. The dishes will not be done in the sink, but in a bucket of sea water.

Another disaster happened. The Genoa came down once more. This time, however, it was for the last time! The sail was trailing in the water and the heavy spinnaker pole ended up on one of the starboard stanchions! The spinnaker pole was bent quite a bit and the stanchion was cut in half. I was able to take a picture of the sail dragging in the water with the bent spinnaker pole. There is no jib halyard anymore. All I can use up front is the small drifter, hanging from the staysail halyard halfway up the mast, or the regular staysail.

DAY 11

June 26, 06:30 hours PDT. Latitude 24°40′ N., longitude 139°25′ W. There were good winds during the night. The boat was sailing on the mizzen and mainsail, going for the wind and yawing terribly. There was not much chance to sleep. The boat was in irons several times during the night and I had to get up to take over the steering. I crossed longitude 139 and am now definitely beyond the halfway point. According to the satellite navigator, I am 1080 nautical miles from Hawaii. The refrigerator started working again after I used my old trick of turning the switch on and off quickly. This shakes up the electronics enough to get the transistors going again and seems a more elegant method than the one where the recalcitrant T.V. gets kicked. My butter is almost gone. I ate it like crazy because it will spoil rapidly without refrigeration.

I was unable to rouse anybody on the VHF radio because I am farther south than anybody else. The big Genoa is now in the bag and out of the way and will stay there until the return trip when the jib halyards are repaired!

DAY 12

June 27, Afternoon. Latitude 24°30′ N., longitude 142° W. I slept all night but am a little discouraged by the lack of wind and consequent low speed. Trying to make sense out of the weather forecast. There seems to be a Hurricane Douglas somewhere, but from what I can make out he seems to be further south and moving east. With these low winds I do not know whether I would mind a hurricane very much!

My barometer reads 1019 millibars, so I should be happy about that and I am theoretically south of the Pacific High. I am not so depressed anymore about not being able to use my headsails. In a way, being undercanvassed makes the sailing easier. During these sudden rain squalls with winds over twenty-five knots, I would have to quickly reef the sails, while now I only have to adjust the wheel.

Talked to my wife, Gondica, today on the single-sideband, but the transmitter got out out of lock after talking for a little while and I had to re-dial about ten numbers to be able to transmit again. The refrigeration is out of commission again. No ship in sight for several days and no contact with the other sailors, which in a way is nice. With my present rig, I still hope to make 120 miles a day, which will get me to Hanalei Bay by July 5 or 6.

There was quite a bit of flak on the single-sideband, ship-to-ship channels. Somebody talking too long. I gather it was the president of some company talking from a transmitter ashore to one of his container ships on the ocean. I presume that if one wants to talk to somebody ashore it is appropriate to go through one of the Marine High Seas telephone operators. At least that is what I do, being a "good boy." They charge thirty-five dollars for the first three minutes, and because of the static one is unable to say very much in that short a time. The ship-to-ship channels are supposed to be used for conversations between different ships. I guess that this company has its own single-sideband radio on land and uses the ship-to-ship channels for its communication. Certainly a lot cheaper, but I wonder whether that is legal? The guy who was trying to interrupt the conversation certainly thought it was more than immoral, though I felt that *his* choice of words was not an indication of a person of very high morals either.

I finally was able to play the harpsichord today, but I spent quite a while tuning it. Harpsichords have to be tuned all the time! They sometimes go out of tune several times a day, depending on the humidity and the temperature. Because the harpsichord case is made of wood and does not have the reinforcement of steel like the modern piano does, it has this drawback when compared with the piano. Or is it a drawback?

First of all, the meticulous pianist always insists on having the piano tuned a few hours before a concert. One of the differences between a piano and a harpsichord is the keyboard, which on the modern piano encompasses over seven octaves. Most harpsichords barely make it to five octaves. Another difference is that over the greatest part of its compass the piano has three strings for each note, while the harpsichord may have only one or two strings for each note. Tuning of the average harpsichord, therefore, can usually be accomplished in less than twenty minutes. However, because of its steel frame the modern piano will stay in tune longer than the harpsichord.

The major difference between the tuning of the piano and the harpsichord is that the modern piano is tuned in equal temperament and at the modern pitch of $A = 440$, while the harpsichord is usually tuned in one of the older temperaments and at lower pitch.

The pitch is the least important and has changed through the times. It varied in different areas and times, but was as whimsical as the arguments about where 0° longitude was going to be established. The British seem to have won again in this respect. Power even has some influence in the arts. (We are are talking now about the latter part of the nineteenth century and early part of the twentieth century.) The French had to come up a little bit in pitch (from 435) and the English had to come down a little bit (from 452). These decisions were made at an international meeting of the "pitch minds" in 1939. Imagine the music authorities of the world getting together to talk about so esoteric and unimportant a subject as the international pitch at a time when Europe was embarking on World War II! It must have been more fun than talking about arms control. Our musical negotiators at least succeeded! a′ = 440 hz was established as the international pitch and this is still so today.

Today's baroque orchestras however, in order to accommodate the historic instruments, often play at a different, and usually lower, pitch. These instruments were designed for the pitch in use at the time and in the geographical area of their manufacturing.

I would like to talk now about the temperament in tuning. This is where the difference between the tuning of the piano and the harpsichord really lies. To explain this difference I'll have to touch on some physics and I will have to go back into history.

When a string is under tension, whether it is a violin, guitar or piano string, it can produce a sound by vibrating at a certain number of vibrations per second. Something has to start this vibration: the violin string is bowed, the guitar and harpsichord strings are plucked, and the piano string is hit with a small hammer. These vibrations produce a note at a certain pitch (vibrations per second). By increasing the tension on the string, the number of vibrations per second is increased, and thus the pitch will be higher and the note will sound higher. When we press down on the string halfway between the beginning and the end of the string, and we pluck either half section of the string, the sound produced will have double the frequency of the sound the whole string produced. This half-string frequency will sound one octave higher than the full-string frequency.

So far so good. The octave interval (C to C′), therefore, relates to its original note as a ratio of two frequencies, or 1:2. But there are other intervals in our present-day music system: the fifth (C to G), the fourth (C to F), and the third (C to E).

The ratio of frequencies of the different intervals is as follows:

> From a note to its octave = 1:2
> From a note to its fifth = 2:3
> From a note to its fourth = 3:4
> From a note to its third = 4:5

As the frequencies are doubled, another octave is produced. However, when we continue to follow the thirds we run into problems. Three thirds should make an octave, doubling the frequency. However, $5/4 \times 5/4 \times 5/4 = 125/64$. If the octave were doubled, the ratio would have to be 128/64. The three thirds, therefore, produce less than an octave. If we want to have our octaves pure, which means having their frequencies at a 1:2 ratio, we will have to adjust the other intervals. The thirds will have to be widened and the fifths will have to be narrowed. In other words, to keep the octaves in tune we will have to adjust, or temper, the thirds, fourths, and fifths. This will force us to tune some or all of these intervals "impurely".

Compromises have to be made. The decision about where to make these compromises has been a controversy for centuries. Just as the computer and its programming is a subject of study and discussion for the modern intellectual, our forefathers deliberated the pros and cons of one temperament versus another. The word temperament comes from the Latin word, *temperare*, meaning proper mixing. What is the proper mix?

I had better mix another Irish coffee, but with more coffee and less cognac this time. I want to keep talking tonight.

The mix depended mostly on what type of music was performed. If many fifths were used, the fifths in use would preferably be pure and the thirds would have to suffer. This describes Pythagorean temperament, which was in use until the end of the sixteenth century. The meantone temperament, which was in use later, favored the thirds. The commonly used thirds were tuned pure in favor of the rarer thirds and the fifths.

In the late Baroque Era, musicians tried to tune the commonly used thirds and the fifths as pure as possible, while the other intervals had to suffer greatly. These were the Werckmeister and Kirnberger temperaments.

Discussions are now underway about which temperament J.S. Bach was using for his well-tempered clavier. The esthetic fascination of these older temperaments versus the modern equal temperament is that the intervals were adapted for the different music to be played. Another way of looking at the problem is to realize that the note G sharp is not supposed to be the same as the A flat. The G sharp is lower than the A flat. On the modern piano they are both played on the same key!

In the past some harpsichords were built with separate black keys for each flat and sharp note. (On the usual keyboard, one black key is shared for two "different" notes; for example, A flat and G sharp share the same black key.) These harpsichords were rather cumbersome to play and only a few instruments with the double black keys were made. I use this as an example to illustrate to what efforts the musicians of the seventeenth and eighteenth centuries went in their attempts to solve the problems of temperament in music. This problem mostly applies to keyboard instruments. The lucky string players only have to move a finger slightly downward on the string to go from A flat to G sharp.

It does not take too long to change the temperament on the harpsichord. If we are lucky enough to attend a baroque concert, and between major pieces we find ourselves waiting for the harpsichordist to re-tune the instrument, chances are that some sharps are being changed to flats, or vice versa. If we inform our friends about this, we will be considered expert baroqueniks.

At the end of the eighteenth century, the trend was to get away from these "temperamental" difficulties. The equal temperament, which was actually known for some time, became the standard for tuning. The octave was carved up into twelve exact intervals. The compromise was made, not by making some intervals better than others, but by making them all equally bad. (This sounds like all the disadvantages of democracy!)

That is how the modern keyboards are tuned now, except for the esoteric harpsichord.

One direct and logical result of the equal temperament is the twelve-tone music system. The major advantage of the equal temperament is that the instrument can be played in all keys without re-tuning. However, artistically we pay a large price for this. There is no differentiation between keys anymore. The fact that we play in C major or in G major makes no artistic difference except for the difference in pitch between C and the G. We lose the temperamental tensions by using the equal temperament. In the older temperaments, when further away from the original key, the temperament would get worse. This was used very effectively to create tension. There is no pure interval except for the octave. The thirds are especially bad and when combined with the fifths (i.e., in the triad CEG), the sound becomes agitated and unsure. As stated before, the modern string players do not necessarily have to follow the equal temperament as long as they are not playing with a modern piano. Maybe that is the reason I like a string quartet so much more than a piano string trio. Another disadvantage of the equal temperament is that it is difficult to tune, at least for me, and I always admire an accomplished piano tuner.

The different temperaments have been only recently re-discovered. Not too long ago the revivers of the harpsichord were playing baroque music in equal temperament. We must be grateful to the scholars who have done all the groundwork and research in finding the baroque treatises regarding the different temperaments. We are waiting for more research that will tell us about the temperament that Bach used!

I will not go into detail about how to tune these different temperaments by listening to the beats of the overtones. It suffices to say that, to my surprise, the sound of the ocean waves does not seem to interfere with hearing the beats. One advantage of the small size of my harpsichord is that I have only one set of strings to tune and less than six octaves.

I tuned my harpsichord in meantone today so I could play some of the oldies of the early seventeenth century. I am looking forward to playing again tomorrow. Great! But now I am too tired and will crawl into bed. Good night.

DAY 13

June 28. Latitude 24°15′, longitude 143°30′ (roughly). Magnetic heading is 250 degrees. That is where I am supposed to go. Wind is on starboard beam, pretty much aft. This is good sailing, because the boat is pretty much on her own. There is no need to adjust the sails, so household chores can be taken care of. I can make music and do my dictation. The only disadvantage is the tremendous rolling.

I am about 900 nautical miles from destination. I went to bed early. However, I woke up at 3:00 a.m. and could not sleep anymore. I have been reading William F. Buckley Jr.'s book, *Atlantic High*. I plan to write him a letter when I return. He writes about his experiences on a sailing trip across the Atlantic during which all his companions were to keep a diary—which he later used for his book. There are so many similarities in the difficulties he had with equipment that it is fun to read. Above all, he is a fine writer. I would like to encourage him to single-hand the Pacific and write a book about it. I will offer him my boat, which is well equipped for this kind of trip. In his book he states he is very conscientious about answering the multitude of letters he must receive daily. Maybe I can influence him to write another book. If he is not inclined to do so, I may try to put something together myself, even though I have never written anything of substance except some sporadic scientific articles. My daily dictations, which serve as my log, might be useful for that purpose.

My refrigeration is now completely out of order. The butter and eggs are still perfectly all right. The more perishable goods are stored in the bow, which is the coolest place, close to the water and out of the sun.

Gondica wrapped each apple and orange separately so that if one rotted it would not spread to the others. Of about fifty fruits, only one was spoiled. That is something to remember for people on long ocean voyages. Each bag has "orange" or "apple" written on it. No abbreviations which might confuse the tired sailor. This gives the reader some notion of the nurturing care my wife can give!

I reviewed the damage to the stanchion and the spinnaker pole. It is unlikely that any of it can be repaired in Kauai. It will not interfere much with the return trip, though, when there will be little chance to use the spinnaker pole. Most of the sailing will be done close to the wind, when the spinnaker is of no use.

One thing that bothers me is the fact that I would love to go for a swim in this hot weather and in that beautiful cool, blue water. Tying myself to the boat would improve the safety, but if just one thing goes wrong it would be difficult to get back into the boat again. By putting the boat in irons she would barely move, but even then it would be risky, and after all this is a race! Instead, I use a bucket of sea water and shower with it several times a day.

I have not seen another boat for several days nor have I been in contact with anybody by radio. I must admit that I secretly enjoy the solitude. Now that the boat takes care of herself it is like being on a cruise, except that I have to do my own cooking, which I do not mind. The loss of the foresail is, in a way, a blessing. I do not have to worry about that big sail anymore, or about winning the race for that matter. It is amazing how many things can go wrong on a boat and not actually interfere with safety. This is in contrast with flying, where even small calamities are often dangerous. On a sailboat one may run out of wind, but the boat will continue to float and the surgery on Monday morning will have to wait! Nothing can be done about that.

Worry is one of the reasons that I gave up flying. When I was taking off I was concerned that I was carrying too much fuel to get the plane off the ground. Once aloft I was immediately anxious about running out of fuel. There was always something to worry about. I loved flying nevertheless. After obtaining my student pilot license as an intern, I ran out of money to rent a plane to fly the required hours necessary to get my full license. To save money, I bought a plane! An ad in the paper said, "Flying club asks members, must be of good character." I felt that I definitely qualified. At the meeting place at the local gas station I entrusted my fifty dollars to the other three members of the club. At the hospital everybody was critical about my naiveté and doubted that I would ever hear from my club members again. A month later they called to inform me that they had bought a P.T. 23, an old Air Force training plane. Up I went, enjoying it immensely. The problem with the plane was that it used so much gas that it was cheaper to rent a small one. No radio, no navigational equipment except for the compass! I later flew in Holland where the weather is a problem. Another problem was that every few minutes I found myself over a different, not always friendly, country. Sailing is surely more relaxing. Several of my colleagues have been lost in non-commercial flying accidents.

Doctors are known high risk flyers. Thinking they are so close to God, they believe that they also know how to fly. They always seem to have some important surgery scheduled for Monday morning, and regardless of the weather they leave Nevada to fly back over the mountains. All the things that have gone wrong so far and may go wrong on my boat in the future do not compare with the emergencies that may develop in the airplane.

I usually have had luck when things did not go according to schedule on many of my trips. It seems that the unexpected makes for positive experiences. I had not foreseen that all three jib halyards would give up, but now I am probably enjoying my trip much more. I certainly am more relaxed because the sailing, even though considerably slower, is a lot simpler this way and leaves me more time to enjoy myself in other ways.

Talking about adversities on trips, in 1954 I was traveling to the United States on an emigrant ship with special rates for exchange students. I had been well prepared for the trip and I was planning to travel from New York to the West Coast by Greyhound bus. My main concern was how to get my huge ship trunk off the boat in New York and across the United States to Berkeley.

Two days out on the Atlantic Ocean I was called to see the captain of the ship who, very embarassed, told me the "bad" news that my trunk had been put on the wrong boat. My trunk was on its way to Halifax, Canada! "Hurrah," I thought—but looked very grim of course. "What can we do to rectify this terrible mistake?" the captain asked. I was glad to help him out of this predicament. When I arrived in Berkeley a few weeks later my *hut-koffer* was waiting for me. The shipping line had sent it by railroad from Halifax to Berkeley! That's the way I feel about my broken halyards and I am having a great time!

I enjoy playing the harpsichord and occasionally I take it on deck. I am not studying any new works, but playing my old friends like Froberger and Sweelinck and Louis Couperin. For later works I run out of keys on my little *kind*. The *kind* ("child," translated from Dutch) is a copy of a seventeenth century Flemish harpsichord that consists of two parts.

The "mother," which was a larger, eight-foot instrument, could be played in unison with another, smaller four-foot (*kind*) instrument resting on top of the mother. The *kind* could easily be removed and taken along in the stagecoach as a practice instrument.

My *kind* probably has the honor of being the first one to cross the Pacific. It was built for me in Berkeley by master harpsichord maker and friend, John Phillips, from the drawings made by Hubbard Harpsichord Builders in Boston. I bought the plans and kit originally from Mrs. Hubbard and John was not interested in working on it until he heard that I was going to build it myself. That was too much for him. He knows what a lousy craftsman I am. This *kind* does not have the brilliance of the Italian harpsichord John built for me, but it has a surprisingly nice sound and it fits in my boat! Instead of the usual flowers as ornaments, John painted some crabs on the soundboard to give it a nautical touch.

My cocktail hour still starts at 18:00 hours PDT. Because of the distance from California, it stays light much longer and I will have to watch that my cocktail hour does not get too prolonged!

DAY 14

June 29, 06:15 hours PDT. Latitude 24°45′ N., longitude 145°45′ W. It is dark so late because I am still using Pacific Daylight Time. I am trying to figure out what my ETA (estimated time of arrival) in Kauai is going to be. If the good winds continue, I might arrive July 4 whch was my prediction. There is a prize for the racer who arrives closest to his prediction, so maybe I'll win that one!

During the night I got up a few times, convinced that the boat was moving backwards! Each time I had to convince myself by going on deck that I *was* hallucinating. Sailing backward is the *non plus ultra* in the art of sailing and used by master sailors to get into a difficult berth. I am not in that category. Maybe I had some *maladie de grandeur*. Anyway, the boat was not going backwards and it would not, under the circumstances, have been appropriate. Up until last night I have not hallucinated on this trip. This has to do with the fact that I have not been overly exhausted. Many people on long, single-handed ocean voyages protect their sanity when very tired by hallucinating, which like dreaming seems to help us survive our subconscious tensions by giving them an outlet.

Sea tales about hallucinations abound. I remember the story of the exhausted sailor who woke up in the middle of the ocean with his anchor having been let out and it was, of course, hanging by its own weight in the deep ocean. He apparently was so exhausted that he imagined he had reached the shore and anchored for some well deserved rest!

On my first trip to Hawaii I also thought I was moving backwards, except that at that time I was not hallucinating. That time the boat practically stopped in the middle of the Pacific Ocean. Near land that usually means that the boat has run aground. But in the middle of the Pacific the average depth is between 2000 and 3000 fathoms. One fathom is six feet and my boat drew about four feet. So running aground was unlikely. There I was, the sails swollen by the wind, but the boat was not moving. When I used my snorkel to inspect the bottom of the boat, I found out that the boat had hit a large log that had almost broken through in the middle, and it was hung up on the keel of the boat in a V-formation. This acted as a huge brake. No wonder the boat was not moving.

With about forty-five pounds of weights around my waist and a snorkel I was able to free the log from the keel. I had taken a course in diving at the University of California, expecting at some time to get into such difficulties with sailing. This time the training paid off. I had decided not to take a compressed air tank along. On the ocean, with all the salt in the atmosphere, there is the worry about deterioriation of the tank. When these compressed air tanks break down, they can become like a rocket and take off right through the hull. My main problems when diving at the University were not only my age (most of the divers were young, athletic students in their twenties), but also my unpleasant habit of swallowing air. The advantage of that is that I float like a balloon in the water. When playing water polo with my younger friends I amaze them with my endurance and power to push them down when playing in the deep. But when diving I have to have many lead weights around my waist to stay down. Without them I shoot up to the surface like a helium balloon. Problems arise when, in some of the exercises, one has to leave the weights at the bottom, surface, and later retrieve them by diving (without weights) and put them on again. I had a definite physiological disadvantage, going down without my fifty-pound weights.

I am looking at the chart from California to Hawaii. This is a large chart, about three feet by three feet. Every day at noon I mark my position with a cross. I am quite a way south from the rhumb (straight) line between San Francisco and Hawaii.

One day's progress amounts to about one inch on the chart, which is frustrating. I am looking forward to using the smaller-scale chart of the Hawaiian islands, on which I will be able to plot every hour's progress. Because most of the chart represents the ocean, the only markings are the depth soundings, and the straight lines of latitude (horizontal) and longitude (vertical). This chart also has the different colored lines to help the Loran navigator. There are many more islands in the Hawaiian chain than I had realized. They go on for another thousand miles farther west of the Island of Kauai. Another surprise! At first I thought I was hallucinating, but this is really no *fata morgana.* There are a lot of seamounts north of the Hawaiian chain. There is nothing unusual about that. Seamounts are mountains rising from the sea floor but not reaching the surface. Their height is indicated in the depth of the sea above them. Remember, therefore, that the shallower the depth, the higher the sea-mount. What is unusual about these particular seamounts is that they are named after western European composers. Here we see Rossini up north, Mendelssohn down south, and another thirty composers in between, floating in the middle of the Pacific Ocean! What are they doing here, of all places? I am spending quite some time, which I now have, trying to make some sense out of this arrangement. Some composers are in bold letters, which might either relate to the importance of the composer or the relative height of the seamount. I am unable to find any correlation that way. Donizetti 1549 compares with Mozart 1004. Donizetti is a lower seamount. (Remember, the higher the seamount, the lower the depth.) Why then is Mozart printed in regular print and Donizetti in bold print? Maybe this has something to do with the particular taste of the oceanographer who had this brilliant idea? Trying to make sense out of the relative geographical location of the composers is also fruitless. The Italian Rossini is the most northern composer and the Russian Prokofiev is in the deep south, close to Oahu! I

Musicians Seamounts

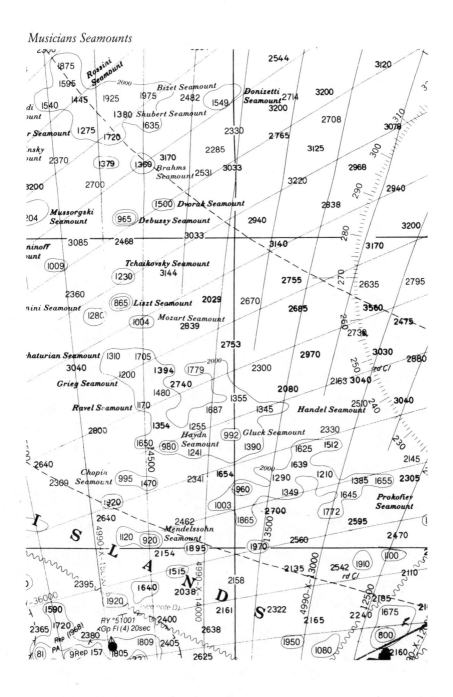

will, however, not forgive our oceanographer for omitting Bach and Beethoven. At least Handel and Haydn are present. Shubert is somewhere up north in small print. Notice that Shubert is written without the "c" of Schubert. I wonder if our oceanographer knew that there was a French composer named Shobert who wrote acceptable keyboard music and who is often played by baroquenicks. However, judging from his choice of composers (eliminating Bach!), our friend seems somewhat averse to that type of music. Another possibility is that he likes mushrooms. The tragic fate of the whole Shobert family was that they all died from mushroom poisoning! I am suspicious that we are dealing with a Russian or at least an Eastern European oceanographer, not only because of the missing "c" in Shubert (Russians do not need the "c" to produce the same "sch" sound!) but also because of the preponderance of Eastern European Composers north of the Hawaiian islands.* On the return trip, sailing farther north in order to go around the Pacific High, these composers must be honored by having their music played when the boat crosses over their seamounts. Special attention will have to paid when crossing the Handel Mount because it will also be his 300th birthday. What a day that will be! We do not have to worry so much about Bach and Scarlatti, who also have their tricentennials in 1985. They have no seamounts!

*To find out how wrong my assumption was, read the "Addendum to Day 14 of Daybook Regarding Musicians Seamounts" at the end of this book. Also, the French composer's name is usually spelled the German way— Schobert! Sorry!

14:00 hours PDT. Fiddled with the radio this morning and talked to race headquarters in Kauai. I got a lady on the phone and gave her my position. Nobody had come in yet, but they expected the multihull to arrive soon.

The answering service on the mainland had no messages except for a question about my having Hawaiian dancing girls aboard? And one message from a patient, letting me know that she was praying for me!

I also talked to my sister, Marijke van Meeuwen, in Holland, so she could reassure my worrying mother about my safety. Of course, the occasion allowed me to show off my ability to communicate with anybody in the world on my SSB radio!

The high seas telephone operator at KMI in Point Reyes was impressed with my making a call to Europe! He probably does not realize that the call to KMI costs $35 for the first three minutes, while the call to Holland only adds about $6. So everything is relative. It is better not to think about a further breakdown of the cost of these High Seas telephone calls, taking into consideration the cost of the SSB and its installation and the paucity of calls that will ever be made. On the one hand, I have put so much money into this unit, including its installation with grounding and a new antenna, that I would like to get my money's worth and use it a lot. But, at $35 minimum a call, that does not become very attractive either!

At least I am lucky that it *works*. Many people, once out on the ocean, find out that their unit does not work. My unit has the unpleasant habit of going "out of lock," which means that after I am finally able to make contact and want to start talking, the station disappears from the readout. I have to start dialing all the numbers over again and in the meantime hope that our little god, the high seas telephone operator, is still standing by.

The high seas operator gave me a hard time this morning and I am still a little shook up because of it. I am very proud of my high seas radio. It is one piece of equipment for which even my wife insisted that no costs were to be spared, so that I would have a reliable radio and be able to communicate with the shore. After trying many different frequencies, I finally got the high seas operator on the line. Then came the usual question, "What is the name of your vessel?" This is already intimidating. They do not talk about a boat. "Vessel" is the word, like the police on land talk about a "vehicle." All of a sudden I realized that I had misplaced a card with the letters of the Alistelle spelled phonetically. "Proceed and spell the name of your vessel." I damned the idea of having given my vessel such a complicated name, but "proceeded" with ALPHA LIMA, while frantically trying to find my cue card to no avail. ISAAC, SIMON.... I knew the last two were guesses and there came the response. "I do not read you, please repeat." I tried again with ISAAC and SIMON, but the operator was heartless and came back with, "Please spell in the phonetic alphabet." I knew by now what the operator was thinking about my I.Q., and the most humiliating option left for me was to spell out the name of my boat, A—L—I—S—T—E—L—L—E.

The rest of the morning I rehearsed: Alpha-Lima-India-Sierra-Tango-Echo-Lima-Lima-Echo. When I made the call to my sister in Holland I had graduated and I got the same operator on the line. He was now properly impressed with my progress and after I told him that I was just a simple solo sailor and not the captain of a big ship, he was forgiving and told me that: "even some captains who have been plying the seas for forty years don't know it." This really made me feel better, although I am now worrying about those captains and I hope they are not plying the seas in my neighborhood.

23:00 hours PDT. Late in the evening, listening to organ music. The sound of the organ reverberates because of all the teakwood. The volume control is set quite high. There are no neighbors here to complain about the loud music so late at night. I had to go on deck a few times because there were some splashing noises in the water. Maybe the dolphins like organ music and I feel like having an audience. The music must carry quite far in the water with my vibrating hull.

This reminds me of my student days when I was playing a nice baroque organ in a seventeenth century church in the university town of Leyden in Holland. I used to play late at night. The streets around the church were about twelve feet wide. The bedroom windows of the houses nearby were about that distance away from the church windows. The neighbors must have been unable to sleep when I was playing, rather poorly I may add. They never complained. Maybe they had lost their hearing by now, or maybe the good burghers of Leyden were still stunned by the decision they had made in 1572. During the war of independence against Spain, Leyden had been surrounded for several months by the Spanish Army, but the city fought off the Spaniards and was never taken. In gratitude for their courage and perseverance, William of Orange gave them two choices: they would never have to pay taxes anymore or they would get a university. They chose the latter! What a quest for learning! I would prefer that the citizens of Berkeley not be given that choice!

It is really blowing now and I am making about eight knots while going where I want to go. There is no need to worry about carrying too much canvas because there are no more halyards left in front of the mast. The only sails left to reef are the mainsail and the mizzen. It is unlikely that there will be that much wind anymore. From the weather report, I have been able to decipher the presence of Hurricane Christina, but she seems nice enough to continue going west and is passing the big island farther south.

Now that I do not have to spend too much time changing sails, I can enjoy myself in a different way. I am now listening to some Beethoven piano sonatas played by Alfred Brendel. My hi-fi system has 120-watt output with separate preamp and amplifier. This twelve-volt system is a better way to play hi-fi, so my technical friends tell me, because there is no need for the heavy transformers to bring down the voltage. I love live music, but am very impressed with my hi-fi system, and the teakwood in the cabin seems to function as a soundboard.

Some time ago when Gustav Leonhardt, the eminent Dutch baroque scholar, was staying at my house, I was very proud to show off my sound system, especially to somebody who had been instrumental in the making of so many beautiful recordings. He was surprised that I listened to it for enjoyment. For him it was more a matter of "reference." Of course, it is different for somebody who is listening and playing with the finest musicians of the world. Anyway, I am happy as a bird with my system. It is highly unlikely that Mr. Brendel, whom I have never met, would be willing to fly down in a helicopter and play on my ship. On top of that, he probably would be as sick as a dog.

DAY 16

July 1. Latitude 23°35' N., longitude 150° W. I was very negligent yesterday. I did not dictate at all. There are two reasons for that. One is that I have been really busy with the sails, going for the wind ... oh, my God, there we go again. The mainsail was backed again. I may try another tack later. I lost another halyard. This time it was the staysail halyard, which came down with the drifter. Luckily, I have another halyard. I had forgotten about that one until I looked up and saw it.

Yesterday I barely made 110 miles! Really disturbing are the rain squalls when all of a sudden the wind comes from a different direction and with different strength. The rain squalls are dense enough to set the alarm off on the radar watch. That is all right when the squall is coming in my direction, so I can be prepared. But most of them pass by without bothering me, except to awaken me with the alarm!

The second reason that I did not dictate yesterday is the fact that I was again in contact with another racer. Ken Roper in the Harrier is a little south of me and at about the same longitude. We talked for a long time on the VHF. Ken comes from an army family. His father graduated from West Point and served in World War II in New Guinea. Ken lives in Virginia near Washington and is, at the age of fify-four, a retired brigadier general who served in Vietnam as an aviator. He leaves his boat in the East Bay. He has done this trip before and will either bring the boat back alone or with somebody else. He is in contact with the Baobob, which is the boat behind him, and with whom I have no radio contact. Ken has a ham radio and will contact some other boats. He heard that the multihull is supposed to arrive today. We will talk to each other again later in the day.

When I woke up this morning, my radar was not working. It turned out that my number-one house battery was drained and

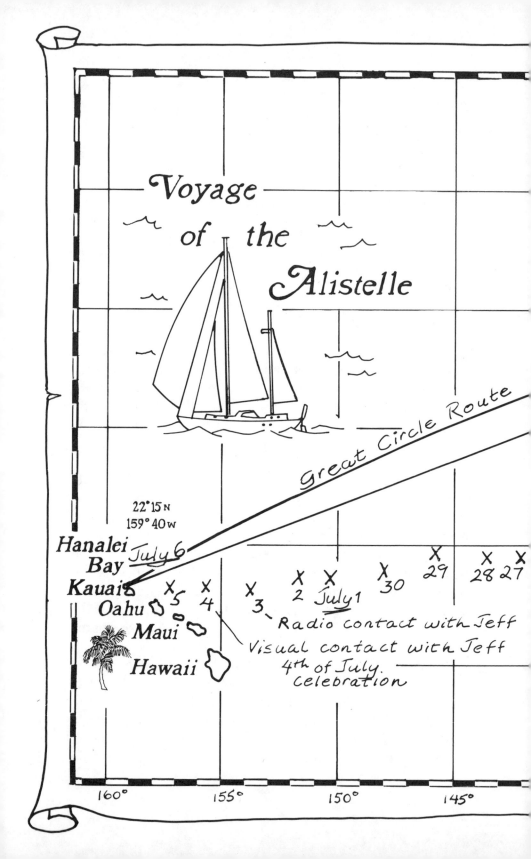

Voyage

of the

Alistelle

Great Circle Route

22° 15 N
159° 40 w

Hanalei Bay — July 6

Kauai

Oahu

Maui

Hawaii

X 5   X 4   X 3   X 2   X July 1   X 30   X 29   X 28   X 27

Radio contact with Jeff

Visual contact with Jeff

4th of July. celebration

160°   155°   150°   145°

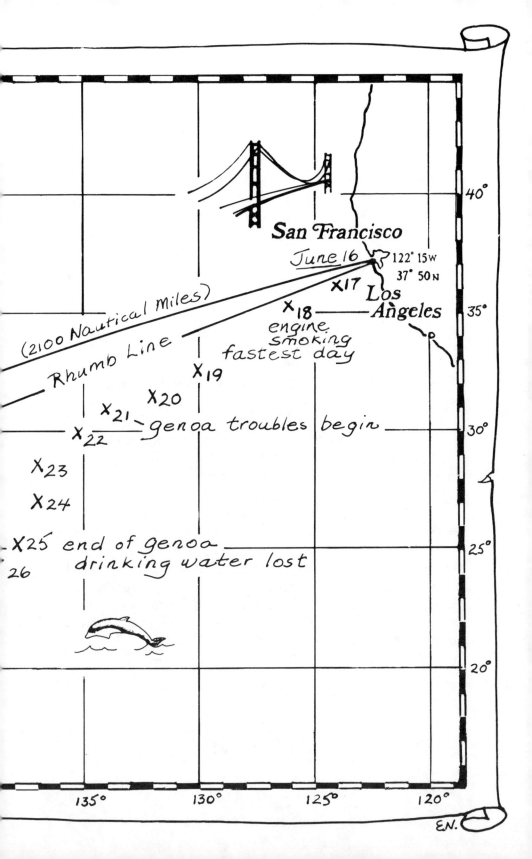

apparently the radar automatically shuts off. My generator charges about sixty to eighty amperes per hour and the batteries are rated for about 200 amp hours. It took about three hours of charging, but all the batteries are again fully charged. Whatever happens, there is now enough "juice" to keep my lights burning during the night for the rest of the trip. I still will be able to use the radar watch, even if my generator should give out.

Made a lot of music yesterday between squalls, but I do not read very much. I am intellectually very lazy and just like to play old favorites on the harpsichord or listen to the hi-fi. My oldest daughter, Julia, gave me her dissertation on the left and right brain, which I promised to read. There is a Conrad book I wanted to read and a Belgian book that Gondica recommended.

These squalls are miserable because I have to get out quickly in the rain before I have a chance to put on some clothes. The rain is good for the boat though. It washes all the salt from the rigging and from the chrome and varnish.

Here I am, twenty minutes later. The tack has been changed to port tack and the boat is sailing much better. Not only is it more comfortable, but I am going 150 degrees off the wind while all sails are on starboard with the drifter boomed out. It is stupid that I did not do that earlier. It makes me realize what poor a sailor I am. If the wind stays in the same quarter, there will be no need to change the sails anymore! That would be great! Well, we'll see....

DAY 17

July 2. Latitude, 24° N., longitude 151°15′ W. Yesterday was another day without wind. The less wind there is, the more work there is to be done. It is really frustrating that the harder I have to work, the less distance I travel. The reason is that the sails go back and forth in these low winds. Only once during the night did the wind pick up, so I had to get up to bring down the drifter.

There was a very poor connection with the ladies of the answering service, but I think they could at least understand my present position, which they will relay to my friends and family. I am still in VHF radio contact with Ken Roper. He is about twenty-six miles away from me, which is about the maximum distance we are able to talk to each other on the radio. He had some more news about the other sailors. Mark Rudiger is ready to come in, but is stuck without wind just off Kauai. The catamaran came in yesterday. The Intrigue is quite a bit ahead of us. I have no contact with the Baobob. She must be too far behind us.

All of a sudden, I realize that there have been no more fixes on the satellite navigator. The satnav picks up a signal from a satellite overhead which tells the present position in latitude and longitude, the exact Greenwich Mean Time and the time and declination of the overpass of the next satellite. At the same time, between satellite readings, it will keep the position updated as long as the sailor feeds in the information of speed, drift, and magnetic course. This information has been very casually updated. I figured that every few hours, with the passage of a satellite, the data would be automatically updated anyway. When there is a satellite overhead and the satnav is reading the data, a red light comes on. There has been no red light for quite a while and it is possible that my position is quite different from the present reading on the satnav. The data have only been updated by my unreliable input. I have, for example, not adjusted for the change in speed and for the different headings. The time of my last reliable satnav fix will remain a mystery. Loran does not give any readings this far off the coast and the Hawaiian stations are directed more towards the Western Pacific. It is important to know my position, especially now that I am getting close to the islands. I prefer not to end up on the wrong island! From the ocean they all look the same.

This reminds me of the story of another sailor who was supposed to meet his wife on one of the islands. After he made the landfall he went to a telephone booth to give directions to his wife about how to walk to the rendezvous. It took quite a few phone calls and confused looking for each other before he realized that he had landed on the wrong island!

No red light on my satnav. I do not know what went wrong. It is probably some short in the antenna on the mizzen mast where there is quite a bit of wear and tear. I am pretty good at celestial navigation and this afternoon will try to get some sights. This is rather annoying because it will take quite some time to plot my position. Now I wished I had bought the Platz computer which has the almanac and all other tabulations in its memory. It would have saved a lot of time, but I did not foresee having to resort to celestial navigation.

14:00 hours PDT. Finally, some better winds. Nothing like yesterday afternoon when there were no winds at all. Tried to reach the Harrier, but was unable to make contact. I talked to the Baobob which is apparently catching up with me fast in these light winds. The Baobob is about fifty miles behind me in longitude *if* my presumed position is correct. The satnav is definitely not picking up signals, and I am now very careful to keep the dead reckoning up to date.

Because of my satnav's refusal to cooperate, I need to take a sun sight today to find out where I am. This requires some time. While waiting between taking the different sun shots, I will try to explain the theory and the technique of the simple noon sight. This noon shot is the simplest celestial navigation. To combat my loneliness and to refresh my memory, I will talk and explain the procedure while doing it.

This loneliness on the ocean encourages monologues. The psychologists tell us that these monologues are a good way of compensating for these feelings. Slocum, the first solo circum-navigator, conversed with the moon and made "the porpoises leap and the turtles poke their heads up out of the sea." At least I am talking into the microphone. My sanity is therefore not that far gone. Some sailors say that it is sometimes good to listen to the tape afterwards and hear oneself. That critical turning point in my sanity has not yet been reached.

We will only talk about the sun, but there are the other heavenly bodies (that phrase does make me feel lonely!) such as the moon, planets, and stars. We will have to refresh our memory about a few terms, such as latitude, longitude, and nautical mile. When Columbus sailed back to the Americas for the second time, using celestial navigation, he was able to predict *where* he would make his landfall, but not *when*. He was mostly sailing west from Spain. He was able to determine his latitude but not his longitude. The latitude, expressed in degrees north or south, tells how many miles south or north one is from the Equator. At the Equator the latitude is 0°. At the North Pole it is 90° north. The longitude indicates in degrees how far east or west we are from an imaginary line that runs through both Poles and through Greenwich (near London, England). Greenwich is longitude 0°. San Francisco is about 122° west. At the International Date Line, somewhere in the Pacific at 180°, longitude turns east. Japan is at about 160° east longitude. We know all this, of course, but the sun is hot and we are tired so let's go slowly. We will talk more about longitude later, but for now, we return to latitude.

It can be advantageous to know where one is in relation to the latitude and longitude. In the near future we will be able to read our coordinates (latitude and longitude) from a tiny wrist satellite navigator. We will then find our position on the local map or chart. If the present trend continues, it is likely that the satellite navigator will eventually come down to that size. But, like my satnav, it will be inclined to break down. We therefore better continue.

It is nice to know the latitude of a place or city. It will inform us about the weather, and if one is a sun worshipper, the less latitude (like a bikini) the better. Why not mention the latitude after the city's name? Vacation planning would be easier. We usually seem to travel either east-west, north-south or vice versa.

Briefly, the latitude tells us how far south or north we are. We will learn how, in a fairly simple way, the latitude can be determined with the help of the sun. The sun has two movements in relation to the earth. Of course it is the earth that is moving and not the sun, but we are tired and want to keep things simple. Every day the sun rotates around the world from the east to the west. This has to do with longitude, and we will come back to that later. We are now interested in the north-south movement of the sun because that helps us in determining our latitude. Through the ages, the latitude has been the easy one to determine. It was the longitude that was the real stumbling block for our forefathers.

We know that through the year the sun moves from the Equator (on approximately September 21) to the southern latitude of 23.5° (to the Tropic of Capricorn) around December 21, back to the Equator on approximately March 23, then to the northern latitude of 23.5° (to the Tropic of Cancer) on June 21. Between those two latitudes are the "tropics." The two times a year when the sun crosses the Equator are called the equinoxes.

Starting on December 21, the sun moves farther north every day until it reaches its highest latitude on June 21.

Through the centuries, December 21 in the northern hemisphere and June 21 in the southern hemisphere have provided an occasion for celebrations because of the return to better weather and longer daylight. The Peruvians, living in the southern hemisphere, celebrate their sun festival, *Inti-Raymi*. When I was in Cuzco a few years ago enjoying this festival on June 23, the people were very proud that their ancestors, the Incas, were better astronomers than their European counterparts. The Europeans, who set the date for celebration on December 25, were four days late in determining that the sun was moving higher in the sky again, while the Incas were only two days late on June 23.

In the tropics the seasons are, if present at all, less pronounced. That creates its own problems. On Manan Island in Papua, New Guinea, I met Nancy Lutkehaus, an anthropologist from Columbia University, who was doing a follow-up study on the work done by a British colleague in the thirties. She wanted to find out what had happened to the Papuans who had been interviewed forty years ago by her colleague. Her problem was that the natives had no method of counting time and therefore had no idea of seasons or years. The only parameters she had with which to establish a time reference were the time of World War II (before, during, or after the war) and the various heights of the children. The war was obvious because of the activity of planes in the air. By painstakingly asking about the heights of the children, and determining the order of births, she was able to create some chronological order. This enabled her to determine the fate and whereabouts of the Papuans interviewed forty years ago. Quite an achievement! Not to mention having to learn their language. It may be nice not to know one's age or have a calendar or clock. For us modern people, this is almost incomprehensible.

Local noon is the time of the day at a particular location when the sun is the highest in the sky. That time will be the same on any spot on that particular longitude. The angle of the sun will be different north or south on that longitude and will reflect the latitude. We should forget the usual noon or twelve o'clock. It is a pity that even the English language with its rich vocabulary does not make the distinction. One has to be careful with double meanings of words. Take for example the word "smoking." When a psychiatrist asked his patient if she smoked after intercourse, she answered, "I haven't noticed." She did not smoke cigarettes and he should have understood.

After being forewarned about the use of local noon let us assume we are on vacation. We drank too much the evening before and wake up on the beach, not remembering where we are. We stand up and realize that the sun is almost overhead because we only throw a little shadow. Half-an-hour later there will be no shadow at all, and half-an-hour later again will be the same amount of shadow as when we woke up. The date on our watch is June 21. The headache is gone, our brain starts working and we realize we are where? On June 21 (at local noon) the sun is straight overhead (at 90°) at the Tropic of Cancer. Latitude is 23.5° north. We have determined our latitude.

But we could be in Africa, Mexico, Hawaii, or many other places around the world that have beaches and are on the Tropic of Cancer. Here comes the determination of longitude. We always have our watches on zone time (Pacific Standard Time) and forgot to change them to Pacific Daylight Time (forward one hour). We do remember that and it makes it easier for us. Our watches read about 11.30 a.m. Aha. In Europe and West Africa they are way ahead of us timewise and are preparing to go to bed. Also, if our watches are at California zone time, (Pacific Standard Time), they will somewhat correlate with local noon at twelve o'clock noon. Our watches read 11:30 hours. We now have also roughly determined our longitude. However, it is not even twelve noon on our watches (it is 11:30 a.m.). So we must therefore be slightly east of the Pacific time zone. The sun moves from east to west around the world. In twenty-four hours it travels 360 degrees or two times 180 degrees. On the globe or world chart we can see where we are. I hope it is clear now how the determination of longitude is "time"-related.

Well, did you figure out where we are? How about Mazatlan, Mexico? Another possibility is Baja California because we have been very inaccurate with our time. Luckily, our watch indicates whether the time is a.m. or p.m. If the time of observation had been 11:30 p.m. Pacific Time, we would be 12:00 hours or 180 degrees further west and we would be looking at the Arabian Sea, somewhere in the western part of India! Without any navigational instruments, we have determined our latitude with the altitude of the sun at local noon and, with the help of our watches, we have now some idea about our longitude.

Now let's go back to the latitude in general. We were lucky that it happened to be June 21 when we did our figuring and that we happened to be on the Tropic of Cancer. If we had been in San Francisco, the sun would not have been ninety degrees overhead, so we would have thrown a shadow at all times, which by the way, would have been the smallest at local noon. At local noon, north of the Tropic of Cancer, the sun will be the highest on June 21 and will gradually go down until December 21. The Almanac tells us the exact latitude of the sun at any given time, so it follows that by measuring the height of the sun with a sextant, we will be able to determine how far north or south of the sun we are or, in other terms, what our latitude is. Between those magic dates, December 21 and June 21, the sun moves somewhere in between those two magic latitudes, the two Tropics. This is where the nautical almanac helps us. It tells the declination (latitude) of the sun (and other heavenly bodies) for every day, hour, and minute of a particular year.

Nowadays we use the sextant to measure the height of the sun. The ancient Egyptians used the shadow of the sun to do this. For example, they used the sun's shadow to measure the distance between two cities along the Nile. The Nile runs pretty well north. They placed two vertical poles of the same length, one in the northern city and one in the southern city. By comparing the length of the shadow of the two poles at the same time they were able, being accomplished mathematicians, to determine the distance between the two cities.* Some high school whiz kid in San Francisco might want to duplicate this procedure over the telephone with his or her cousin in Los Angeles; however, this might not work too well. Better do it between Omaha, Nebraska and Houston, Texas. These cities are roughly on the same longitude.

Let us discuss latitude further. As stated before, the latitude at the Equator is 0° and at the north pole 90°. Each degree represents sixty nautical miles. It is indeed helpful to know our latitude roughly. If we live in San Francisco, for example, at latitude 38° north, we know right away that we are 2,880 ($38 \times 60 = 2{,}880$) nautical miles from the Equator and 3,420 ($90 - 38 = 52 \times 60 = 3{,}120$) miles from the North Pole. Now isn't that nice to know? So, for north-south, up and down, that works great. Going east-west can only be done at the Equator. That is actually where the nautical mile is derived from.

The earth, being roughly round, is divided at the Equator into 360 degrees. 360 times sixty nautical miles is approximately 21,600 nautical miles. That works pretty well and there is no need to worry that nautical miles will be changed into kilo meters. A nautical mile is slightly longer than a statute mile. A statute mile is about 1.6 kilometers, while the nautical mile is about 1.8 kilometers.

*See drawing on page 277.

One degree longitude is only sixty nautical miles at the Equator. Further north or south the circles get smaller. To measure off a nautical mile on the nautical chart, we always use the degrees and minutes indicating the latitude on the left or right side of the chart. These figures are not exactly correct since the earth is a little pear-shaped, that is, flattened at the poles and bulging at the Equator. All this has fascinated scientists through the centuries, but for us simple souls, the earth is round.

Now a little more about longitude and time and I will explain what I have been doing meanwhile here in the hot noon sun with my sextant, watch, pencil, paper and nautical almanac. I will then be able to tell where I am without a tequila hangover. As we discussed before, every day the sun moves westward around the world in twenty-four hours. The problem is, where do we start counting? Why not in Greenwich near London? At the longitude of Greenwich, which is 0°, local noon corresponds with twelve o'clock Greenwich Mean Time. (Midnight is either 0 or 24 hours.) This premise has been internationally accepted. Actually, in the last century some nations still had their own "world time"! The Portuguese started their "world time" in Lisbon and guess who started it in Paris? Through the ages it has been a battle of national ego trips because each nation considered itself the only world power. Even the French have accepted Greenwich longitude and time! However, we are not supposed to call it Greenwich Time anymore, but International Standard Time! (There were also some difficulties with the acceptance of the English-American international S.O.S. (Save Our Souls) sign. The French wanted *m'aidez*, which means "help me" in French. To the unilingual Americans that sounded like "May Day." Tolerant as they often are, the Americans deferred to the French preference—so May Day it is.)

People all around the world like to have their local noon correspond as much as possible with twelve o'clock noon.

Therefore, the world is divided into one-hour time zones. It was not always that way. I remember that in Europe the time zones between the different countries were measured in minutes. It is obvious that local noon does not jump east every hour, and that this is a gradual process. When we look in the nautical almanac, we find the Greenwich Hour Angle (GHA), which tells us up to the second at what longitude local noon is in Greenwich Mean Time. For that purpose, in navigation we use Greenwich Mean time, or International Standard Time, as it is called now.

At the Equator the circumference of the earth is, as we should remember now, 21,600 (360×60 nautical miles $= 21,600$) nautical miles. The sun goes around once in twenty-four hours, which equals 86,400 (60 seconds $\times$ 60 minutes $\times$ 24 hours $= 86,400$) seconds. That amounts to roughly four seconds for a mile, which means it takes the sun four seconds to move a nautical mile. In other words, if our watch is forty seconds off, the error in longitude will be a minimum of ten miles. At least at the Equator. That ain't no hay! Further north or south the error will be even greater. And our friend Columbus was working with hourglasses! That is why the longitude took so long to be mastered. It was barely practical on the heeling sailing ships to take along one of those grandfather clocks with its long swinging pendulum and heavy weights. It was not until 1714 that the Board of Longitude at Sea was set up. Sir Isaac Newton and Edmund Halley were consulted and their final recommendation was to offer a prize of 20,000 pounds to the person who could make a timepiece allowing the navigator an accuracy of thirty miles after the usual six-week voyage to the West Indies. The prize was finally given to John Harrison in 1764. It is ironic that only recently have accurate clocks been made, now that the chronometer has almost become obsolete with the advent of the radio.

Radio station WWV in Fort Collins, Colorado, sends out the exact time, day and night. On my satnav, the time is adjusted every few hours when a satellite is overhead.

Another way to look at time: If it takes four seconds for the sun to travel one mile at the Equator, one can travel with (or without) the sun at 900 (15×60 nautical miles/hour = 900) nautical miles per hour. If one hates daylight, charter a supersonic plane and there will be no need to put on goggles. Further north or south from the Equator, there is no need for that high speed. If afraid of high speed, one might want to walk around the North Pole. As a matter of fact, not too long ago when the supersonic plane Concorde was not doing well, British Airways offered a New Year's Eve trip from London to Rio de Janeiro in order to prolong the ecstasy of celebrating New Year's midnight. There are other slightly less expensive ways to prolong the ecstasy, but they have nothing to do with navigation, though they may have something to do with the law!

However, if we think we will not age this way, there is bad news when we arrive at the International Date Line. Suddenly one day has been added. If we really don't want to age, we will have to travel at the speed of light, but this is a whole different matter, beyond the scope of my monologue today in this hot weather.

By now we should understand latitude, longitude and, above all, local noon. We will first look at the sextant and then at the nautical almanac before I give my position away. The sextant is used to measure the angle between a heavenly body and the horizon. Remember as a kid making a periscope with two parallel mirrors in a tube for you to look over the neighbor's fence? The major difference with the sextant is that its upper mirror can move and that movement is recorded on a scale in degrees and minutes of arc. One looks through a small telescope into the lower mirror which is only half-mirrored, fixed at a forty-five degree angle when the sextant is properly held in the vertical position and aimed horizontally towards the horizon. The left half is transparent glass. The right half is mirrored and reflects the upper mirror. When the angle of the upper mirror is in the forty-five-degree angle position, the indicator on the arc will be at zero degrees. In this case, when looking through the telescope, we will see the horizon line up through the transparent and the mirrored glass. If the two images do not line up, the angle of one mirror of the sextant will have to be adjusted. Usually, the sextant comes with instructions on how to do this.

Sextant

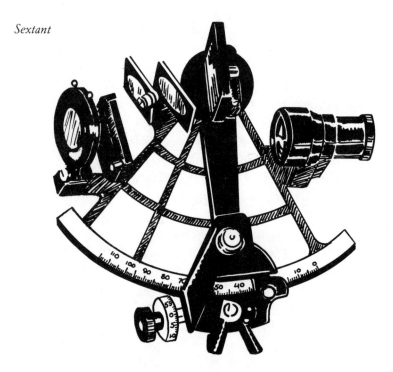

Now let us presume that the sun is fifty degrees above the horizon. The upper mirror will have to rotate, so that the index arm points to the fifty-degree mark on the arc. If that is the case, we will see the lower edge of the sun through the telescope in the lower mirrored part "kissing" the horizon in the transparent part. We usually use the lower edge of the sun and the sextant has to be completely vertical. The degrees of the arc are read off the scale. Remember, a degree at the Equator represents sixty nautical miles. The minutes then are read from another, finer (vernier) scale on the sextant. The minute is then divided into tenths. The tenths are roughly estimated between the two minute marks. For example, 10°20.8′ means ten degrees, 20.8 minutes. We do not use the seconds, but divide the minute into tenths. If we are able to guess our position to within a tenth of a mile, we are doing pretty well. Later on, we will see that the same system is followed in the nautical almanac. One more little reminder. When we start adding or substracting degrees and minutes, remember that 60° and 00.0′ equals 59° plus 60.0′.

Both mirrors of the sextant have dark glasses in different strengths to protect the eyes from too strong a light, so as not to burn a hole in the retina. The price of a sextant varies from a few dollars for a plastic one, up to several hundred dollars for a fancy one. Davis makes a very good one for the beginner and for emergency backup.

Taking a Sextant Sight

What have I been doing in the meantime? I first checked the time on my watch and compared it with the International Standard Time of radio station WWV and adjusted it up to the second. Then I turned to the daily page of July 2 in the 1984 nautical almanac. The sun is pretty high and I know that it soon will reach its highest point in the sky before coming down. That moment is going to be local noon. I want to find out two things. How high in the sky the sun is going to be, and secondly, at what International Standard Time the sun is going to be highest. To have the greatest accuracy, I start taking sights early before "noon" and I take a few sights after the sun has started lowering in the sky. For every sight I take, I write down the angle of the sun with the horizon obtained with the sextant. The highest reading obtained was 88°58.3′. Almost 90°, and almost straight overhead. Makes sense because we are probably in the Tropics (below 23.5°) and the sun has been moving south since June 21, about two weeks ago. The time that the sun was the highest was exactly 22 hours 12 minutes 0 seconds International Standard Time. The fact that the sun is almost ninety degrees high in the sky makes the accuracy of our sight rather unreliable. We have, however, taken several sights and this noonshot is done mostly as an exercise. Now we look at the almanac on the page of July 2, 1984,* at 22 hours and 23 hours GMT (Greenwich Mean Time). I read off for the sun: At 22 hours GMT the GHA is 148°58.4′ and the declination is north 22°58.4′. At 23 hours GMT the GHA is 163°58.3′ and the declination north 22°58.2′. Our time of observation was 22 hours + 12 minutes which, corrected for the Greenwich Hour Angle (GHA), adds one-fifth of the difference for the hour (15/5 = 3 degrees). This means we have to add three minutes to the GHA:

148°58.4′ + 3°00.0′ = 151°58.4′.

Believe it or not, this is supposed to be our longitude! The

---

*See page 274 for copy of page in almanac.

longitude is basically read off from the Greenwich Hour Angle which is the longitude of the sun at local noon. You saw how quickly it changes in that one hour. That is why the longitude obtained this way is not highly reliable. The sun moves around the world from east to west that fast. But look at declination, which is going to help us in determining our latitude! It hardly changed between 22 hours and 23 hours.

The declination tells in degrees how far the sun at local noon is from the Equator. Our sextant told us what the angle of the sun was in the sky as compared to the horizon. If the sun had been perpendicular above the Equator and we were at the Equator, the sextant would have given a reading of 90° and our latitude would have been 0°. Suppose the sun was at the Equator, but we were north of the Equator, and our sextant measures the sun at local noon at, let us say, 60°. Our latitude would be 30° (90° − 60°). But the sun is not at the Equator, it is further north at its declination as told in the almanac, so we have to add the declination and we have our latitude when the declination is north. To find our latitude we subtract our sextant-observed sun angle from 90° and add the declination as found in the almanac, which will be northern in this case. In the almanac we find that on July 2 at 22 hours G.M.T., the sun's declination is N 22°58.4′.

90° is 89°60.0′. This means 89 degrees plus 60.0 minutes. We divide the minutes into tenths and not into seconds. A degree represents sixty nautical miles, and one minute represents one nautical mile, which then is divided into tenths because we cannot be not more accurate than a tenth of a mile anyway. The seconds are therefore replaced by the tenths.

   89°60.0′ (90° degrees)
 − 88°58.3′ (sextant reading)
 + 22°58.4′ (declination)
 = 24°00.1′ (latitude)

Noon Sight

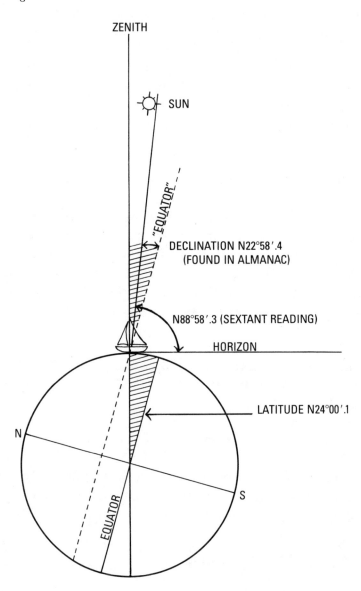

ZENITH

SUN

"EQUATOR"

DECLINATION N22°58'.4
(FOUND IN ALMANAC)

N88°58'.3 (SEXTANT READING)

HORIZON

LATITUDE N24°00'.1

N

S

EQUATOR

Is that not simple? I did not discuss some minor adjustments and corrections I had to make. All I wanted to spell out was the principle.* I am a little further south than my dead satnav has decided for me. This makes sense because I had been going farther south for a day or so before that information was fed into the satnav computer. My latitude is 24° north, and the longitude is supposedly 151°58.4'. We are almost at the 152° longitude west. Hallelujah. The fact that I can do celestial navigation does not mean that I am particularly excited about it. Will try tomorrow to get the satnav to cooperate again.

20:00 hours PDT. What an evening! The boat is going about six to seven knots, but on the ocean there are hardly any whitecaps. The wind is blowing very steadily and the boat is moving as smooth as can be. Maybe I will still arrive on July 6. I am going before the wind. The boat is going as fast as and in the same direction as the wind, and so I experience no wind. If I would have to turn around and go into the wind, the wind would roar and the boat would heel roughly against the waves. I wish I could go only with the Trade Winds, continuing from Hawaii on to Polynesia and farther. But, alas, I'm not retired yet!

Twice a day I try to reach the other sailors on VHF radio. The Baobob and the Harrier came through very poorly, but Jeff and Ken could understand me very well. (Who says I have a Dutch accent?) The Harrier is ahead of me and the Baobob is still behind me.

Ate my last *nasi-goreng.* This is an Indonesian rice dish with lots of hot spices which goes well with this hot weather. The temperature of my Heineken beer was a little above the recommended fifty-five degrees, but without the refrigerator it is impossible to get it below the temperature of the Pacific Ocean!

---

*For more detailed information about the noon sight consult the "Addendum to Day 17 of Daybook," at the end of this book.

The wine is running out. There is only one bottle of Beaujolais Nouveau left. Somewhere in one of the fifty storage places on this ship there must be more wine. I have been sleeping in the main cabin lately to be closer to the wheel. Especially with the light winds, I have to be able to see the sails and have to get on deck more often to adjust the sails or the wheel. I wish I had installed in the cabin a remote station of my Combi unit which gives the depth, wind speed, wind direction, and boat speed. The unit is in the cockpit and I spend much more time in the cabin than I had anticipated. These tiny little petty winds drive me crazy with their frequent changes in direction. During the night I have to put on the spreader lights to see what is going on.

DAY 18

July 3, 00:30 hours PDT. Cannot get myself to go to sleep. It is such a beautiful evening. The ocean is getting a little wilder. I hope it will not get too wild because that would mean I would have to go to work and adjust the sails.

I am sitting without any clothes on, watching the stars, the glittering sea, and the dark-looking sail that covers the moon once in a while. The moon is in its first quarter. Luckily, there will be moonlight when I make my landfall at night. They told me that Hanalei Bay is not that easy to find from the ocean. When sailing to Hawaii for the first time with a crew we were anxious for the landfall days ahead of time. I do not feel that way at all this time. Of course, I am looking forward to putting my feet on shore again. On the other hand, I dread the thought of ending this ecstasy. Maybe I am more of a loner than I thought!

Just found a short article about me in the magazine *Longitude 122*, June 15. Headline is "Don't forget the harpsichord!" It was obviously written by somebody who read the article about me in the *San Francisco Examiner* because the same words are used, words like "fact-finding trips in Ethiopia and New Guinea." My competitive pride is hurt by the sentence: "Ah, with a beautiful sunset and a glass of 1974 La Tours special reserve by Cabernet Sauvignon, guess who may come in last?" I am afraid, though, that I indeed will be the last one to come in. They must have been surprised to find out that on day two or three, I was probably ahead of everybody else! I wonder whether that was reported in the press. Also, I probably made the longest distance in one day. Of course, all this happened before I lost my headsails.

It is amazing how one gets publicity. Walking around naked on Broadway one is bound to get some newspaper coverage.

Same with me. Take a harpsichord along on a Transpac race and all of a sudden one becomes just a little more interesting! My main reason for being interviewed was to get publicity for my pet project, the Philharmonia Baroque Orchestra of the West. That is of a lot more interest to the reader than my harpsichord!

Still listening to music. Besides the beautiful evening, maybe it is the Irish coffee that keeps me awake. Tonight is baroque night for me. All music tonight is from the Baroque Era.

I first became interested in baroque performance about ten years ago. A well-known East Coast harpsichordist, Tim Read, was giving a concert in Berkeley at the time and invited me, knowing my interest in music and especially keyboard music, to a private recital the day before the concert. Prior to this recital, I had listened to the European baroque recordings and had even built a harpsichord myself.

That evening, when I heard an unmeasured prelude of Louis Couperin played on that beautiful French harpsichord, I realized what I had been missing. I became aware that my harpsichord had nothing to do with the real thing, and that I had missed much of the beauty of the music and the instrument when I listened to it on my state-of-the-art stereo set. Tim's recital inspired me to study baroque music. This was *it*. For the next few years this was going to be my great avocation.

For most of us the Baroque Era begins somewhere in Germany with J.S. Bach, Handel (also in England), and Telemann. In Italy the prominent composers were Vivaldi, A. Scarlatti, and Corelli. Rameau, the Couperin family, and Lully, to mention a few, were composing music in France. Domenico Scarlatti, after leaving Naples, became the prominent court keyboard player in Spain. All these composers flourished around 1700.

Earlier, around the year 1600, in what we may loosely call the early Baroque Era, we find Sweelinck in Holland, Byrd in England, and Monteverdi and Frescobaldi in Italy. J. S. Bach's sons and W. A. Mozart are at the borderline of what we can call late Baroque. Soon after the late Baroque Era, big changes developed rather abruptly. After the French Revolution in the early 1790s and western Europe entered the nineteenth century, the whole approach to the performance of music changed rapidly. Music-making became, in a way, more democratic in France and Germany. In Italy music has always belonged to the people. That may have something to do with the fact that all Italians seem to be able to sing!

In France, before the revolution, sophisticated music-making was done mostly at the courts and, to a lesser extent, in the churches. The greatest honor for the French musician was to be *musicien ordinaire du Roi*. The nobility in those days considered it part of being well bred to be proficient in the making and writing of music. Also, the art of dancing "in good taste" was part of a well-rounded education. The different courts competed to have the finest musicians. The dance master was also an important feature and each court sometimes had its own dances, which were often recorded on paper. The dance steps were meticulously explained in drawings. This not only is helpful in researching the dance itself, but also in interpreting the music written for it.

The suite, with its allemande, courante, minuet, gigue, and other dances became a popular way of formatting music. In the second half of the eighteenth century the suite was replaced by the sonata form with its allegro, adagio, presto, etc.

The French noble family *had* to have a harpsichord, preferably built by one of the famous French or Flemish builders. With the excesses of the French Revolution this all changed dramatically. To keep one's head above the shoulders it became imperative not to touch the *clavecin*, that symbol of French aristocracy.

When Balbastre, the French keyboard player and composer, heard Taskin, the harpsichord builder, play an early English piano in 1770 he remarked, "... *Jamais ce nouveau venu ne detrônera le majestueux clavecin.*" (That new upstart will never dethrone the majestic harpsichord.) However, in 1792 when he composed variations on the Marseillaise, he wrote, *"Arrangés pour le forte piano par le Citoyen C. Balbastre."* (Composed for the piano by citizen C. Balbastre.)

That is the reason that relatively few of the French harpsichords have survived. It has also contributed to the paucity of French keyboard music in the following years. There was very little piano music written in France immediately after the French Revolution. Germany and Austria were where the action was. The music of the Baroque Era continued to be performed during the nineteenth century (i.e., Handel's music), but music-making had changed so much that the original baroque ideas became muddled by different styles and, very importantly, by different "improved" instruments. Music had become serious business and an end in itself.

In the previous centuries music was played by the musicians for their own enjoyment, for dancing, for religious services, or to enliven the dinner of the king. Music was usually made in small groups and heard by a few people at one time. There were some exceptions, especially in Italy and England, such as a coronation or other rare occasion.

Usually each musician had his or her own unique part to play, not like in the large nineteenth and twentieth century orchestras of over a hundred musicians, where most of them play the same melody with twenty or more of their colleagues. So much for individuality in the art of music.

The audiences had become larger and, to fill the larger concert halls, the orchestras had to sound louder. Music had become more serious and the musician had become an artist, often with long hair to make the point. There was no more eating, drinking, or coughing while sitting in the uncomfortable seats of the concert hall. The institution of soloist became common! Before the nineteenth century a musician would

mostly play his own music. If he borrowed from another composer, he would make variations. The difference between a
performing artist and a composer hardly existed.

Are we beginning to see the similarities between twentieth
century jazz music and the baroque music-making? Both types
of musicians write and play their own music, often for the
church or dancing. They often improvise at the moment and
add their own embellishments. They do not take themselves too
seriously and the audience is allowed to talk and drink. Much
of the music played is never written down. Music is not written
for posterity, but more for the moment. Music is not played in
large groups and each musician has his or her own particular
melody, which is not duplicated by any of the other players.
Rhythm is an important part of the music and tempo changes
are rare.

It is interesting to note that most modern day baroque performances reflect the serious music-making of the twentieth century. That is one respect in which they are not authentic. This
may have something to do with the awesome respect we have
for the baroque masters. Maybe this is because they have been
dead for such a long time.

Is it possible that in another one hundred years university
scholars will be busy writing their treatises about the performance practices of the Beatles? Maybe "late comers will not be
seated" during the centennial Beatles celebration.

The eighteenth century composer did not see himself so
much as an artist. The word itself has taken on a new meaning
in the last hundred years. It comes from the word artisan,
meaning craftsman. The baroque musician was for the most
part writing "on order" for a particular court occasion or a
religious service. In that respect he resembled the architect who
was ordered to design a building or the painter who had to
paint a portrait that was supposed to have some similarity to
the subject. *L'art pour l'art* (art for art's sake) had to wait until

the end of the Baroque Era to enter the music-making world.

We can notice a similar change in the nineteenth century world of painting, especially when photography, in a way, took the wind out of the portrait, landscape, or event (e.g. a battle) painting. Some of the functions of the painter had been taken over by the photographer, so the painter now felt freer to develop his way of looking at things. He had now become a "real artist." When black and white photography became threatened by color photography, the black and white photographer started thinking of himself as the new artist on the scene, leaving the recording of people or places to his junior photographer with the color film. The color photographer, in turn, is starting to move up in the world of art and is delegating his routine work to the person with the polaroid camera!

Did Bach think of himself as an "artist" on Friday evenings when he participated in jam sessions at the Leopold Coffee House, or when he had to quickly finish another of his circa 250 cantatas for performance in church on Sunday? He thought of himself as only an ordinary musician, although he knew he was a good one! I do not think he ever imagined how serious we would become about studying his music. He wrote for the moment and not for posterity.

In his last *Goldberg* variation for harpsichord, when Bach quietly throws in as one of several voices a popular and risqué tune, *"Kraut und Rüben haben mich vertrieben"* (cabbage and turnips have put me to flight), we get some insight into the fun Bach must have had improvising and using popular tunes polyphonically with the rest of the family when singing or playing instruments. What a difference with modern, especially twelve-tone, music, where in some cases it takes a few years to compose a short piece of music. All the compositions of twelve-tone composer Anton Webern can be performed in one afternoon. Serious business!

But it was not only the philosophy of music-making that was

different. Let us look, for example, at the musical instruments. Few people realize that of the modern instruments in a symphony orchestra, each one (except the triangle) has changed considerably, since as recently as Beethoven's time. We are all for progress, but at the same time is it not possible that in this process (making the instruments either easier to play or making them sound louder) some of the sonority or other qualities have gone by the wayside? Does it not make sense to at least occasionally listen to the music we love so much played on the instruments the composers were using and hear the music performed in the style the composers were playing it?

How do we know how this music was played in those days when there was no recording technique? A lot of research and many papers on this subject have been discovered and studied, mostly in recent years. For almost any instrument, several treatises have been found with elaborate instructions about how to play it. Any serious student of the harpsichord will want to read *L'art de Toucher le Clavecin* by François Couperin.

There still are, of course, discussions going on, and there are many controversies to keep the scholars busy. How different and dull will our great-grandchildren have it when they study our contemporary composers? There will be very little controversy because they will have contemporary recordings of our composers, whether it is Schoenberg conducting a symphony orchestra or the Beatles.

Sometimes it is nice to have doubts. This reminds me of the Inca ruins. The Incas had no written history for the simple reason that they did not write. What heaven for the guides of every building. They can use their fantasies and make up their own stories (and do) because nobody can contradict them!

It is true that because baroque music is so universal and so great, it has been able to survive after all we have done to it. Some of my best friends listen to Bach on the synthethizer. If I could just get them to a live baroque performance!

What are some of the different performance practices? Let us look at the modern orchestra, for example. When I was involved in building the first baroque orchestra in the western United States, we had fund-raising parties at my home. For our prospective donors we would play two different recordings of a minuet from a *Brandenburg* concerto of J. S. Bach. One was performed recently by a famous contemporary conductor (and sailor, to give a clue to the insider!) with a major European symphony orchestra, and the other, for comparison, by a well-known Dutch baroque orchestra. The audience was surprised by the difference, and some did not even recognize the two recordings as the same piece of music! That is not to say that everybody preferred the authentic baroque recording! *De gustibus non est disputandum!*

The uninitiated person is often surprised by the different sound, which has to do with the different temperament. This has its origin in the tuning techniques developed in the baroque era, which I talked about a few days ago. To some new listeners the baroque sound even seems out of tune because our ears are used to the equal temperament of modern tuning. It is true, however, that it is much more difficult to keep the old instruments in tune. This is one of the concessions we must make to get that beautiful sound.

The sound of the old instruments may surprise the novice. In music we like to hear the familiar to a certain extent. But after continued listening to the mellow sound of the wooden flute and the gut strings of the violins, the music lover with *bon gout* will not be disappointed. The major difference is the style in which the music was played. The big symphony orchestra in our fund-raising demonstration recording played the minuet like a very serious, almost Wagnerian, sad piece. Few recognized that it was a minuet, a favorite dance of the Baroque Era. The baroque composers took those dances very seriously and Bach is known to have taken dance lessons to learn them! To my delight, I noticed that during the "baroque" recording some of the listeners were getting restless and tapping their feet as if they had the urge to dance! I knew that I had them on my side!

What happened to the instruments? The string instruments were often "improved" in the past century. Metal strings were used instead of gut strings. The Stradivarius violins are now being rebuilt in order to undo the changes made during the nineteenth century and restore them to their original shape! Similar changes occurred in many of the Roman and gothic churches in Europe, where it took considerable work to undo all the painting and other "beautification" processes done to the churches during the nineteenth century. We are playing the wind instruments again without the valves added in the last century. How difficult it is to play these instruments and how few can do it; but how rewarding to hear that pure sound!

One of the difficulties of an authentic baroque orchestra is that there are perhaps only a few hundred players in the world with the right instruments and ability to play in that style. For example, if one of the horn players becomes ill before a performance in the Bay Area, there may be no one in the whole country to replace him! There is no possibility of borrowing from the San Francisco Symphony. That is why many of the players travel as "gypsies" around the world, going from one baroque area to another.

Authentic baroque performances began attracting my attention only about ten years ago. I grew up in Holland and was exposed to the harpsichord even before World War II. Holland is, and has been for many years, in the forefront of baroque performance. Although I was playing the piano, I heard the harpsichord many times. I remember that even before the war, a harpsichord was used for the yearly performance of the *Saint Matthew* passion. I was not terribly impressed at that time and continued to leisurely play Bach on the piano.

I recently realized why I had not been impressed with the

harpsichord. The harpsichords built in those days had all the disadvantages of the harpsichord and none of the advantages of the modern piano. They were usually built by the piano factories that were trying to develop a market for an up-and-coming instrument.

By meticulously studying the instruments that have survived and by copying them carefully, using the the same type of wood and other materials, we now have the opportunity to play on instruments with the same tonal quality as the instruments the great masters of the Baroque Era were using. This type of handmade harpsichord is a far cry from the factory harpsichords, which are still in use by many occasional baroque players. We are lucky that now in western Europe and in the United States a generation of excellent harpsichord builders has developed. These builders can be compared with the famous builders of the seventeenth and eighteenth centuries. The exchanges between the builders and the players has to a great extent contributed to the increased knowledge about baroque performance practices.

The harpsichord followed in the footsteps of the lute, which was a plucked instrument. The lute had become so complicated with so many strings that it was difficult to play. Keyboards were known at that time—people had been using the psaltery for many years—so it seemed quite logical to adapt the keyboard and use it to pluck the strings.

The keyboard family (organs excluded) can be divided into two types. In one type the string is struck with a hammer, as on the clavichord, forte-piano, and modern piano. In the other type the string is plucked, as on the virginal, spinet, and harpsichord proper. The clavichord was in great use at the time of Bach and Mozart. It was a small instrument with one string per note and it had a direct action. By pressing the key down, a lever beneath the string comes up and a brass wedge at the end of the lever comes up and hits the string. In this way the player was able to strike the string loudly or softly according to the force used to hit the key. In this respect, the clavichord was the forerunner of the forte-piano, which later developed into our modern piano. The clavichord was unable to produce a lot of sound and was therefore used only for private use. The baroque music lover who does not want his neighbors or even his spouse to hear him play, might like it.

Clavichords are available in kit form and are not that hard to build. The major difference between the clavichord and harpsichord is that on the clavichord we can give each individual note its own volume, albeit not very loud.

The harpsichord was a relatively loud instrument which could easily be heard in the resounding baroque halls or churches and in the large baroque rooms. The harpsichord had its greatest glory in the days of Couperin in France and at about the same time in Germany. From a simple, one-keyboard instrument, it had become a sophisticated and rather elaborate instrument, often with two keyboards. Anybody with a harpsichord made by the famous Flemish and French builders had it made! Most instruments had stops which allowed the player to use one or two sets of strings. This allowed the player some differences in timbre and in loudness for certain parts of the music, but not for the individual note.

The largest number of keyboard works was written for the harpsichord and the organ. The organ has a similar disadvantage as far as the individual loudness of a particular note is concerned. This disadvantage is, of course, relative. In any art form some restriction is essential, whether it is the rhyme or rhythm of a poem or the time and place of a Greek drama.

The main limitation of the harpsichord is inherent in its mechanism. When the player touches the key, a mechanism is set into action that will pluck the string in an all-or-nothing way. This restriction forced the composer and player, in order not to sound dull, to use special writing and playing techniques, which were so typical of the baroque period. This restriction was the reason for the marvelous use of embellishments and articulation in baroque keyboard music. It was also the cause of the harpsichord's abrupt disappearance from the musical world for over one hundred years. The forte-piano had appeared on the horizon and it did not have this restriction.

Are we not lucky then that all these baroque composers had to struggle with that one restriction! What did they do about it? The music was to be lively. How do we bring out accents and let important notes stick out if we do not want to sound dull? Here we have to deal with the different baroque styles, such as Italian, French, etc. The methods that the composers and players used are multiform, and we will touch on just a few of them.

To make our spoken words lively, we use the techniques of articulation, pausing, or raising and lowering our voices on certain words, etc. We can use all these techniques on the harpsichord except the least civilized one, which is raising the voice! To accentuate a specific note we can, as in speech, halt for a moment to make the note stand out more. We can also come in with our note just a little bit before or after the beat to surprise the listener. We will have to articulate each measure carefully so that it stands on its own. Above all, we can embellish the note with a trill or any of the other multitude of ornamentations of the Baroque Era. This is the main reason that harpsichord music, especially French, is supplied with so many little niceties such as coulé and trill.

We should be thankful about the restriction of the harpsichord. Without it, the music of the baroque era would have been quite different. This is the reason that performing French harpsichord music on the modern piano makes no artistic sense. The need for embellishments is not only superfluous, but they are also more difficult on the modern piano, which requires a much heavier touch.

The French Revolution caused the *coup de grâce* for the harpsichord in France, and in Germany the harpsichord also became quickly *démodé* with the rise of the Austrian and English forte-piano builders. Mozart and the sons of Bach quickly became forte-piano players. The restrictions of the harpsichord, which made it and the music written for it so great, became in itself the reason for its (temporary) downfall. Musicians wanted more ability to directly express their musical emotions and did not want to be tied down. They wanted to be able to play crescendo, and loud and soft (forte and piano). The term forte-piano became the advertising slogan for the new generation of keyboard builders, and the word piano, originally meant to promote this new invention, is now used as the name for today's most popular keyboard instrument.

Nobody should claim superiority of taste in the arts, but it is interesting to note that the modern symphony orchestras are getting on the bandwagon and are ordering harpsichord and forte-pianos and at least are trying to become "authentic."

The relative lack of loudness of the harpsichord and forte-piano is out of balance with the hundred-member symphony orchestra, and this has created some unusual performances. Now we see that our modern orchestras are beginning to cut down on manpower when playing baroque music. At least it is a beginning. The more difficult next step, besides changing the instruments somewhat, will be to learn the baroque style!

The controversy about whether to play baroque music on the modern piano vs. the harpsichord is favoring the harpsichord, and more and more I hear soloists and orchestras using the harpsichord as accompaniment in their baroque pieces. This does not mean that they are playing in the baroque style. This is an accomplishment that would require much more than simply buying a harpsichord, and playing it as if it were a piano.

The futile discussions about whether to play Bach on the modern piano or on the harpsichord will continue ("If Bach had had a piano he would have played on it," etc.). These discussions make no sense, as Bach was exposed to the forte-piano but he did not see the necessity of owning one. Play Bach on the synthesizer, mouth harmonica, or whatever, but play it. I prefer to play Bach on the harpsichord, but if necessary I will be happy to play Bach on the modern piano, especially the not too polyphonic pieces, such as the concerto in the Italian style. If I could play the harmonica, I would play Bach on that. I am sure Bach would not mind.

The future will tell us how esoteric we are going to be with authentic performances. The trend now is to go almost to the absurd and play the music only on the instruments the composers were using. That means that to play Mozart we would need a Mozart piano and for an early Beethoven sonata an early Beethoven piano. It would be difficult for practical purposes to be that specific. The recording companies, however, seem to be taking note and following along those lines.

Only a few people have been exposed to the live sound of baroque music in this country. In Europe, especially in England, Holland and Belgium, it is already a way of life. Currently, there is also a revival in Germany, France, and Italy. Why do we see such a revival of baroque music?

Twentieth-century man has become so inundated with mass production and the "bigger is better" syndrome that he longs again for the intimacy of baroque music. The big orchestra may have a difficult time in the future, while the small chamber music groups are going to have great appeal. Of course, the standard "big band" music of Beethoven, Brahms, and Bruckner, written for the symphony orchestra, is so well-known that people will continue to like it and listen to it. I am no exception. But if we look at Holland, the forerunner of the present-day baroque music world, we see a diminished attendance at the big symphony orchestras, while some of the often esoteric harpsichord or other early music recitals are well attended.

Much of the classical music is now heard on fancy hi-fi sets in the living room, and this has somewhat replaced the need for people to hear the big sound in the concert hall. The modern listener may want to hear that one individual or few individuals playing together.

During the Nazi occupation of Holland, the members of the orchestra in my hometown had to join the German *kulturkammer*. This was an obligatory musicians union. The great majority of the members refused to join out of principle, and that was the end of the orchestra until the war was over. To help the musicians financially, *huisconcerten* were arranged. There was also an ordinance that gatherings of more then twenty people were *verboten*. The end result for me was that I had marvelous small-scale concerts to attend in private homes. I hope that in the future our society starts getting out of the TV room and begins reviving music-making at home!

How are we able to hear the live baroque sound in this country? In many of the big cities in the United States there are now flourishing early music societies. The members of these societies are usually small groups of musicians and instrument makers, dedicated to the teaching and performance of baroque music in the style and on the instruments of the period. Call them, join them, or at least go to their usually intimate concerts and *listen*!

The chance to hear a full baroque orchestra is more remote. In the United States there is at the moment only one full baroque orchestra playing regularly and the number of Americans who have been exposed to this sound is very small.

My first experience with a full baroque orchestra occurred a few years ago in Berkeley, where with the help of friends, we started the first baroque orchestra in the western United States, Philharmonia Baroque Orchestra.

The San Francisco Bay Area happens to be a place where many of the rare American baroque players reside and it was therefore a logical place to begin. With the energy of our artistic director, Laurette Goldberg, and the devoted musicians, as well as help from a hard-working board, we were able in a few years to have an orchestra that is now well established. It has given many people on the West Coast their first opportunity to hear the full sound of the baroque orchestra. The orchestra has traveled all along the West Coast and is making its first recording with the well-known French recording company, Harmonia Mundi. Many of the orchestra musicians are Americans who were living in Europe, where they had a chance to study and play baroque music. It is good to see them back and doing here what they like to do so much. For the people on the West Coast there is now a chance to hear a baroque orchestra live. There is no substitute for live music. In recorded music we often fill in with our fantasy what we have heard earlier in the concert hall. We remember the sonority of the instruments and even though we may not hear it on the record, we fill it in from memory. Without ever having heard the baroque sound live, it would be impossible to fill the gap between a recording and a live performance.

Even though many of the baroque performances are sold out, there is always the need for more money to run an organization of this caliber. Without the generous donations from corporations, foundations and private donors, the orchestra would not be able to exist.*

What a pleasure it is now, after about ten years of studying the Baroque Era from beginning to the end, to go back and study the early nineteenth century composers. As a product of the twentieth century I listened to Beethoven, for example,

---

*If the reader feels inclined to follow in the footsteps of the patrons of the arts of the eighteenth century, such as Prince Leopold of the court of Cöthen for J.S, Bach, and Louis the XIV for François Couperin, he can send his check to Philharmonia Baroque Orchestra, P.O. Box 77344, San Francisco, CA 94107.

with an ear attuned to the nineteenth and twentieth century composers. It was more like looking backwards. Now, after working my way forward from early baroque, I find new vitality in the same music and sense the progress that was made, and how the contemporaries of Beethoven, and for that matter he himself, must have looked at the modern music of that time. It is like reliving history. Being able to look forward gives new life to the music, and the performance consequently takes on new meaning.

One begins to realize that the modern performer or musical group has a tremendous job to do when trying to perform music from these different periods and styles. In this respect our forefather musicians had it easier. They mostly played the music of the current time, and they played and composed in the local manner, except for some occasional composition that was written in a style from a different country, such as French style or Italian style, etc. Have we been trying to achieve the impossible? The future may bring many more performing groups specializing in the music of many different periods. The early music groups and the baroque orchestra may be just a beginning.

That Irish coffee got me again. This time there should have been more cognac and less coffee in it! I really should get some sleep because one never knows what might be ahead. My reading has been minimal. I have been listening to music so much that not much time is left over after all the daily chores are done. Sometimes I listen to the same piece several times. Music is, after all, memory. If we know the composer but not the piece, we suspect what is going to come and then, surprise, the music is just a little different from what we expected. Admittedly, I may have been a little too passive intellectually on this trip. This may relate to the fact that all other things like cooking, cleaning, doing the dishes, changing sails, and navigating, certainly are not done passively. There is nobody else to do it! I feel therefore that I have a good excuse not to read a difficult book or to study a four voices Bach fugue, but to play and listen to my favorite and familiar music!

Some people (guess who is among them) started this solo sail hoping and expecting to find clarity in some of their soul searching. The solo sailor is either too busy, too tired, or too elated to do any meditating. A drive during rush hour in an automatic automobile is probably more appropriate for meditating. There is a situation where there is *nothing* one can do. Turn off the radio and that is the time to meditate. For many of us civilized western people it is the only time that we have no piped-in music or bosses, wives, children, telephone, singing birds, or beautiful nature, food, drinks, exercises, sex, etc. to distract us. The only thing we have to do is steer the car. That is enough distraction to create an atmosphere for meditating. To have to concentrate on meditating can be in itself very distracting. There are some people who even want to take that single moment of tranquility away from us and who advise such things as "share a ride" or increased public transportation. Let's do the meditating or soul-searching behind our two hundred horse-power, but do not single-hand to Hawaii for your answers! Anyway, I am not going to talk into this tape recorder about my soul. That is my private business as long as I am alone on my boat. It is early morning. I had better try to get some sleep now. Sleep well.

08:00 hours PDT. Latitude 23°15′ N., longitude 153°45′ W. I had hoped to be able to sleep in this morning after my long monologue, but I woke up because the radar alarm went off. There was a big rain squall about four miles aft. This time, to be prepared I put my foul weather gear on, closed all the portholes and went up to the cockpit. Of course, now that I was really prepared, the rain squall passed south of me. The radar showed that it was going to hit Jeff, but I did not dare wake him up. He probably had his radio off anyway. I had to get up once more, this time to get the boat out of irons. It is amazing how one learns to recognize the different rattles. Some noises necessitate my getting up, other ones are perfectly acceptable. Not acceptable is the absence of rattles, because then the boat is usually in irons or heaved to and stopped. It is difficult to learn to wake up to the absence of noise!

There are plenty of problems with the chain of the automatic pilot breaking. I am glad to have two self-steering devices so that when the vane has to be repaired I can use the auto pilot and vice versa.

The night was exhausting, but progress was good. I forgot to mention that at 03:30 hours I woke up for no reason at all (?) and saw a ship behind me. The captain answered immediately when called on channel 16 on the VHF. It was a Chevron tanker, the Arizona, on her way to Honolulu from Richmond. It overtook me on the stern and port so I must be crossing the shipping channel from San Francisco to Honolulu. This makes sense because I am coming back from having been further south of the Great Circle Route and going to an island further west.

The Harrier is now out of radio reach, both for the Baobob and for me. I am now in regular twice-a-day contact with the Baobob.

17:10 hours PDT. We are getting close! The different Hawaii radio stations come through very clearly. I am using the Honolulu radio station as a homing station for my radio direction finder to check out my position. The type of music on the stations is rather disappointing compared to what we are used to in the sophisticated Bay Area, but it is good enough for direction finding! This homing-in reminds me of the delighted faces of the Japanese fighter pilots in the movie *Tora, Tora, Tora* when they flew their Pearl Harbor mission and were picking up the signals of Radio Station Honolulu, which were to guide them to their target on that infamous Sunday morning in December 1941. I am glad I do not have these hostile intentions, although the type of music I am hearing does not make it any easier! Listening to Hawaiian music is not my favorite pastime.

Some good news. My satnav is working again. After taking it off the wall, I noticed that the antenna connection in the back of the unit was rather feeble, and after trying a little juggling and putting the unit back into place, I got a red light with the passage of the next satellite! Great! No need to do celestial navigation anymore. I also learned, now that I am very careful in checking the satellites, that some satellites are out of commission! It is amazing that these multi-million dollar gadgets break down like anything else.

I find myself talking all the the time with Jeffrey Hartz of the Baobob. We must be pretty close because the reception is very clear. Both of us are trying to make up for all the time that we were alone at sea and we spill out all our stored up conversation. Maybe I am not such a loner after all. We are talking to each other about all kinds of personal things, knowing full well that nobody else is able to hear us. I cannot remember what Jeff looks like. I must have met him at our pre-race meeting, but he was one of twenty other people there. We talk to each other most of the day. When I am busy doing things, he keeps talking and vice versa. When he is unable to keep his finger depressed on the microphone, I pour my heart out. The topics of our conversations seem inexhaustible, and include politics, money, love, marriage, cars, and sailing. One of us occasionally forgets to use the "over" phrase. Sometimes we both continue talking to each other at the same time. This is a situation that is hard to do in an ordinary conversation. The radio, unlike the telephone, is set up in such a way that when transmitting one cannot listen! At one time we both were probably talking to each other at the same time for over fifteen minutes. I wonder whether anybody else with a VHF radio in the neighborhood was listening to this cacophony. The listener must have doubted the sanity of these two people talking to each other at the same time about different subjects without any apparent interest in what the other party was saying.

DAY 19

Glorious Fourth of July! 16:00 hours PDT (13:00 hours Hawaii Time). Latitude 23°14', longitude 155°49'. I am about 200 miles away from Hanalei Bay. This means that if the wind stays at least moderate, I should arrive during the day of July 6.

Spent part of the day opening cans. This should be no problem, but my can opener has rusted out during its long life on boats. My Swiss army knife has served mostly as a can opener. Each nation seems to have its own type of cans. I find the French cans the most difficult to open. This is too bad, because their contents are usually the most appetizing, at least in my case (i.e., pâté de foie gras). The French do not give any instructions on how to open the cans. *Je m'en fous.* The Americans are different. They blatantly announce that their cans are "easy to open." Then you *know* you are in trouble. It is the same reasoning I see in my young patients brought in by mothers who tell the children, "Doctor is such a nice man." Children know when their parents are lying and that is when they really start screaming. When I tell them that I am not so nice they usually calm down immediately. This honesty re-establishes some guarded trust.

Talked this morning again to Jeffrey on the Baobob. The reception was so clear that we decided to switch to the lower amperage transmitter, which only carries a few miles, and we were still very clear. Jeff scanned the horizon and spotted me first. "I can see you!" He has his spinnaker up and is catching up with me. He had some bad news. He had run out of "juice" and on the Fourth of July! In the meantime I have taken stock of my inventory and found more wine and a bottle of gin. Jeff will try to catch up with me. I promised to furnish a Fourth of July surprise package.

It took Jeff four hours to catch up. He still surprised me and took some pictures of me *au naturel* before I had become adjusted to the fact that my solitude of several weeks had ended. I was lucky enough that he had set the diaphragm of his camera the wrong way and that these pictures were ruined.

I had prepared a water-proof "care" package. This was wrapped with a lot of duct tape and connected to a buoy. The buoy had a sixty-foot line which was attached to my boat. After having lost a boat hook on the first try, Jeff was luckier the second time. We took some pictures of each other's boats. I took the harpsichord on deck for the occasion, but Jeff could not hear me because he was up wind from me. With his spinnaker Jeff was considerably faster than I and he soon left. He had to come back to take more pictures, though, because he found out about the mistake he made when taking the first ones. Serious racing! By this time we knew pretty well who would be the first to arrive. I was worried because our boats were very close at times and it would have been terrible to have a collision on this big ocean! I recognized his face now that he was so close.

Two harpsichord keys are a little sticky because of the humidity, so I may leave the harpsichord in the sun for a little while. There is a saying among the Transpac sailors, "When you hear harpsichord music on the ocean you are not hallucinating, but you are certainly one of the last!"

DAY 20

July 5, 20:00 hours Hawaii Time. It is getting dark now, the moon is half-full and the stars are brilliant. My position this morning was 157° west and about 23°15′ (miles) north. I cleaned the boat, vacuumed, and did all the laundry, including the bed sheets. The kitchen is spic and span, even the oven. It looks like I will arrive in Hanalei Bay tomorrow morning. I want the boat to look her best when the Racing Committee boards her tomorrow. I also want to impress the three ladies who will be sailing my boat back. Maybe they will be enticed to deliver the boat to me in the same shape. However, I am not worried about that. Linda Rettie, who will be in command, is a much better sailor than I and has raced extensively. She came in sixth in her single-handed race to Japan, and she was the only female and only Caucasian in an all-male, all-Japanese group of racers. Sue has sailed with Linda and has considerable long distance experience. The third of "Peter's Angels," as they call themselves, is Claudette, who apparently also loves sailing.

I continued to yak away with Jeffrey on the VHF low power. Last night Jeff and I celebrated the Fourth of July with our own fireworks. We used different types of emergency flares and found out that there is no relationship between the price of the flares and their relative visibility and durability! I also used a lot of outdated flares, which all ignited easily. Better not to have an emergency at sea on the Fourth. Nobody would believe your emergency flares.

Jeff saw some dolphins yesterday, but I was not as lucky. It is amazing how little wild life I have seen on this trip. The only fish I caught was a flying fish that landed spontaneously on my deck.

It took considerable time to untangle the topping lift which was twisted around the higher spreaders. This is something that never happened to me before.

I am about seventy to eighty miles from Hanalei Bay and going about five knots. I am using the Hawaiian chart and it is exciting to move several centimeters in one hour versus the few millimeters on the large Pacific chart. Jeff is using his Loran to navigate. He does not have a satnav. He is able to get some readings now from the western Pacific Hawaiian chain. Yes, Californians, you do live near the eastern part of the Pacific. I cannot get any reading on my Loran, but feel very comfortable with the working satnav.

I poured the ten gallons of reserve water into the big water tank and will have the luxury of having a fresh-water shower tomorrow morning before arrival! This last evening is so beautiful. The winds are good and the sea is calm. I do not feel like going to bed and will enjoy my last evening with a glass of cognac. The coast of Kauai cannot be too far away. I am sailing alongside and not too far off the northern coast, but am unable to see land or lights.

It has occurred to me that no one can help me on this trip, but I have suddenly realized I am also unable to help them. Not my family, friends, patients. Maybe this is the most fascinating aspect of my voyage—the sense of being uninvolved. Will I be a better person for this experience? At least a more interesting one, I hope. Wonder what it will be like to be ashore and to make the first phone call to my family? It's interesting playing the harpsichord knowing no one can hear me. I like to play for myself, but, like other musicians, I very much enjoy touching others with my music.

Tonight I definitely will use the radar watch. Not only has Jeffrey warned me about possible fishing boats, but I would rather not have a collision with Jeff himself! He is faster, but often when he falls asleep, his boat gets into irons, while my boat slowly but steadily keeps moving. Also, for the first time in twenty days I am approaching a coast and I would rather not end up on the beach or the rocks while asleep. I have two safety devices to wake me up if I get too close to the coast. The radar watch will wake me up when I get to within twelve miles of land, and the depth alarm will sound when the depth is less than twenty fathoms. In the 1982 around-the-world BOC Race Richard McBride fell asleep and slept longer than anticipated, during which time the wind had changed direction. He ended up on the beach of the Falklands, but was lucky enough to refloat the boat! Less lucky was Desmond Hampton who, in the same race, hit the rocks on the southern coast of Australia. He lost his boat. I had better turn on my alarm clock and check my fathometer and radar before I go to sleep for the last time on this trip.

DAY 21

July 6, 06:00 hours Hawaii Time. I slept a few hours. It is still dark and I can see a flashing light on port, which probably is the beacon east of Hanalei Bay. There is also a white light ahead of me, which is probably Jeff. He must have fallen asleep and been in irons. There is no other traffic and the the coast is not visible yet. Will try to get more rest and maybe even more sleep.

Woke up at 08:00 hours and I can see the Kauai coast and also Jeff's light. How different from my first trip to Hawaii when we tried to see the coast for hours. I think the difference comes from the fact that, at that time, I navigated using only celestial navigation. I was never one hundred percent sure about my position, always doubting my calculations and sextant sights. Here I made a landfall and did not even wake up!

At 08:30 hours I dared to call Jeff on the VHF without the chance of waking him up. I wondered why I had caught up with him. He apparently had fallen asleep and had been in irons. That, however, was not his main problem. He had become unsure of his position and was wondering whether the ten-second flashing light on our port was the marine beacon close to Hanalei Bay or the airport beacon of Lihue Airport. He had decided to go slow and wait for daylight. He was already in contact with the Racing Committee which was monitoring channel 68. They have two stations, "high society" at headquarters and "low society" at the harbor and committee boat.

July 6, 23:30 hours, Hanalei Bay. Latitude 22°15′ N., longitude 159°40′ W. Jeff came in at 11:00 hours and I talked to the Racing Committee, announcing that my arrival would be at noon. The finish racing buoy was easily found. I had put on my yachting outfit and looked like a gentleman in my pressed trousers which had been hanging in my closet and were saved for this occasion. The committee boat was there to welcome me. The committee members boarded my boat and took over the wheel! I tried to offer them a whiskey, but they had cold beer. I had to blink away a tear and was wondering why. Maybe it was because for the first time in almost three weeks somebody else was doing something for me! For twenty days I had done everything myself. I was never able to ask somebody for advice or help. All of a sudden here were these nice men who took over the wheel, offered me a drink, brought in the sails and planned dropping the anchor. I could sit back and watch without feeling guilty. They were deliberating for me where to place the anchor. What luxury!

Or was it the thought that I had *done* it? We had climbed our Everest, as Jeff had put it in one of our conversations on VHF yesterday. Years ago it had seemed such an accomplishment to single-hand the Pacific, and now, in retrospect, it seemed that it was such a simple thing. Or was it seeing the beautiful green and still unspoiled Hanalei Bay after seeing only water for twenty days? Was it because I had made no progress in my soul searching?

We were brought to shore by a Boston whaler and we went immediately to the race headquarters, where lunch was being served. Here I heard about the whereabouts of the other sailors. I knew about the three sailors who fell out in the first few days and returned home. Banks Henward in the Pippin, for reasons unknown, had decided to make his landfall in Maui. The Racing Committee had, to no avail, tried to encourage him to continue to finish the race to Kauai. Peter Bird, the veteran solo rower who had oared from California to Australia, was missing. He had been out of radio contact for days. There was some concern about him. However, we all knew how experienced he was and none of us was terribly worried.*

Many sailors had indeed experienced difficulties the first few days with the rough seas and strong winds. That was when I was having such a great time with my larger heavier boat. Grace Simes, the only female competitor, had "not a very pleasant sail," to moderate her language. She had suffered some burns on her foot from boiling water. She was one of the first ones to arrive though. Frank Dinsmore, the veteran Transpacker and overall winner, had *his* problems, and I quote him from the report of Christine Klampe. Christine is a free-lance writer who was covering the race from beginning to end. Frank: "Really big waves and a lot of wind. The boat is in total shambles. I went out to put in a triple reef in the main and everything got fouled up. The brass bar on the wall has been totally bent out of shape with objects hitting it. I've never seen anything like it. I've taken one severe knockdown where everything came totally across the cabin. I've never seen anything like that on a boat, where everything goes right over the top. It is very scary. I hope that does not happen again. Anytime you get knocked down out there, there is a grave reason for concern. A little bigger wave would have put me under, I'm sure."

In retrospect, I cannot complain about the performance of my boat. I was indeed the last to come in within the allowed time, but I was only one hour or so behind Jeff. The boat was at her best in heavy weather, especially with the wind on the beam. Just when the other sailors had their toughest time, my boat was going comfortably in the thirty-plus knot winds, while I was below enjoying relative comfort and listening to music. During those days I probably did the longest distance in one day. The reason for the three broken jib halyards that had been chafing is not clear to me, and this needs to be further investigated to prevent this from happening on my next solo sail

---

*The next day the message was received via a commercial ship that Peter had lost his self-steering vane and that he would arrive late, sailing during the day and heaving to at night.

(around the world?). Without the use of my largest sail, the Genoa, it is surprising how well I did after all. Furthermore, when solo racing one mostly sails against oneself, does as much as the boat and sailor can do, and that is enough. In the single-handed races the finisher is by that fact alone a winner. My main purpose, which was to prove that solo sailing can be done safely and in great comfort (even though I lost my refrigeration and most of the fresh water), was accomplished.

I was indeed the last one to arrive within the limits of the race, but I did finish and was the eleventh to come in out of sixteen starters.

A room in a nice little hotel called The Sandgroper, located close to the racing headquarters, has become my *pied à terre*. I am dictating my final notes about the trip in a nice room, with a view of Hanalei Bay, lying in a comfortable bed with clean sheets and an ice-cooled drink next to me. I spent the afternoon in a daze after too many Mai tais in the local joints with my competitors, exchanging sailing stories. Later in the day, while driving a rental car in Kauai, I had to keep reminding myself that the car did not have a self-steering vane or auto pilot.

In good tradition, in a restaurant this evening I saw a wallet on one of the tables which resembled mine. I made a remark to that effect to the people at that table and they said that they had been wondering to whom it belonged. I looked then at the contents and, of course, it was mine. I had not even missed it because everybody else had been paying the bills! There were quite a few greens in it and I was glad to have these honest people on the island!

Sue arrived in the afternoon. Linda and Claudette are apparently on their way. Arrangements have been made to have some of the other sailors repair part of the damage to the boat and prepare her for return to the mainland by "Peter's Angels."

The evening was spent dancing in the bar of the hotel. There was a nice cassette tape collection of Greek folkdance music.

The attractive female bartender pleasantly surprised me when she, between the dance music and as favor to me, put on a tape of Bach's *Goldberg* variations played on the harpsichord by my friend Gustav Leonhardt. I had a hard time concealing how moved I was by this beautiful music. There are many surprises in Hawaii, even in the field of music!

Medicine
PREVENTIVE MEASURES

Several books have been written about first aid at sea. However, as far as I know, no one has particularly addressed the potential medical problems of the single-hander. Becoming ill or injured when alone at sea can produce unique problems. There is no crew available to lend a helping hand or give medical advice. And the fact that sometimes the solo sailor is not able to get any help, even by radio, is rarely addressed in these books.

This section does not pretend to be a complete medical guide, but it will focus on how the solo sailor should handle medical emergencies. More elaborate general medical books to have on board will be mentioned when we discuss medical provisions. This chapter will also be useful for the skipper with a crew, and for people on land in situations far away from medical help. My experiences as "expedition doc" in remote parts of the world, such as Ethiopia, the Andes, New Guinea, and Nepal, enable me to give the lonely explorer, whether at sea or on land, some useful "pearls." If this medical section helps some lonely sailor, even in a small way, please let me know. It will make my day! Any comments or suggestions that might help other sailors are welcome.

What are the chances of a major medical catastrophe? It will depend mostly on how careful the sailor is and the state of his health before leaving on his voyage. Anybody in reasonably good health is much more likely to sustain an injury than to be struck with a severe illness. Most injuries and many illnesses are preventable. I will discuss how to diminish the chances of becoming ill.

The individual risk factors should be studied and discussed with a doctor so that appropriate action can be taken in advance. The medical history of the sailor should be taken into consideration. If, for example, there is a history of a duodenal ulcer, appropriate medicine should be on board to treat this eventuality. Recently, great new medicines have come on the market for ulcers. A bleeding ulcer on a voyage could be quite a nuisance! It is interesting to note I do not remember ever having a sailor as an ulcer patient. This must have something to do with the sailor's temperament. On the ocean there are no nasty bosses to give ulcers; at the same time the solo sailor cannot give them to anybody else. (Franklin D. Roosevelt once said to one of his secretaries: "Don't get ulcers, give them!")

There may be some increased risks by being alone on the ocean, but there are also some advantages. Allergy problems often improve on the ocean because of the absence of pollens. I think it is rare to get an illness on an ocean voyage. There are no nasty bacteria or viruses. No polluted air! As a matter of fact, after a few days out, and especially when single-handling, life could be compared medically to being inside a sterile bubble! Extra care, however, should be exercised during those farewell parties prior to departure. Our friend or sexual partner may have given us a surprise that will take some time to mature on the ocean!

It is wise to take some special care to prevent an infection during those busy days before leaving. It is at that time that exposure is most likely to occur. It is quite different being at home with a simple flu, than it is being out on the ocean where one cannot conveniently crawl into bed for a few days. This is certainly an impossibility for the solo sailor. Infection could be the cause for having to abort your solo sail, or perhaps race! Think about the time and money spent on preparations. You would not want to have some silly bacterium ruining your trip! It is a good idea to avoid people with an illness, even if it is only a common cold, for about a week prior to departure.

Watch that bon voyage party on the boat! It may be that the boat was quite sterile before the party, but with all those people it may have become more like a cesspool. Many germs are transferred by eating utensils. At home in a hot dishwasher germs are usually eliminated. If that bon voyage party is a condition *sine qua non*, the minimum precaution should be to use disposable utensils, such as paper cups and dishes, plastic glasses, forks, knives, and spoons. Even the Armed Forces are now using disposable utensils instead of the old aluminum cans.

It is advisable, on a trip with crew, that everyone, particularly the first few days, has his own utensils which are separately washed. Nobody should use the same wash water because it is often the lukewarm water which will encourage bacterial growth. In this way the germs are transferred to other dishes. There may be one crew member who comes aboard with a germ which will then be transferred from one member to another. There is plenty of ocean water available so that each crew member can wash his dishes separately. Rafting down the Omo river in Ethiopia many years ago, most of the approximately twenty expedition members got their turn becoming ill with the same diarrhea. The only ones who did not become ill were those who had followed my advice (of course!) and used their own utensils! Recently, in the hospital where I work, almost the whole crew of an ocean freighter was admitted after one sailor infected the rest of the crew with tuberculosis during a trip from the Orient to California! Their quarters were certainly larger and less cramped than on the average sailboat. Let the captain be forewarned! Watch that new coughing crew member, especially if he came aboard in a foreign port.

The sailor should go to the doctor and establish his individual risk factors, taking into consideration past medical history, present aches and pains, family history, and bad habits like drinking, smoking, and eating too much. The sailor should have a thorough physical examination. Blood and urine should be analyzed. Blood pressure, cholesterol and electrocardiogram should be normal. The mariner may undergo a treadmill test to evaluate the status of his coronary arteries. He should have some idea about his chances of developing a heart attack on the way! The urinalysis should be normal, as a kidney stone or bladder infection might be unpleasant on a trip. The captain of a ship with a crew who is planning an extended offshore cruise should insist that all crew members have a thorough physical. He should have a detailed, confidential report from the crew's doctors about their physical and mental condition and particular risk factors. It is amazing that even in this day and age some people do not want their medical ailments to be known.

While studying medicine in Leyden, The Netherlands, I once traveled to the U.S.A. on an ocean liner, and I shared a cabin with another student who was quite seasick. He got worse and worse until, finally, he lost consciousness. Then I discovered his syringe and needles. It turned out he was a diabetic and had been giving himself the usual amount of insulin while not being able to keep any food down because of his seasickness. He was in an insulin coma! This was easily corrected with an injection of glucose.

Some crew members may be hesitant to discuss their problems out of fear they might not be accepted on board. The skipper might want to contact their physician who, if he has his patient's permission, can give advice. The whole crew might profit from it. The medicine cabinet should contain the special medications that might be needed for this individual.

The sailor still might develop an attack of appendicitis (see disscussion of *appendicitis* in Infections and Antibiotics section). Some people have the appendix taken out *á froid* (a French term meaning "when cold"), as we call that in the medical jargon. This seems quite foolhardy but may not be such a bad idea when planning a long solo ocean voyage or solo circumnavigation, especially for the relatively young, who are at risk of getting appendicitis. If for some reason the doctor is exploring the abdomen (for gall bladder, hysterectomy, etc.) of a potential circumnavigator or land explorer, it might be advisable to take the appendix out at the same time. Years ago, before the common use of the airplane, it was not unusual for Dutch people, before going to what used to be called the Dutch East Indies, to have the appendix removed if they were going to be stationed in the more remote areas.

Let us presume the sailor is in excellent health. He exercises every day and is of normal weight. His urinalysis and blood tests are normal. He does not smoke or drink excessively. He has never been seriously ill, and his parents lived to the age of ninety. What can go wrong? Overconfidence! As mentioned above, for somebody in reasonably good health, the major risk factor is not going to be illness but injury. To be on a wet, bouncing boat, often wrapped around in knots by the lifeline like a dog on a leash while missing a good night's rest, or to be sick with *mal de mer*, has its risks. The first few days seem to be the major obstacle. Later, everything gets into a certain routine and the danger of mishaps gets smaller.

For the 1984 single-handed race to Hawaii, we were required to make a qualification sail at least one hundred miles offshore and at least four hundred miles long. It was during this sail that most people had their difficulties, and it was one of the reasons that out of twenty-eight contestants only sixteen ended up at the starting line. My experience during that trip confirms that the first few days are the most difficult. I was constantly seasick in the qualifying sail, while by the time of the race itself I had become adjusted. The prudent sailor should go out on the ocean a month before the big voyage, preferably in some rough weather, to test the boat and to get conditioned for the *mal de mer*.

In April and May (the Hawaii race took place in June) the weather off the coast near San Francisco is usually pretty rough, but it is better to find the weaknesses of the boat and equipment (not to mention the sailor!) while close to shore, when deficiencies can be easily corrected. After my qualifier, during which I spent some of the most miserable hours of my life, I was ecstatic because I knew that after having experienced being sick and tired on a leaking, cold boat for four days in a gale, sailing to Hawaii was going to be a breeze.

Several weeks before departure, the solo sailor should start thinking about everything that might go wrong and immediately take action to prevent potential problems. If he has ever banged his head while the boat is in dock, he can anticipate banging it twice as hard while on the ocean. Some protective padding should be applied to the dangerous areas. What will fly around in the cabin if the boat makes a full 360-degree roll? The batteries and floorboards should be tied down. The galley is a dangerous place, not only because of the fire hazard, but because of the potential for burn accidents. There is rarely a need for boiling or very hot water! There is no need to boil the water for tea, coffee, or soup. Too many people have had their trips ruined because of hot water burns.

The alcoholic intake should be moderate. Statistical studies on drowning victims have brought some interesting information to light. Many victims were 1) males, 2) had alcohol in their blood, and 3) had their flies open! Alcohol apparently played a dual role in this set of events by increasing the victim's urge to urinate, and secondly, by causing him to lose his balance when urinating overboard.

Most mariners have seen the novice macho male sailor. He is finally not sick anymore and has been able to hold the alcohol in his stomach. He feels pretty good about himself and is thinking about applying for a modeling job for Marlboro cigarettes. He now has the urge to urinate and while hanging on to a shroud with one arm, is admiring his urinary stream, which seems even longer because of the ocean wind, provided he follows the Golden Rule of doing it over the leeward side of the boat. It does not require a big wave to throw *him* overboard. It is not demeaning for our male sailor to "lower" himself to sit on the head. He should remember the old dictum, "Sailor at sea sits to pee."

Seasickness remedies should not be tried out for the first time during the trip. It is safer to experience the side effects while on land and with other people around. The instructions should be studied! Many a sailor has hallucinated because he thought that the scopolamine patches should be applied every day instead of every three days.

The mariner should realize that immediate action is rarely indicated. This applies not only for medical problems, but also for sail changes, etc. On my solo race to Hawaii I took a photograph of every calamity before I did anything else. This tended to put things in perspective. It pays to spend some time in evaluating a situation. In my medical practice I have often seen that more harm is done in the first few minutes after an accident because of the tremendous urge we have to do something immediately. We have become conditioned by sirens, ambulances, and gadgets.

Many years ago, I recall, a man was caught under a tree he had cut down on a lot across the street from my home. I heard the sirens and ambulances, and when I arrived at the scene, the fire brigade, with a large crane, was frantically trying to lift a huge tree from the unfortunate man. It was evening and searchlights were everywhere. I was asked to examine the "patient," who by now was completely terrified. I calmly talked to him and found out that he was not in pain nor had he any difficulty in breathing. He was just plain *scared*. I reassured him and asked the crane operator to stop and re-evaluate the situation. My main concern was that the crane might move the tree which in turn might crush the victim. It turned out that we could remove some leaves and pine needles by hand from under the man and free him in that way. He came out of the accident unharmed!

It seems that in our modern days we grab automatically for

the most complicated methods and tools available. We physicians are no exception. We have been made to believe that it will be difficult to survive medical crises without a physician and the physician believes he will need all the tools of modern medicine. People around the world survive pretty well without the benefit of a coronary care unit. A study in England showed that uncomplicated heart attacks treated at home compared favorably with heart attacks that were treated in the hospital coronary care unit. It seems that the added stress and the definite risks of being in a hospital in many cases outweigh the peace of mind that comes with being at home in a familiar environment. So it may not be any more dangerous to have a heart attack in the middle of the ocean than in the "safety" of a hospital—although neither is desirable, or course. And remember that the many modern breakthroughs in medicine are to a great extent also available to the sailor. He can take along antibiotics, anti-hypertensives, and other medicines for whatever ailment he may be suffering.

The solo sailor may be concerned that there will be nobody to give him CPR (cardio-pulmonary resuscitation). There is an old dictum in medicine, *primum non nocere*, which means first of all, do no harm. With this in mind, I encourage everybody to get training in CPR, as there is no question that it has saved many lives. Problems develop not usually in the execution of the procedure by the layman, but in determining whether cardiac and/or pulmonary resuscitation is indicated. I have been in primary care medicine for over twenty years, and I have given CPR many times. Even in the relative quiet of an office or hospital, and with a stethoscope around my neck, it takes me some time to determine that a patient's heart has stopped beating. On the ocean, without a stethoscope, with the wind blowing hard, and on a boat which is rocking back and forth, it will not be easy to feel a pulse quickly. When the patient is in shock and has low blood pressure, it will be even harder.

Cardiac resuscitation is not harmless even in experienced hands (e.g., broken ribs can result). People who have had a cardiac arrest because of heart disease and who have been followed afterwards turn out to have a poor prognosis. In the case of a cardiac arrest caused by an electric current, asphyxiation, or drowning, the indications are more appropriate because we presume that we are working on a healthy heart. One of the reasons to give cardiac resuscitation is to try to get the patient to the hospital alive for further treatment. CPR is often most gratifying if the patient sustains a relatively minor heart attack with only a small amount of heart muscle damage, but, because of the particular location of that injured part of the heart, suffers a potentially lethal irregularity of the heart rhythm. The electric conductors that regulate the heart rhythm are in that case obviously right where the heart damage is located. This may lead to fatal heart rhythm irregularities such as ventricular tachycardia or fibrillation. These often respond to the use of a defibrillator. It is consequently crucial to keep the tissues, especially the brain tissue, oxygenated with CPR, until treatment with the defibrillator is possible. A defibrillator is usually not available on a small ship! Let us therefore be careful and be aware of the risks of CPR.

Pulmonary resuscitation is another matter. Here there is much less danger of doing harm and a relatively much better risk-benefit ratio. Injury to the patient (except to infants, by blowing too much air in their small lungs) is less likely and the diagnosis of "not breathing" is easier than in the case of cardiac arrest.

The solo sailor should familiarize himself with the Heimlich maneuver, to be used in case food becomes lodged in his windpipe. This maneuver can be done by the single-hander to himself. It behooves the sailor to learn this procedure because he is at increased risk of getting food lodged in his trachea when trying to get his food down while standing in strange positions, struggling to keep his balance, or eating while sleepy.

It should be stressed again that the section on medicine in this book should not be considered a regular medical manual for sailors. The prudent sailor should have on board a more extensive medical book such as the *Merck Manual,* or the *Ship's Medicine Chest and Medical Aid at Sea.* (See Medical Provisions section.)

A word of warning: The often controversial suggestions given in this book are meant only for the *solo* sailor far away from shore or other boats and unable to make radio contact to get medical advice.

Medications in this section are referred to by their most commonly-known name, whether generic or trade. Generic names are lowercased (i.e., erythromycin); trade names are capitalized (i.e., Empirin). When there is reason to use both the generic and trade name for the same drug, the generic name appears first and the trade name follows in parentheses. The names of most medications available only by prescription are followed by the ℞ sign.

SURGICAL INJURIES

We will now discuss general surgical injuries such as cuts, bruises, bleeding, foreign bodies, etc. A surgeon needs good light and good vision. The light must be strong and concentrated on one small point. Preferably, both hands should be free to work. There are small, strong penlights available which can be taped to the forehead. During the day one can go outside and let the sun come in over the back, but usually a strong, artificial light is more satisfactory. If the person is over forty-five years old, magnifying glasses may be needed, but even for younger people a set of these glasses is helpful. They should be available in different strengths, in order to have a choice for all types of work.

Suppose you have sustained a four-centimeter cut on the left arm. The cut is about one centimeter deep, and there is a lot of bleeding. Remember, when donating blood, one-half liter of blood is withdrawn without too many bad aftereffects. That puts things in perspective. Now sit down with the arm on the table and evaluate the situation.

The first thing to do is stop the bleeding. No need for tourniquets. Use a towel to dab the cut area and try to find the source of the bleeding, which could be a vein or an artery. The bleeding source may be hard to pinpoint. It does not matter too much. Now start applying fairly firm pressure on the cut for at least five to ten minutes. That will allow some time to calm down and at the same time give the blood a chance to clot. Maybe it will even provide time to read this section again. Normal bleeding or clotting time is usually below five minutes, but you want to take your time because there is no rush. The systolic blood pressure is presumably around 120 mm of mercury. If the bleeding source is arterial, the pressure applied should be a little above 120 mm. Take the pressure off the wound and see what happens. If, by now, more than 500 mL (one-half liter) of blood have been lost, the application of a tourniquet might be considered, however unlikely this is to happen. The problem with tourniquets applied by lay people is that they often are not put on tight enough and/or they are used unnecessarily. The pressure of the tourniquet is then below the systolic pressure, which makes the venous cuts (the most common ones) bleed even more. This is the same situation as when the lab technician draws blood after applying a rubber band around the arm to make the veins stand out. The use of the sphygmomanometer (blood pressure meter) is a good way to apply a tourniquet because the pressure can be read off the gauge. The pressure should be ideally a little higher than the systolic blood pressure.

But again, the chance that it will become necessary to use a tourniquet is very remote and in my practice it is indeed a rare event. If, for some reason, major bleeding cannot be stopped by simple pressure alone, it is worthwhile knowing that in a healthy individual one can leave a tourniquet on for over an hour. This method is often used in surgery on the extremities to obtain a clean, bloodless field. After releasing the tourniquet for several minutes, it can be reapplied if necessary.

You should have been able to find the source of the bleeding by looking carefully. Venous bleeding should have stopped by now, but an arterial "pumper" might not. The artery may have to be clamped with a small surgical clamp called hemostat and, if necessary, sutured and tied. It is advisable to carry a small hemostat on board for that purpose. Also available are small, disposable, battery-operated, sterile coagulators which are sometimes used in surgery. A coagulator has a small wire at one end, and, when one pushes a button, the wire glows and stops small bleedings when applied. Local anesthesia will likely be needed when using these battery coagulators. A small amount of adrenalin combined with the local anesthetic will sometimes contract the smaller blood vessels enough to stop the bleeding. Adrenalin should not be used on the hands or feet. (See Medical Provisions section for further discussion.)

Some of these medical instruments are great for purposes other than medicine! One of these is the hemostat. When making electronic repairs it can hold small objects and help to place them in difficult spots. Simple tools for many purposes are wooden tongue blades and wooden cotton applicators. The latter can serve to stop little leaks, clean the nails, open small valves, etc. Take plenty of them along. I always seem to run out of them on my boat.

After the cut has stopped bleeding, there are several things that can be done. One is to leave the wound alone and cover it with ointment and/or a bandage. This may seem crude, but in general surgery it is not unusual to leave large areas open. For example, if a large incision has opened a few days after surgery, it is often left that way and not resutured. In surgery on a pilonidal cyst at the sacral area (the part of the back where it loses its decent name!) the lesion is only excised and the wound left open to heal by nature. I hope this will reassure the sailor that in the event of sustaining a huge open wound and being unable to get the edges together or to suture the wound, he very likely will survive anyway! This also applies to wounds which cannot be reached by the solo sailor, for example, wounds on the back.

To bring the wound edges together it is important to make sure there is no foreign material imbedded. The wound should be cleaned as much as possible and rinsed with sterile water. To try to approach normal saline, one teaspoon of table salt can be added to a quart of fresh water before boiling it. If trying to save fresh water and salt, add one part of sea water to three parts of fresh water. All that is needed for suturing are a needle holder, forceps, a pair of scissors, some different sized suture material, and a piece of foam rubber to experiment with the suturing. The larger-sized cutting needle with the swedged-on surgical silk or nylon is preferred for the uninitiated. I advise the larger-sized needle because the smaller wounds are more easily treated by the beginner with Steri-Strips. (Steri-Strips are discussed further along in this section.) The plastic result may not be as good as with suturing, but these are special circumstances. The beginner should use silk to approximate the edges and plain catgut for the deeper tissues. There are better, less irritating materials such as nylon, but they are slippery and harder to work with for the beginner, and the knots untie easily. Again, suturing with silk is not that difficult to do.

In July 1954, freshly arrived from Holland and starting my internship in a Berkeley hospital, the call schedule was made up for service in the emergency room. We were asked who wanted to be on call on the fourth. "What is so special about the Fourth of July?" I asked, new to this country. Guess who was on? I had no experience in suturing even the simplest wounds. I asked the nurses in the emergency room for help and they supplied all the material. I quickly learned all the knots and suturing on foam rubber and was ready for the Fourth.

My first patient was a gentleman with a rather superficial cut on his hand, so there was no need to ask the surgical resident for help! With a lot of time and much perspiring, I finally got the job done in about forty-five minutes. This simple procedure should have taken less than ten minutes. When I wrote on his chart, I discovered he had an M.D. title behind his name. I was rather embarrassed, but he was very accommodating. It had taken "a little long" but he realized that "it is the beginning of July and the new interns have just started!" As a newcomer to this country I was startled by this American tolerance and it may have been one of the earliest impressions that made me decide to make these United States my home.

There is an amazingly simpler way than suturing to bring the wound edges of even large wounds together. All that is needed is tincture of benzoin and Steri-Strips. The Steri-Strips are sterile strips of paper with one sticky side. They come in different sizes to correlate with the size of the wound. The tincture of benzoin is indispensable to make the strips stick on moist or oily skin. Put the tincture of benzoin above and below the edges of the wound with a cotton applicator, let it dry, and apply the Steri-Strips while pulling the wound edges together. Leave the Steri-Strips on at least a week.

If there is further bleeding, a pressure dressing should be applied over the wound with gauze and elastoplast. Use the tincture of benzoin again to make the elastoplast stick and draw it as tight as possible over the wound so that there will be constant pressure to prevent further bleeding when you start moving the arm. Remember, look for the bleeding source and do not keep putting clean towels on the wound. That may give temporary mental relief as long as the towel is not blood-soaked, but in the long run it will not help.

If it is a large wound that has become contaminated, you might want to take some antibiotics. Antibiotics are discussed in more detail in the Infections and Antibiotics section.

Cuts on the scalp have a tendency to bleed heavily and may look worse than they really are. They are hard to evaluate because of the hair, which makes the wound messier. Good pressure directly over the area will stop the bleeding from these cuts in most cases. Use a clean handkerchief or gauze, or something similar. Rarely is there a need to do anything else as these wounds normally heal without infection and without any visible scars unless the patient is bald. The presence of clotted hair may be disturbing, but it does not seem to enhance the growth of bacteria very much.

Another common source of bleeding is the nose. Over 90

percent of all nose bleeds have their origin in the inner (medial) forward part of each nostril. Here again, firm pressure against the septum of the nose for several minutes will most likely stop the bleeding. Forget the cold compresses on the neck. It is not advisable to take pain medications containing aspirin (acetyl-salycilic acid) if there is a chance of bleeding because aspirin prolongs the bleeding time. On the other hand, if there is a high risk for vascular accidents such as clots in the coronary arteries (heart attack) or in varicose veins (phlebitis), it might be advisable to use one aspirin a day as a blood thinner. This should be discussed with your private physician who will be able to weigh the advantages versus the risks in each particular case.

Foreign bodies do not always have to be removed, but if it seems easy enough to do, it is certainly worthwhile trying. Again, make sure to have good light and use magnifying glasses. A splinter removal instrument is also very helpful.

With rectal bleeding bright red blood is usually coming from the end of the rectum. When it is mixed with the stool it often has its source slightly higher. If the stools are tar black and the patient is not taking iron or vitamins with lots of iron (either of which can cause the black color), it is possible that it is coming from higher up and possibly from the stomach (i.e., a bleeding ulcer). Most commonly, if the blood is on top of the stools or especially on the paper, its source is most likely a bleeding hemorrhoid. When in the bowl it may look like a huge amount of blood, but a few drops of blood may make the bowl bright red. The ladies lose much more blood during menstruation every month. No need to panic, like I did on a motorbike trip from Holland to Denmark. I was sure that my end was near and it ruined the fun of the trip quite a bit. Hemorrhoids are very common on camping or sailing trips because of changes in hygiene habits.

Blood in the urine is mostly caused by infection or trauma (i.e. kidney stone, injury, etc.), or less commonly by a tumor or a bleeding disorder. The most common cause in women is a bladder infection. (See urinary tract infections in the Infections and Antibiotics section.)

A common, not serious but painful injury is a subungual hematoma. This is a formation of blood under the nail after it has been hit. The easiest and least painful way to handle this is to straighten an ordinary paperclip, make the end red hot by holding it with a hemostat in an open flame of the stove, and then carefully burn a hole in the nail, stopping as soon as blood comes out. This may sound a little scary, but the blood has moved the nail from the underlying nail bed and if you go about it carefully, the hot paperclip will not touch the underlying skin.

Fire and burn prevention cannot be stressed enough. One of the most common causes of loss of a boat is fire. The usual precautions with the use of propane and gasoline are essential. Cooking on the ocean with all of its hazards is often a culprit. Even if the stove is suspended in gimbals and the pots and pans are fastened to the stove with clamps, a safety belt for the cook is recommended to prevent him from falling. Boiling water, if used at all, should be handled with respect.

The first emergency procedure for the victim with a not too large burn is to cool the area of the burn for at least twenty minutes. Cooling the burned area has been shown to reduce the depth of the damage done. The coolest material available for the Pacific sailor who does not have ice aboard may be the ocean water. The salt water should not be directly applied to the burn, but the coolness of the sea water should be transferred via a bottle or another type of flexible container. Ice, if available, must not be applied directly to the burn as this might crystallize the tissues.

The next step is to prevent the occurrence of infection in the burn. There is as yet no ideal topical antibiotic available for the treatment of burns. Silver sulfidiazine (Silvadene) is currently the most popular antibiotic cream for burns. If Silvadene cream is not available, another antibiotic will have to suffice, such as Bacitracin ointment. Nature's own blisters are the best cover to protect the wound, and only if the blisters have become dirty or contain pus rather than the clear yellowish body fluids, will it be advantageous to open the blisters and remove the dirty debris. Again, being alone on the boat and not in the rather bacteriologically dangerous hospital environment may be an advantage, and under these circumstances it is prudent to leave the wound uncovered except for the use of a thin layer of the Silvadene cream.

Non-traumatic dental emergencies can often be prevented by a visit to the dentist before departure. After he has done a thorough examination and has taken full mouth X-rays he will be able to treat early potential problems such as cavities and abcesses. For the young sailor he can predict future difficulties with wisdom teeth. A professional cleaning of the teeth may prevent gum problems.

Once underway, the sailor should treat dental infection (swelling, pain, and sometimes fever) with respect. Infections in the upper jaw may spread to the sinuses and even to the central nervous system, while infections in the lower jaw can cause swelling in the neck. Antibiotics are indicated and most dentists recommend erythromycin, though penicillin, ampicillin, or other antibiotics will also be helpful. (See section on Infections and Antibiotics.) One problem with the use of antibiotics for tooth infections is that the antibiotic does not penetrate well in this area and long term treatment may be necessary as long as professional dental care is not available. Almost all dental afflictions will benefit from warm, saline mouth rinses (in this case use half a teaspoon of salt in half a glass of water). Rinse the mouth for five minutes at least five times daily. Lost fillings or broken teeth can be temporarily treated with Cavit. This is a putty, available in a small tube and can be obtained from a dental supply house. Lost crowns, fillings, or teeth should be saved, if possible, for conceivable future reference. Crowns can be temporarily re-glued using chewing gum. Sugarless gum is of course preferred. Before use, the gum should be chewed and be ready to blow bubbles!

It is advisable to have spare dental appliances. In rough weather it is easy to loose or break these. The lack of dentures will not improve the sailor's morale and might interfere with his caloric intake. Dental emergency kits are available. Your personal dentist should be able to advise.

ORTHOPEDIC INJURIES

The solo sailor is reminded again to set up his boat, before departing, in such a way as to diminish the chance for mishaps. Once at sea he should try to remain careful and alert as much as possible. The waxed fiberglass deck becomes very slippery when wet. Walking should be done carefully on the boat, without rushing. The sailor should sleep when possible. The next twenty hours may require his constant attention. Everything that can fly through the cabin should be tied down. I taped my shoe laces down with duct tape to prevent tripping. Lee-boards should be in place to prevent falling out of bed. The rugs in the cabin must be firmly tied to the floor. The boat should be considered to be your living quarters during a chronic earthquake.

It takes some training to get used to the life harness. It will prevent falling overboard but it is by no means without disadvantages. In the excitement of working on deck in a rough sea we may forget it and will be rudely reminded when we find ourselves at the end of the line or wrapped around it like a puppy dog on a leash.

Despite our precautions, orthopedic injuries may occur. They are divided into sprains, dislocations, and fractures.

Sprains are injuries to ligaments and are usually caused by stretching a ligament beyond its normal range. This causes a tear and sometimes bleeding. The area involved becomes painful, swollen, and warm and discolored because of the underlying blood. There is no major medical breakthrough for treating these injuries. Our pain threshold will tell us what we should or should not do!

The non-traumatic joint or ligament problems such as arthritis, bursitis, and tendinitis, will be discussed in the Miscellaneous Medical Problems section. The use of anti-inflammatory drugs will be discussed in more detail in the same section.

The ankle sprain is common. Usually it is the outside ligament which is involved. The treatment for sprains is mostly the same regardless of the location of the injury. Pain medication should be taken as indicated. An Ace Bandage will minimize the swelling and give support. Anti-inflammatory drugs (see discussion of arthritis in the Miscellaneous Medical Problems section) may reduce swelling, relieve pain, and shorten the disability. After the initial stage, when cold compresses should be applied, heat may speed the recovery. Applying heat may, however, be impossible under the circumstances. In case of an injury to the lower extremity it is helpful to keep the leg elevated. Since Homo Sapiens started walking on two instead of four legs and since the laws of gravity apply, the blood from that injured foot has to work its way back up to the heart which, when we stand up, may be four to five feet higher than the injured area. That is why varicose veins occur more often in the legs than the arms. And that is why it takes so long for foot injuries to heal, whether they are sprains or sores. Therefore, the leg should be elevated as much and as long as possible. This can be accomplished by lying down on the floor with the leg resting vertically against the wall.

When one of one of the joints has become dislocated (out of the socket), it is advantageous to reduce it (put it back in place) as soon as possible. This not only gives quick relief of pain, but it can be done more easily immediately after the injury than a few hours later. If too much time elapses before a dislocation is reduced, swelling, edema, and fibrous tissue will set in, making it much more difficult to reduce the dislocation.

One of the most common dislocations is a dislocation of a finger. When compared with the same finger of the other hand, the difference will be obvious. To reduce a dislocated finger, it should be pulled away from the hand with long and steady traction. It probably will not be very painful to do this and, as a matter of fact, it might give some relief. The pull should be maintained for several minutes. A sudden click will be felt when the dislocation is reduced. In addition to a dislocation, there might be a fracture in that finger. Even if there is a fracture, traction would very likely do no harm. It might even reduce the displaced fracture! This is also true for other kinds of fractures.

Another common injury is the dislocation of the shoulder. If it has occurred on previous occasions, the patient should be trained to self-reduce a dislocation. Even if this happens for the first time, there is normally little difficulty in diagnosing a dislocated shoulder. After an unusual movement the shoulder "pops" and becomes very painful. When palpating the shoulder and comparing it with the other side, the difference will be noted. The injured person should now start pulling the afflicted shoulder by holding onto something (e.g., a door knob) with the hand on the injured side and pushing his body away from the door. Only the hand muscles and the weight of the body should be used. The shoulder muscles should stay relaxed. A long and steady pull may accomplish the reduction. A commonly-used method to reduce the dislocated shoulder is to have the patient lie face down on a table with a pillow under the afflicted shoulder, while the shoulder and arm hang over the side. A bucket containing water, weighing ten to fifteen pounds, is then attached to the wrist with bandages. The weight of the arm plus the bucket will, usually after fifteen to thirty minutes, overcome the tight muscles and pull the shoulder back into position. The disadvantage of the last method is that it will take the solo sailor at least ten minutes to set up this scenario, having the use of only one arm. In these ten minutes some spasm may already have begun. I advise using the first method immediately and, if that fails, using the method with the bucket. There is a chance that the solo sailor can reduce his own shoulder, even if this is happening to him for the first time. It is harder to dislocate a shoulder than to reduce it! Afterwards an arm sling should be used and the arm should be wrapped to the waist for protection from re-dislocation.

Through the years I have reduced fractures and dislocations in the field, far away from X-ray and other medical conveniences. I was always surprised how easily reduced many of these dislocations were, even without local anesthesia, if reduction was done soon after the event. There is always the remote chance of making a displaced fracture more displaced. However, it is rare that straight traction on a fracture or dislocation will do harm, and the chance of reducing it is so great that I feel comfortable advising the single-hander to at least try. The same applies to fractures of the forearm. If there is an obvious deformity and expert medical help is weeks away, immediate reduction should be tried. The chance of doing harm by straight long and steady pulling is relatively slight and it will help to better align the two fractured parts. In this case, the hand has to be pulled away from the rest of the arm. This can be done with the help of the other arm or the injured arm can be wrapped in an Ace Bandage and, using the bandage, the hand can be attached to something solid, like a doorknob. Traction can then be performed by pulling away from the point of attachment with the whole body. Another way is to have the hand of the injured arm grab hold of the doorknob directly, without benefit of an Ace Bandage, and then pull away from the doorknob with the rest of the body. The difficulty in this case is that the patient probably will tighten the forearm muscles, which need to be relaxed and not fight the traction. For the trained person it would be reasonably safe to inject a few mL of a local anesthetic in the fracture site to give some pain relief and better relaxation. These forearm fractures have a tendency sometimes to displace again after reduction. After reduction the arm should be placed in a firm splint with a relatively tight Ace Bandage. If the fracture or dislocation cannot be reduced, the patient very likely will survive, albeit slightly less comfortably. Later, on land, there will be plenty of opportunity to put everything back where it belongs under anesthesia.

Fractures of the lower extremities are harder to reduce if they are displaced. It may suffice to immobilize the fracture with a splint and wait for further treatment ashore. Fractures of the toes are common, but usually not of any major significance. The affected toe can be taped and splinted to the neighboring toes. A shoe with a firm sole and with the part covering the toes open will enable the patient to hop around with only minor discomfort. In case of an open fracture, where there is a direct connection between the fracture and the open wound, a problem of potentially dangerous bone infection exists, and the use of antibiotics is highly recommended.

The voyager should be able to "jury-rig" a forearm splint on the boat. I recommend taking along some flexible metal finger splints. My experience with the inflatable splints has not been very satisfactory. The extremity should be placed in the "functional" position. On a finger, for example, the splint can be bent so that the finger will be slightly flexed. Ace Bandages can be used to keep the finger or extremity applied to the splint.

Fractured ribs are a very common injury, especially on a bouncing boat with a tired sailor. The ribs are pretty well protected and secured by muscles and ligaments and therefore rarely get out of place. Fractured ribs may not be a source of major complications as a rule, but it is a rather uncomfortable event for several weeks. Elastoplast can be applied to the chest wall for some relief; however, this is by no means necessary. Before applying the elastoplast, it is a good idea to use the tincture of benzoin so that the elastoplast will stick. It will also make the removal of the tape more comfortable. One of my fellow contestants used duct tape when he broke a few ribs on the qualifying race. I am very glad I was not there when the tape was removed!

Neck and low back problems should be treated with heat, rest if possible, and with some form of support. If no braces are available for support, a pillow can be used, held in place by an Ace Bandage or duct tape. If muscle relaxants are on board they should be used with caution by the solo sailor in order not to interfere with his mental ability. For other remedies, see discussion of arthritis and musculotendinous diseases in the Miscellaneous Medical Problems section.

INFECTIONS and ANTIBIOTICS

Infections can be divided into four categories, bacterial, viral, fungal, and protozoal infections. For practical purposes we will address only the first two in the beginning. Viruses are much smaller than bacteria and are not visible with the ordinary microscope. Viruses cannot be cultured on simple media, in contrast to most bacteria such as the bacterium streptococcus. Common viral diseases are the common cold, influenza, and viral hepatitis. The virus can also settle in the throat or lungs, as with viral pharyngitis or pneumonia, respectively.

Even in a modern laboratory it may not be so easy to determine immediately whether an infection is of viral or bacterial origin. Most viral illnesses do not respond to antibiotics. However, when we realize the dangers of becoming ill while single-handing and being forced to continue sailing, and compare that with the situation on land where there is somebody to take care of us and where we can rest in bed when necessary, it becomes obvious that the possible and rather academic risk of taking antibiotics unnecessarily at sea is rather insignificant, unless there are known contraindications such as allergies, etc.

My advice, therefore, if there is fever caused by an infection and the sailor is alone and far from shore, is to take antibiotics as soon as possible. The sailor will have to study which antibiotics to take for what conditions and be aware of some of the risks. If the solo sailor has been in a malarious area and the fever may also be due to malaria, he might have to take some anti-malarial medicine or an antibiotic that attacks both the plasmodium of malaria and the bacteria of the other infectious diseases. (See discussion of malaria in the Medical Problems in Foreign Countries section).

As long as we are alive our body is slowly burning to produce our energy. This burning process makes our body warm to

about 98.6° Fahrenheit or 37° Celcius under normal circumstances. This base temperature may differ from one person
to another and it will fluctuate during the day. Usually at 4 p.m.
it is slightly higher. Before going on a long trip it might be
advantageous to find out what your normal temperature is
through the day. During the second part of a woman's menstrual
cycle the temperature is about three-fourths of a degree higher.
This occurrence is sometimes used to prevent pregnancy, and
is commonly referred to as "Vatican Roulette."

The temperature is a diagnostic tool that cannot be underesti-
mated by the single-hander because it is readily available and
can help him make a presumptive diagnosis and decide what
course of action to take. Make sure to have more than one
thermometer aboard, as thermometers break easily.

A thermometer is especially helpful in a situation where the
fever is only moderate. The only way to check the temperature
in this case is to measure it with a thermometer. If the fever is
102° it is obvious, but if the temperature is at 100° it may not
be noticed without checking it with a thermometer. The presence of fever indicates that there is very likely an infection
somewhere. If there is, for example, some mild lower abdominal
pain and the temperature is 98.6°, the chance of starting an
acute attack of appendicitis is much less than if the temperature
is at 100°.

In our modern medical offices all kinds of other testing
would be done, such as blood tests and cultures, to find out
what bug is the likely source. But on the boat we, as the Dutch
say, "paddle with the paddles we have."

Many infections do not cause a fever because the infection is
not generalized, as in the case of a bladder infection or a small
boil. Some viral infections cause the body temperature to actually drop.

Most antibiotics can be taken by mouth. Injected antibiotics
are not necessarily more potent, as so many patients seem to

think. For practical purposes, the oral route is the preferred way of administration, though it might be advantageous to have injectable antibiotics on hand.

The main reason to inject antibiotics on the ocean is that because of nausea and vomiting, none of the oral antibiotic may reach its destiny via the bloodstream but may end up at the leeward (we hope) side of the boat. Vomiting can be caused by seasickness; however, the disease itself may be the culprit, as in the case of appendicitis.

One can learn how to give an injection in an hour. The problem is that many injectables have to be refrigerated and refrigeration is a luxury few sailors have. Injectable antibiotics remain active much longer in powdered form. Immediately before use, a sterile saline fluid is added, as indicated on the package insert.

For reasons I have never been able to understand, the administration of medications through the rectum has never been very popular in this country. In Europe the use of suppositories is much more widespread. Recent studies showed that when phenobarbital was administered rectally to children with fever convulsions, the blood levels of phenobarbital reached therapeutic levels faster than when the phenobarbital was given intramuscularly.

In case the sailor is not able to keep antibiotics in his stomach and he has no access to injectable antibiotics, he might try to dissolve the contents of the capsule in a small amount of water and give himself a small enema. Again, this is meant only as a last resort because the absorption through the rectum and large intestine is rather unpredictable. For long ocean passages take injectable antibiotics along!

There is one advantage the sailor has over his sick counterpart in a hospital on land. It is very unlikely that he will have any of the exotic infections seen so often in our modern hospitals. Once out on the ocean, one is more likely to encounter the "garden variety" of bugs.

Here are some guidelines for choosing the "ordinary" anti-biotics that I suggest the single-hander have available on board. First of all, consider the antibiotics that have been taken before without bad side effects and with good therapeutic results. If there have been a few attacks of cystitis and one of the sulfas worked, take the sulfa along. If the mariner is allergic to sulfas or penicillin, those drugs, of course, are to be avoided. Check for cross-allergies of antibiotics that are chemically closely re-lated and to which you may have been previously allergic. Check the generic name, as it may have a different trade name, but be the same antibiotic! When I talk about allergy I am referring to reactions such as a rash, hives, or breathing difficul-ties. I am not referring to unpleasant side effects such as nausea or a yeast infection. The last complication is very common after almost any antibiotic, especially in women (yeast vaginitis). Many antibiotics cause photosensitivity reactions, especially tetracycline and its derivatives. Stay out of the sun when taking antibiotics and prevent sunburn.

The risk of taking ordinary antibiotics is relatively small. Remember, these are unusual circumstances. Thousands of kids with acne have been taking tetracycline for years without any trouble. However, it is well known that tetracycline should not be given to children under eight years of age, as it will stain their teeth.

It is good practice to ask the pharmacist to include the package insert. This enables the user to become aware of the side effects and the usual dosage. The expiration date should be noted and the antibiotics should be stored in a cool place. Some antibiotics can be harmful, in addition to being ineffec-tive, after their expiration date. The dosage of ordinary antibio-tics is often not very critical, but in general it is advisable to follow the insert's usual dosage instructions.

In modern medicine, before giving the patient antibiotics,

the doctor will often take a culture. That will tell him which organism is causing the infection. If indicated, a sensitivity test is done. The organism is then subjected to all the different antibiotics to determine which antibiotic is most likely to annihilate this germ. This method is, of course, of no help to the single sailor on the ocean, but this testing and the previous experiences in using antibiotics have yielded some general rules about the selection of antibiotics for different illnesses.

The solo sailor should especially watch for side effects as there will be no one else to see him if he gets confused, sleepy, or disoriented. If in doubt, start with a lower dosage to ascertain the particular effects the drug may have on *you*.

If there is no obvious improvement after a few days of using an antibiotic, another type should be tried. It is advisable to read the package insert to be aware of side effects. If new symptoms develop after taking a medicine, the decision must be made whether to continue or stop using it. The wise sailor will then carefully balance the relative need to continue versus the risk of more side effects. It will be prudent to change to another antibiotic if available.

In the United States, oral antibiotics require a doctor's prescription.

For upper respiratory infections (sinus, throat, nose, ears, trachea, bronchi, and lungs) most commonly used antibiotics, such as ampicillin and Bactrim will work. Erythromycin also would be an excellent choice for treatment of upper airway, bronchial, and even some alveolar (pneumonia) infections.

Intestinal infections are often caused by viruses such as intestinal flu. Under the unusual circumstances of the solo voyager however, it may be advisable to try ampicillin, Flagyl, Vibramycin, or Chloro-mycetin. Vibramycin is especially effective in Montezuma's revenge. "Chloromycetin" is not used very often because occasionally after prolonged administration it can have the side effect of bone marrow depression. It has the advantage that it (and Flagyl) work on anaerobic bacteria. These are bacteria that do not require oxygen to thrive. It might be the drug of choice in a case of impending appendicitis where the relative risks are outweighed by the dangerous situation.

For urinary tract infections such as bladder, kidney, urethra, and prostate, use Bactrim or ampicillin.

More detailed information about the choice of antibiotics for the different sites of infection will be given in the rest of this section.

Throat infections when associated with fever, are often caused by bacteria. Under those circumstances it is probably advisable to take antibiotics, such as ampicillin, erythromycin, or penicillin.

The names for other upper respiratory infections, pharyngitis, laryngitis, tracheitis, bronchitis, and pneumonitis, indicate the anatomic site of the infection down the respiratory tree. It will be more relevant to know *which* virus or bacterium is invading than to know in *what* part of our anatomy. Again, especially if there is fever and coughing up of yellowish or green sputum, antibiotics should be started. Ampicillin and erythromycin are indicated as antibiotics, particularly if a bacterial pneumonia is suspected. Symptoms of bacterial pneumonia are high fever, chills, productive cough with colored sputum, and sometimes chest pain. The effect of antibiotics in case of a viral pneumonia (less fever, less sick, sputum more whitish) is of course small. It might prevent a secondary bacterial, superimposed, infection. Without a culture and without the help of a blood count, it is always going to be a guess as to whether an antibiotic is indicated. In case of a bacterial infection the decision will have to be made which antibiotic might be the most appropriate.

Bronchodilators, either in pills or in spray form, are helpful to open the bronchi if there is a lot of wheezing. The sailor who is prone to bronchitis or other respiratory ailments (smoker, asthmatic, or emphysema patient) should discuss this with his physician. The ordinary cough syrups are of little avail and they sometimes suppress the cough reflex so that it is harder to get the lungs cleaned from the phlegm. Drinking lots of liquids may help to liquefy the sputum.

Ear infections are divided into two different entities. Internal (middle ear) and external otitis. Middle ear infections are located inside the drum and usually travel from the throat through the eustachian tube from a sore throat. This type of ear infection is often seen when a cold swells the eustachian tube and the middle ear becomes plugged up and the bacteria have a field day. Besides taking antibiotics it is worthwhile to take antihistamines to help clear the passages. Swallowing with mouth and nose closed may open up that passage. Closely related is a sinus infection, for which the same treatment is indicated.

External ear infections are actually infections of the skin of the ear canal. The skin in the canal is very tight over the underlying bone structure. If there is a small boil in the skin of the canal it could be very painful. It is usually painful to touch the ear canal in this case, while in a middle ear infection it is not. Treatment is again Bactrim or ampicillin and local therapy with VoSol ear drops or Lotrisone cream. Apply Lotrisone cream with a Q-tip. On land one usually tries to clean the ear canal very carefully, but that is not practical at sea.

For eye infections special drops have to be used, such as Garamycin eye drops. These eye drops can also be used for external infections of the ear when ear drops are not available Do *not*, however, use ear drops in the eyes!

The symptoms of upper gastro-intestinal tract infections (esophagitis, gastritis, and gastro-enteritis) are usually heartburn, nausea and vomiting, occasionally with diarrhea. These symptoms can be caused by hyperacidity per se and do not necessarily indicate an infection. If there is also fever, the diagnosis of an infection is more likely to be correct. The causative organism in this case is often a virus. When alone on the ocean the use of antibiotics might be considered. Treat the nausea with sea sickness pills and the heartburn with appropriate antacids. Use small amounts of liquids frequently to prevent dehydration and vomiting. A liquid diet is indicated in almost any illness but especially in the case of gastro-intestinal infections where clear liquids (orange and apple juice) are beneficial.

Acute diarrhea is caused by infectious viral, bacterial, and parasitic agents, poisons, toxins (spoiled food), and drugs. Drugs that may cause diarrhea on a trip include antacids containing magnesium hydroxyde and laxatives. Sometimes antibiotics themselves may cause diarrhea because of overgrowth of bacteria that are not sensitive to that particular antibiotic. In case of this type of diarrhea, the decision whether to continue to use the antibiotic will depend on the relative need.

In this country, viral or bacterial diarrhea usually runs its own course naturally and rarely requires therapy, other than the usual regimen of clear liquids and sometimes the replacement of lost potassium with fluids high in potassium, such as orange juice. In the adult, severe dehydration is rare in these cases. If there is associated nausea and vomiting, the sailor should try small amounts of liquids frequently. Start with a tablespoon every ten minutes and if this is tolerated, increase the amount gradually. If the diarrhea starts in one of the "developing countries" one should be more alarmed, as the chance of this diarrhea being caused by salmonella (typhoid fever) or shigella (bacillary dysentery) is considerably increased. The other cause of diarrhea, again more prevalent in the developing countries, is the parasite (amebiasis and giardiasis, etc.). These intestinal infections usually require antibiotic therapy.

What should the single-hander do when he develops a case of severe diarrhea after having left a foreign port in a primitive country? It is impossible to make an accurate diagnosis without a laboratory. Most probably the diarrhea was caused by the garden variety of bacteria, or toxins in the different type of food in that country (i.e., Montezuma's revenge). For prevention, only bottled water should be used for drinking. Carbonated water is preferable to make sure the bottle has not been filled out of the kitchen's faucet! Avoid uncooked vegetables, fruits without skin, fatty and heavy meals. Eat light and small meals (rice, tea) and peel the skin of fruits yourself.

Statistically, one out of three American travelers in the developing countries will get traveler's diarrhea. The diarrhea remits without treatment within two days in 55 percent of people, within four days in 70 percent and after one week only 10 percent of the afflicted are not well yet (data from the National Institute of Health). There is a tendency for the traveler to put pressure on the physician to give prophylactic antibiotics to prevent the *turista*. The doctor's reputation is at stake when his patient finds out that the other members of the group have some prophylactic drug he did not prescribe! If the traveler insists on taking some prophylactic antibiotics before the fact he should at least read the label to be aware of the side effects. This may suffice to change his mind. Remember that prophylactic treatment can bring on the development of bacterial resistance and may increase the likelihood of the *turista*. The use of Entero-Vioform was popular several years ago and it is stil available in some countries. It has been taken off the market in this country because of serious neurological side effects. So beware.

Besides the usual clear liquids some mild antibiotic such as Vibramycin, Bactrim, or ampicillin, might be tried when the diarrhea is severe or is prolonged for more than three or four days. If typhoid fever is suspected (headache, cough, abdominal pain with diarrhea or constipation, stepladder increase in temperature every day which stabilizes after one week, "pea soup diarrhea"), increase the dosage of ampicillin or Bactrim, or better, start chloramphenicol (Chloromycetin) at least 500 mg every six hours. If there is enough choramphenicol on board, that dose should be doubled.

The use of the popular Lomotil in cases of diarrhea is definitely contra-indicated. In general, the use of anti-diarrheal agents such as Lomotil, opium, paregoric, and kaopectate tend to prolong the illness while indeed giving temporary relief. They lower the gastro-intestinal motility so that the causative organism tends to stay in the gastro-intestinal tract longer, thus prolonging the illness itself. My advice to the patient is to use them only if unable to reach the bathroom in time and if this is, for one reason or another, socially unacceptable.

If the sailor is known to have gallbladder stones, he probably should have them removed before going on a long solo voyage. Severe pain in the right upper quadrant of the abdomen, radiating into the back, along with nausea may indicate disease caused by stones in the gallbladder, often leading to infection of the gallbladder.

If there is associated fever, antibiotics will be definitely indicated. If there is obstruction in the bile ducts yellow jaundice may become apparent. Liquid diet and pain medications will help.

Appendicitis often begins with discomfort in the mid-abdomen which moves later, in the classical case, to the right lower abdomen. There is diminished peristalsis (noises of the moving bowel which should only be heard with the stethoscope). There is usually pain on pressure on the abdomen more marked on the right side and aggravated when the hand is removed suddenly. Lifting the leg straight up often gives pain over the right lower abdomen. Bowel movements usually stop and there is often a low-grade temperature. Often there is nausea.

The use of the stethoscope is very helpful. It is worthwhile to listen to your heart with it under normal circumstances and to listen to the noises in the stomach when well. In case of appendicitis all will be "quiet on the abdominal front." The stethoscope can also be used for practical non-medical purposes. One can pinpoint an unusual noise easily with a stethoscope. This is often helpful in diagnosing which valve in the engine is making that awful noise, etc.

What are your chances if there is no possibility of expert help in a few days? Reliable statistics about appendicitis treated non-surgically are not available. However, there are some indications that the chances for survival in modern days with antibiotics are not that bad at all. It is not that uncommon, in children especially, to miss the diagnosis of an early appendicitis. The patient is treated for some general infection with antibiotics. The appendicitis keeps on smoldering or the appendix ruptures and forms an abscess which then becomes incapsulated. When the appendix ruptures, the patient feels temporary relief, but now the infection spreads to the peritoneum, causing peritonitis. With the continuing administration of antibiotics this process can often be fairly well controlled. Later, it will most likely become necessary to remove the abscess surgically.

Dr. Alvan G. Foraker in "A Reluctant Surgeon at Sea" (*J.A.M.A.*, Vol. 245, No. 22) describes how he reluctantly prepared to do an appendectomy at sea during World War II. When the patient was put on the operating table he said, "Doc, my belly does not hurt anymore. Maybe you won't have to cut on me." The patient had ruptured his appendix and now had peritonitis. He was treated with intravenous fluids and sulfa. In the next few days he developed a mass in his right lower abdomen. Six weeks later the patient was transferred to an army hospital, where skilled surgeons with good facilities excised his appendix and the surrounding abscess. All was well. It is now common practice that isolated medical officers on small ships do not attempt an appendectomy for ordinary cases of acute appendicitis.

Out in the countryside in China, the patient with a suspected appendicitis has to receive three days of acupuncture treatment before he is allowed to be operated on. This will often eliminate unnecessary appendectomies but apparently increases considerably the incidence of ruptured appendixes. I wonder how cost-effective this policy really is.

The quintessence of all this is that there is a good chance of survival in case of acute appendicitis even if the patient is a solo sailor. To increase chances of survival, it is advisable to have antibiotics on board.

If the unlucky solo sailor suspects acute appendicitis, he should start on a clear liquid diet. Intravenous fluids are for practical reasons an impossibility for the solo sailor. Never take laxatives. As long as there is no vomiting, oral antibiotics such as Chloromycetin, metronidazole (Flagyl) should be taken for a long time. These antibiotics also cover the anaerobic bacteria. Ampicillin can also be used, but does not cover most "gut" anaerobics. Ampicillin plus Flagyl would be a good combination. In case of vomiting, injectable antibiotics may be preferable if they are available. If injectable antibiotics are not available, the antibiotics may be administered rectally. If the appendicitis-afflicted sailor happens to be a well-trained surgeon he might be eager to operate on himself—this has been done! I would prefer to treat myself conservatively as outlined above. Also, I am afraid that the bending during my "own" appendectomy might throw my back out!

Diverticulosis is a very common occurrence in the elderly population and most people are asymptomatic. Diverticula are pouches in the wall of the colon. From the inside of the colon they look like small openings and from the outside they resemble grapes attached to the wall of the colon. They become increasingly frequent after the age of forty. Because stool can be retained in them they can become infected and lead to diverticulitis. This may manifest itself by lower abdominal pain, often left-sided with cramping. It is frequently relieved by a bowel movement. The course of this illness is usually mild, though occasionally a diverticulum ruptures and sometimes requires surgical intervention. If there is diverticulitis, the treatment is the administration of antibiotics, such as tetracycline and ampicillin. Chloramphenicol or Flagyl, if available, would be preferable.

Urinary Tract Infections include infections of the bladder, prostate, urethra, and kidney. The most common one, especially in women, is the bladder infection. This infection is usually accompanied by a burning sensation when urinating and a feeling of urgency. This happens often during vacations because of increased chance of vaginal irritation. In bladder infections there is usually protein and often blood in the urine. Most commonly the bladder infection is not associated with bleeding, but often the urine looks cloudy because of the pus (white blood cells) in the urine.

To facilitate the diagnosis of urinary tract diseases it is helpful to have some Uristix on board. These are small strips of paper, each with different colored stripes. Each color represents a certain substance to be measured in the urine. The color changes are compared with a standard chart. Some strips only indicate the presence of sugar and acetone to help diabetics control their blood sugar. To check the color change for glucose one can try out the Uristix in regular Coca Cola, which contains glucose. No need to urinate in the Coca Cola bottle, which a little old lady patient of mine found hard to do. She had misunderstood my instructions! The fancier Uristix also indicate the presence of protein and blood in the urine, as well as the Ph and specific gravity. Dip the Uristix in the urine and compare the colors with the color chart provided on the container. This product is available at the drugstore.

Because women have a shorter urethra (the little tube from the bladder to the outside), they are much more susceptible to bladder infection. Bacteria can easily come from the outside into the bladder. Often bacteria arise after intercourse (i.e., honeymoon cystitis) and therefore it sometimes may be advantageous to urinate after intercourse to wash the bacteria out and not give them a change to multiply all night in that nice warm urine in the bladder. Most women have had cystitis sometime in their lives, which somewhat correlates with urethritis or prostatitis in men. Most infective organisms respond well to the sulfa drugs such as Gantrisin, Bactrim, and Septra). Not infrequently some of the tetracycline drugs are more effective, especially in the male prostatitis.

Because these lower urinary tract infections are so common, I will repeat the main feature: painful, frequent urination, with a feeling of urgency and a burning sensation. The response to antibiotics is frequently obvious in one to two days. The urine often looks cloudy and the Uristix is commonly positive for protein and often for blood too. One should take plenty of liquids. There is usually no fever, in contrast to kidney infections when there is often fever associated with chills. With kidney infections the pain is often more constant and in either the right or left flank. Again, there is protein in the cloudy urine, but rarely blood. The response to antibiotics is slower and the patient is in general sicker.

For gynecological infections the reader is referred to the Medicine for the Female Solo Sailor section.

Infections of the Central Nervous System invade the lining of the brain (meningitis) or the brain tissue itself (encephalitis) and manifest themselves with severe, constant headaches, high fever, vomiting, and neck stiffness. If the infection is caused by bacteria, the use of of high doses of ampicillin or, if available, chloramphenicol is usually very effective.

For severe skin infections with pus formation or boils which often are caused by the bacterium Staphylococcus, erythromycin would be the first choice between the antibiotics on board. In the case of skin infections it may be helpful to also use some antibiotic ointment, such as Bacitracin ointment. Cellulitis and erisypelas are diffuse spreading infections of the skin. In erisypelas the infection is more superficial while in cellulitis the underlying skin is involved. In erisypelas we see a sharply circumscribed, red, hot, painful skin area with or without blisters. In cellulitis the borders are more diffuse and the skin is more swollen. Both afflictions often occur after a small break in the skin becomes infected. The use of warm compresses and antibiotics (erythromycin) will often ameliorate the condition.

Boils should never be squeezed and warm compresses are the best local therapy.

Some additional information about skin infections may be found elsewhere under burns and in the following chapter, Diseases of the Skin.

DISEASES OF THE SKIN

The most common skin problems the sailor may encounter will be either contact dermatitis or skin infections of bacterial, viral, or fungal origins. The generalized rash over the whole body caused by infections such as measles or the skin eruption like hives caused by allergic reactions to ingested foods (shellfish) or medications (penicillin) normally does not benefit greatly from local skin preparations. In these cases the systemic infection should be treated with antibiotics if indicated or the allergy should be treated with oral medications such as antihistamines or cortisone by mouth.

In the case of contact dermatitis, the skin is irritated by the saltwater, sun, or stronger heat, such as with a burn. Or there may be allergic skin reactions to a contact allergen, such as chemicals or plants. These diseases all need different treatment and the type of skin lesion regardless of its etiology, may need not only different medications, but may also require a specific vehicle, such as cream, lotion, ointment, or gel, to have the maximal therapeutic effect. Only a very superficial outline for treatment will be given because it will be unlikely that there will be more than one or two dermatological preparations on the boat.

The sailor's hands exposed to sun, wind, and salt water often become very dry and can develop fissures. Dry skins require lubricating or softening ointments or creams. Moist or oily skins profit from greaseless drying agents (gels). Acute, red, blistering, oozy, and wet lesions should be treated with wet dressings or soaks or lotions. The more chronic skin diseases with thickened and crusty lesions profit more from medicated ointments and creams. Sunburn, a common affliction among Pacific sailors, is to be avoided at all costs. Staying out of the sun, wearing protective clothing, and the use of a strong sunscreen are recommended. The sunscreen should have a sun protection factor (SPF) of at least 15. PABA may cause allergic reactions, so it is probably advisable to use an over the counter sunscreen that does not contain PABA, but that has an SPF of 15 or higher.

Bacterial infections of the skin are often started by small, traumatic skin lesions such as scratches. Often there are blisters filled with pus (pustules), or the pus becomes dried out and forms a crust (scab), as in impetigo. Local treatment with an antibiotic ointment, such as Bacitracin ointment, may be sufficient. If the crust rubs off easily, it should be removed. The antibiotic ointment applied to the red and sometimes oozy area below it will then be more effective. The bacteria are located below the crust and the ointment does not reach that area unless the crust is removed. If this does not improve the situation, systemic antibiotics such as erythromycin may be indicated, especially if the skin infection is associated with the formation of pus or boils.

Fungus infections (for example ringworm) are not unusual on sailing vessels because of the changes in clothing and bathing habits. They are often characterized by round, itchy, scaly lesions with a clearing in the center. Use anti-fungal creams such as Micatin, MycelexR, or LotrisoneR. Lotrisone cream, which is included in the minimal medical provision kit, contains clotrimazole and a cortisone derivative. Clotrimazole is effective against both fungus and yeast (candida) infections.

Yeast (moniliasis or candidiasis) infections are very common in the area of the vulva, vagina, anus, in the body skin folds below the breasts, in the groin area, and in the external ear. The main characteristic of these red skin lesions is itching. Almost any person, especially a woman, has at one time or another been afflicted with this annoying, but mostly not serious, skin problem. Yeast infections are very common after the use of antibiotics. Use Lotrisone, Mycolog ointment, or Mycelex cream.

In the United States topical cortisone preparations are now available over the counter without a prescription (½% cortisone cream or Cortaid). These are helpful for lesions not obviously caused by infection, allergic skin reactions such as contact dermatitis and poison ivy, or more chronic skin diseases of unknown origin, such as psoriasis. These over-the-counter cortisone creams are quite a bit less effective than the cortisone in the prescription drug Lotrisone cream.

To simplify the treatment of skin diseases on the boat, only two dermatological preparations are included in the minimal medical provision kit: Bacitracin ointment and Lotrisone cream.

In the case of a bacterial skin infection the skin is crusted, pussy, or tender. Use Bacitracin ointment locally and, if indicated, an antibiotic such as erythromycin.

In the case of a contact (allergic) dermatitis, fungus, or yeast infection, the skin is red, itchy, and scaly and Lotrisone cream should be used. In this case the cortisone in the cream will take care of the allergic skin rash and the clotrimazole will annihilate both fungus and yeast. One of the two ingredients in the cream may be superfluous, but without a definite diagnosis and under these unusual circumstances this is acceptable.

The economically minded sailor may, instead of using Lotrisone cream, prepare a mixture of two over-the-counter preparations. Micatin cream will cover both fungus and yeast infections and Cortaid cream contains cortisone. The Cortaid cream may advantageously be replaced by a more powerful but not necessarily more expensive generic prescription such as triamcinolone 0.1% cream.

Like some infectious skin diseases that may require systemic antibiotics, some allergic skin ailments may require oral (systemic) cortisone. Before using cortisone by mouth, antihistamines, such as Benadryl, Phenergan, or Actifed should be tried. Antihistamines often induce drowsiness, which the single-handed sailor can well do without. There is, however, a substantial range in tolerance for the diverse antihistamines. It is advisable to try them out before the trip to find out which one works best for the user.

A commonly used dosage for cortisone is prednisone℞ 5 mg tablets; six tablets on the first and second days, four tablets on the third and fourth days, and two tablets on the fifth and sixth days. This amounts to twenty-four tablets.

Other indications for cortisone, besides allergic skin reactions, are asthma, other life-threatening allergic reactions, bites from insects and sea creatures, or bee stings, especially when there is swelling of the trachea and breathing becomes difficult.

For people with previous allergic reactions there should be the usual medicines aboard, such as epinephrine for injection, and Sus-Phrine℞. The sailor should be aware of the side effects of prolonged use of cortisone. Cortisone can cause sodium and water retention, leading to an increase in blood pressure, loss of body protein and consequent osteoporosis, increased chance of peptic ulcer disease, and lowered resistance to infections. This drug may be life-saving for the sailor in rare instances, but the risks of its use should be compared with its potential therapeutic effect. (See discussion of asthma and allergic reactions in the Miscellaneous Medical Problems section.)

The use of soap combined with the lack of an abundant amount of water often causes problems. In our "civilized" world we are used to taking showers and we use a lot of water. On a boat we probably use less than a gallon of fresh water per shower, or we have to rinse with a bucket of salt water. In this situation we must use our soap sparingly and use a moisturizing cream afterwards. It is often the soap which gives the rash or skin irritation. We probably remember how small an amount of soap is needed to cover a large pond with bubbles. The modern soaps are that powerful. To remove all traces of soap we need extensive rinsing with a liberal amount of water, especially at the skin folds, in the groin and buttocks areas, and below the female breast. Many of my sailing friends agree with me that liquid Prell is easy to use when only salt water is available for washing. I have used it for years on the ocean not only as a toilet soap but also to do the dishes and wash clothes. When washing clothes it is important to rinse extensively to get all the soap removed from the clothes. The salt, however, will remain!

To soften the guilty feeling of charging so much, the manufacturer of expensive soaps often adds some unnecesary ingredients. I prefer the most commonly used soaps which have been used by so many other people that bad side effects would have been obvious. After Christmas time, I often see an increase in skin problems because of the expensive soaps given as presents during the holidays.

MISCELLANEOUS MEDICAL PROBLEMS

In this chapter we will first discuss the diseases of the arterial blood vessels and the involvement of the coronary arteries that supply the heart muscle with blood. Damage to these arteries may lead to a heart attack. We will further discuss arthritis and related diseases, peptic ulcers, kidney stones, asthma and allergic reactions, heat exhaustion and stroke, varicose veins and phlebitis, headaches and seasickness. In the "typical" heart attack there is pain in the chest sometimes radiating into the arms or neck. Sometimes the heart attack presents itself as indigestion. Sometimes the coronary is hard to diagnose even with an electrocardiograph and blood enzymes. This is not the place to go into details of the symptomatology of the heart attack. The candidate for a potential heart attack (because of age or other risk factors) might benefit more from information about diagnosis, treatment, and prognosis. There are no major medications or procedures for the solo sailor at sea who has suffered a heart attack. You should realize, however, that the prognosis for the coronary patient is not that much improved in the coronary care unit. The main treatment given in the hospital is the administration of oxygen and pain medications, the observation and treatment of undesirable rhythm irregularities, and assistance to the heart to help increase its output.

The survival rate in the coronary care units may very soon improve with the advent of the new drugs to lyse, or dissolve, the coronary clots within about six hours of onset, i.e., before there is too much damage done to the heart muscle. So the high coronary-risk sailor had better start taking off soon, for in a few years it might be considered irresponsible for him to do this. Perhaps it will be possible for the sailor with a coronary to inject these new drugs into his own veins to lyse the clots or to combat the heart irregularity. Who knows?

When one or more of the arteries to the heart muscle (the coronary arteries) are blocked, the electrical conduit that regulates the heart rhythm may be interrupted. This can cause potentially fatal irregularities of the heart beat. Drugs are usually administered intravenously (i.e., lidocaine) to prevent this from happening. There are new drugs on the market which almost have the same potential, and have an advantage in that they can be taken orally. Apparently their side effects prevent them from being ideal oral substitutes for lidocaine. The high coronary risk sailor is advised to discuss with his doctor the possible advantage of having them in his medicine cabinet. It might also be advantageous for him to learn to feel his pulse and recognize his usual rhythm so that he will be forewarned if there are any changes.

What makes somebody statistically a candidate for a heart attack? Having had a coronary in the past increases the chance of a second one considerably. Other contributing factors are strong family history of heart attacks, untreated hypertension, smoking, high blood level of cholesterol, diabetes, being overweight, and lack of exercise. It is unusual for women during childbearing years to have a heart attack!

If one or more of these risk factors apply to the solo sailor, he had better pay special attention and discuss these with his doctor. A treadmill test is a good way to evaluate the relative risk of a heart attack. If the sailor is in a high-risk group and insists on going anyway, he might profit from some instructions and he should take some anti-arrhythmic and other cardiac drugs along.

On the other hand, some patients undergo heart attacks without ever noticing them until sometime after the fact (silent infarct). This is usually picked up on a routine electrocardiogram. In retrospect, the patient can often recall some vague chest pains. In a way he is very lucky, now that he has survived.

He saved himself a lot of "heartache." He did not have any of the anxiety associated with "normal" heart attack recovery in what is to many people a frightening coronary care unit. And of course there are the financial advantages!

The above-mentioned risk factors apply also for other vascular "accidents" such as strokes (cerebro-vascular accidents) and clots in the arteries of the legs (peripheral vascular disease). These vascular accidents are the main cause of death in the adult and are more common than cancer. Study the risk factors carefully. There is the possibility of increasing the quality and length of your life if you so desire! Other diseases of the heart such as rheumatic or valvular heart disease and heart failure fall outside of the scope of this book. The sailor with a high risk for these afflictions should consult his personal physician before departure. Thrombosis and embolus in the vessels are discussed under varicose veins and phlebitis.

The sailor who is suffering from arthritis or other musculo-tendinous diseases (rheumatoid arthritis, osteoarthritis or gouty arthritis, bursitis, tendinitis, myositis, low back pain, neck pain, etc.) will benefit in most cases from the old fashioned treatment of rest, heat, and aspirin, regardless of the cause or site of the pain. Aspirin in relatively low doses has primarily an analgesic (pain killing) effect. In higher doses administered over some period of time, it will also have an anti-inflammatory effect. This way the aspirin will not only diminish the pain but also reduce the swelling and redness. In high doses there may be gastric irritation (heartburn, leading in susceptible individuals to stomach ulcers) and toxic effects on the equilibrium organ in the middle ear (cochlea), manifested by dizziness and ringing in the ear or aggravation of sea sickness. The sailor should have an adequate supply of aspirin on board in case there is the need for high dose therapy. I agree with many of my colleages who, according to the T.V. advertisements, would choose aspirin if they were allowed to have only one drug on a deserted island. Other non-steroid anti-inflammatory drugs are indomethacin (Indocinℝ), ibuprofen (Motrinℝ, Advil, Nuprin), naproxen (Naprosynℝ), tolmetin (Tolectinℝ), suldinac (Clinorilℝ), piroxicam (Feldeneℝ). The response to these drugs is often individually different. Besides aspirin, one other anti-inflammatory should be on board.

In more severe cases, when aspirin or other anti-inflammatory drugs are ineffective, a short course of a steroid such as oral cortisone might benefit the sailor. (For instructions how to use cortisone, see the discussion of allergic skin reactions in the Diseases of the Skin section.)

Peptic ulcer manifests itself with a persistant upper abdominal pain. Again, for a more extensive description of the symptoms of an ulcer, I must refer to more extensive medical books. Anybody who has had an ulcer in the past will remember the symptoms and signs, and will take along one of the H_2 antagonists, such as Zantacℝ or Tagametℝ, just in case.

If there is no history of an ulcer in the past and no strong family history, the old-fashioned antacids like Gelusil (which tends to constipate), Maalox (which often gives soft bowel movements), and Mylanta, or the popular Tums, may be helpful in case of heartburn or ulcer disease. These are unusual medicines in that they not only relieve the heartburn, but at the same time they also neutralize the acid and protect the stomach wall.

The importance of diet in case of peptic ulcer has not been clearly established. However, for the patient with signs of an ulcer it's worthwhile to avoid food that has upset his stomach in the past and to abstain from alcohol and coffee.

If he passes tar-like stool, he may be bleeding from his ulcer. Luckily, in most cases the bleeding will stop spontaneously. Perforation of an ulcer is associated with sudden severe abdominal pain and will only rarely heal over, but, fortunately, this is less common.

Though asthma and other allergic reactions may be less common on the ocean because of relative lack of allergens away from terra firma, it behooves the allergy-prone sailor to have some medications for this eventuality aboard.

If regular antihistamines do not work he may have to use cortisone tablets. For use of oral cortisone and its side effects see discussion of allergic skin reactions in the previous section. For a severe allergic reaction the sailor might have to give himself an injection of adrenalin (Susphrine℞, see Medical Provisions section). The asthma-prone individual should also have bronchodilators either in tablet or spray form on board (Theodur℞ tablets, Proventil℞ inhaler).

The passing of a kidney stone is usually associated with a lot of pain in the flank, radiating into the groin. The urine might not look bloody to the naked eye, but a few red cells in the urine will make the Uristix positive for blood. This is the time to use pain killers, not only to relieve the excruciating pain, but also to stop the spasm in the ureter where that small stone may be lodged. Strain the urine through a handkerchief or gauze to find and save the stone, which often is only a few millimeters in size. Analyzing the stone will help in determining what diet or medications should be used to prevent further stone formation and hence further attacks. If the stone has not been passed after a few days (persistent pain and blood on the Uristix), it is advisable to start on antibiotics (tetracycline, sulfa, or ampicillin) to prevent concurrent infection.

The elderly, male sailor with a history of an enlarged prostate might consider having a catheter on board and should be trained to use it on himself in case of urinary retention.

When the veins become dilated, knotted, and tortuous we talk about varicose veins. They usually occur in the leg and are more likely to get infected than normal veins. When the veins become infected we call it phlebitis. Besides varicose veins, there are other factors which predispose one for phlebitis, such as trauma and the use of contraceptive drugs. The use of elastic stockings by patients with varicose veins will diminish the risk of phlebitis.

In the case of thrombophlebitis of the deep veins, the calf of the affected leg become painful and sometimes swollen and hot. When the foot is bent backward there is often increased pain in the calf. This condition should be treated with respect and the sailor should, as much as possible, elevate the leg and apply heat if available. Standing still or sitting on a chair with the leg down are worse than walking. When the deep veins are involved there is a chance of clot formation with the possibility of a lung embolus (clot in the lung). Aspirin has an effect on the clotting mechanism and the use of it, even in low doses, may decrease the chance of a lung clot.

Thrombophlebitis of the superficial veins is characterized by redness and tenderness along the superficial veins. There is usually no swelling of the leg and no calf tenderness. There is no tendency to clot formation and the use of aspirin is not indicated. The treatment is otherwise about the same as for the deep phlebitis, but the course of this condition is usually brief and less dangerous.

Edema of the leg manifested by swelling ("pitting edema") is not necessarily due to varicose veins or other more serious afflictions. Working hard on the boat all day with some sunburn on the leg may lead to some swelling of the foot in any person. Elevating the leg will decrease the load on the veins carrying the blood back to the heart. Lying down on the floor with the legs in a ninety-degree angle resting against the wall for some thirty minutes several times a day, is often of great benefit. The use of diuretics (water pills) may occasionally be helpful.

If headaches are a problem on land, it does not necessarily mean that they will occur on the boat. There is often an emotional overlay in this affliction, more than in many other diseases. The change of environment and the reduction of social stress may actually reduce the occurrence of headaches. Fatigue and lack of sleep, however, may bring about a headache and one would be wise to take along whatever medication has helped in the past. If there is a history of classical migraines with relief after the use of ergotamine, the sailor should have plenty in the medicine cabinet. For most headaches the supply of a normal amount of analgesics, especially the prostaglandin inhibitors such as ibuprofen (see medical provisions) should suffice.

Heat exhaustion is a reaction of the body to prolonged exposure to heat. It is caused by dehydration, sodium depletion, or both. When the exhaustion is due to lack of water, which is not unusual on long Pacific crossings, there is often thirst, weakness, headache, and lack of muscular coordination. Frequently the body temperature is elevated. If not corrected by the administration of water, this syndrome may deteriorate into heatstroke.

The other cause of heat exhaustion is sodium depletion, mostly resulting from loss of salt through sweating. There is muscular cramping, no thirst, and the temperature is, as a rule, normal. The solo sailor should go to the coolest place on the boat and drink salted liquids. Tomato juice with at least one teaspoon of table salt is often very well tolerated.

The solo sailor in this condition often feels nauseated. Small amounts of liquids should be taken frequently, one teaspoon every five to ten minutes to begin with. Enteric coated salt tablets, which are absorbed in the intestines and not in the stomach, are often better tolerated and rarely cause vomiting by themselves.

Heatstroke is such a medical emergency that the only practical treatment for the solo sailor is prevention and early recognition. Remedial measures should be taken at the early onset of symptoms. With heatstroke there is a fairly sudden failure of the heat regulating mechanism. It often follows excessive exposure to heat and strenuous physical activity in hot weather. The use of tranquilizers, seasickness pills, and alcohol may play a contributory role.

At the onset there may be some headache, dizziness, and visual disturbances. Coma sets in later. At the earliest signs of this potentially lethal medical event, the sailor should rest in the coolest place or cool off with ocean water while checking his body temperature to make an early diagnosis. If the body temperature is above 100° he should be suspicious. As discussed before, he should be aware what his body temperature is under normal circumstances. Do not wait until the temperature starts rising. The temperature may reach 109° Fahrenheit (40° Celsius) in extreme cases.

Simple fainting after exposure and excessive exercise in the heat is luckily much more common than heatstroke. In fainting the skin is usually cool and moist and the body temperature is normal. After rest and lying down there are no further problems.

It becomes obvious how dangerous it is for the unseasoned solo sailor, who is often already exhausted and requiring anti-seasickness remedies, to be working on the deck in the hot sun.

Most people will experience some degree of seasickness the first day out in the new season, but most of them will get over it after one or two days at sea, depending on their individual susceptibility and the status of the sea. Once they have become adjusted, their acquired immunity to seasicknes may last for weeks after the sail. For the first few days of solo sailing, which are usually spent near the coast and the shipping lanes, it is a handicap for the solo sailor to be ill with *mal de mer* or to be drowsy from the anti-seasickness remedy. Before setting out on a solo sail it is prudent to have sailed in the immediate past and have some degree of "sea legs."

We perceive movement in space through impulses from the equilibrium organ (cochlea), which is part of the inner ear. Three tiny circular canals in three different planes contain fluid that moves when there is a change in position. This fluid, when moved, in turn moves tiny sensors and a signal is sent higher up to the brain. When there is more movement than usual, as on a ship, motion sickness appears. When there is an infection of this organ (labyrinthitis), similar symptoms ensue.

It is often helpful to counterbalance this reaction by concentrating the eyes on a stationary object like the horizon, thus creating a conscious sense of our place in space. When we look at an object in the boat, our eyes are telling us that we are not moving, while our semi-circular canals are busy moving the little sensors all the time because of the movement of the boat. This contradiction aggravates the illness. That is the main reason that when people go "below," the nausea almost always becomes worse. I like to have the sick crew member stand at the wheel and watch the horizon. Standing makes it possible to sense the movement of the boat and rectify it by balancing with the legs so that the head stays relatively stable. Looking at the stable horizon will also add to the sense of stability.

It is important for the sick sailor to try to keep his fluid balance in order and to frequently take small amounts of fluid to prevent dehydration.

There are many medicines on the market for seasickness. Each sailor or doctor has his preference. Still popular is Dramamine. One 50 mg tablet every four hours is the usual oral dose.

For the person who, because of vomiting, is unable to take

tablets, one 100 mg suppository can be inserted rectally every eight hours. Dramamine causes drowsiness, which for the single sailor is a disadvantage. For the crew member who is feeling so sick that he would like to commit "temporary suicide" and lie down below, it may be advantageous to take a double dose.

Promethazine (Phenergan℞) 25 mg, often in combination with ephedrine to counteract the drowsiness caused by the former, is popular with many sailors. Other medications are meclizine (Antivert℞) 12.5 or 25 mg tablets, Benadryl, and Bonamine. Some people recommend starting the medications the day before rather than a few hours before departure.

Scopolamine patches (Transderm℞) have become very popular and are effective. I used them the first few days of my sail. They are sold by prescripton only and should not be used except with utmost caution. The patch is applied to a hairless area on the skin behind one ear. The medication is then slowly absorbed through the skin after about two to four hours and will continue to be absorbed for a period of three days. It is important not to get any of the material on the fingers. If this happens anyway, the hands should be washed thoroughly. If the contaminated finger touches the eye accidently, a trace of scopolamine will completely dilate the pupil. Even without direct contamination, the pupils might dilate, often only on the side of application. Side effects are dry mouth, blurred vision, drowsiness, and in case of an overdose, delirium and delusions. If because of delirium and delusions, the user presents himself to an unsuspecting physician who finds one dilated pupil, he might be misdiagnosed as having a major brain disorder! The physician should be notified about the previous use of a scopolamine patch! The dose is one patch applied behind the ear every three days. Take the other patch off when applying a second one, in order not to overdose.

For centuries it has been suggested that the root of the ginger plant has an anti-nausea effect in the case of seasickness. Recently, triple blind studies have objectively demonstrated that ginger is more effective against the nausea of seasickness than Dramamine. (Daniel B. Mowrey and Dennis E. Clayson "Motion sickness, ginger, and psychophysics," *The Lancet* [1982] 655-657.) Ginger can be obtained from a herbalist or health food store. For the person who does not like the taste of ginger root, it can be obtained in capsules. Recommended dosage is 900-1000 mg powdered ginger root in a capsule every four to six hours.

MEDICINE FOR THE FEMALE SOLO SAILOR

Though sailing, especially single-handed sailing, throughout the years, had a "macho" male connotation, I would like to address the specific medical problems that may be encountered by the female sailor. Some of my best sailing friends are women. As a matter of fact, the only persons I trusted enough to bring my boat back from Hawaii were three lovely female sailors. I was pleased and honored that they called themselves "Peter's Angels." They *were* angels for delivering my boat back to the San Francisco Bay Area in good shape. I hope this section will be of help to the many courageous women who are solo sailors.

Being of the opposite sex puts me at a disadvantage when advising women on female medical matters, but since no female physician or nurse solo sailor has written about the subject, I do not feel I am stepping on any woman's toes.

I delivered some two thousand babies during my younger years, but I still have no idea how it feels to be pregnant with child. To avoid being too harshly criticized by my female readers, I asked for help from two female sailors, Linda Rettie and Karin Hughes, R.N. Karin, like Linda, has been on long ocean crossings and has experienced the typical adversities women have to put up with under such unusual circumstances. The three of us met with my colleague, Risa Kagan, M.D., a Berkeley gynecologist. The following is a summary of the subjects we discussed.

The importance of preventive care was stressed. Each individual woman has her own set of problems that might arise during a trip. These problems should be discussed with her own doctor before taking off and a list of medications to take along should be made up for the woman's particular needs.

The medication should be tried out on land first to see how it will be tolerated. The chances for infection during the farewell festivities should be kept to a minimum. This will prevent that nasty venereal or any other infection, which might surface after only a few days out on the ocean!

Careful contraception is a must. The nausea of pregnancy does not ameliorate with the up and down movement of the boat! A miscarriage without medical help can be dangerous, and the amount of blood loss, though usually not too significant, can at times be life-threatening. An ectopic pregnancy at sea would be a disaster for the solo sailor. If there is any possibility of being pregnant, it is advisable to have a pregnancy test shortly before leaving. Nowadays, these tests are reliable very early in a pregnancy.

If menstrual periods are regular and of normal strength on land, it does not necessarily follow that this is going to be the case at sea. The timing and amount of flow are mostly regulated by the ovarian hormones, estrogen and progesteron. These hormones in turn are regulated by the hypophysis, the master gland, which again is under the influence of the hypothalamus which receives stimuli from the rest of the brain. Some "all girl" crews report that they synchronize their menstrual cycles. Psychological factors have a profound influence on the timing and flow of the menstrual period. The excitement of a big event like a solo ocean crossing may throw off the hormonal system and often does, as many women sailors will concur.

There may be heavy bleeding or there may be no periods at all during the trip. The cycle may become irregular all of a sudden. It is therefore important to remember not to become too alarmed when this happens. We can see how necessary it is to prevent pregnancy before leaving so as not to be confused and worried about the absence of a menstrual period. If the sailor plans to use birth control pills to prevent heavy menstrual bleeding during the voyage, she should start taking them several months before departure so that individual side effects have become evident. There are so many different birth control pills containing different hormones that one must discuss the different options with an expert.

Birth control pills will accomplish several goals. They will make an unplanned pregnancy highly unlikely. They usually make the periods not only regular, but light or even absent. This last effect is a blessing for the woman for whom circumstances such as foul weather gear, difficulty in changing clothes, sleeping dressed, lack of showers and other land amenities make the period really unpleasant. Another beneficial effect of the birth control pill is that in some cases it helps to lessen the symptoms of premenstrual tension. Another advantage of using birth control pills is that it prevents ovulation. This will not only prevent pregnancy, but also will remove the discomfort which many women experience in the middle of the cycle. This *mittel schmerz* (German for "middle pain") can be confused with an attack of appendicitis, particularly if the ovum being shed is in the right ovary. Woman have been operated on for appendicitis when the pain, slight fever, and elevated white blood count were actually caused by ovulation. The woman sailor might, like the surgeon, have difficulties in differentiating between these two conditions!

A lot of blood can be lost during the menses and this is the most common reason for women to become anemic. Plenty of iron pills should be in the medicine chest.

If menstrual cramps and headaches during the period have been common before departure, the sailor should use whatever method or medication was effective before. Prostaglandin inhibitors ibuprofen (Motrin℞ 400, 600 or 800 mg tablets, Advil or Nuprin 200 mg tablets) often are effective in giving relief.

Before going on a long solo voyage a thorough self examination and professional examination of the breast is indicated in order to prevent unpleasant surprises under way. A mammogram might be helpful. Generalized breast discomfort can be helped with analgesics or sometimes with diuretics if there is considerable premenstrual fluid retention. Mammary dysplasia (fibrocystic disease) is a common cause of painful and lumpy breasts often aggravated premenstrually. Avoid trauma and wear, day and night, a bra which gives good support. Many centers and individual patients report improvement after the discontinuance of coffee, tea, and chocolate.

Breast abcesses are relatively rare outside the post partum period. They should be treated, like any other abcess, with hot compresses and antibiotics.

Infection of the uterus, tubes and sometimes of the ovaries, manifests itself with lower abdominal pain, chills and fever, vaginal discharge, and menstrual irregularities. Every day farther away from the coast the chances for this event will be diminished for the solo sailor. High doses of antibiotics should be taken (Keflex, tetracycline, ampicillin). Pain should be controlled with analgesics, and a liquid diet will be helpful, especially when the fever is high. The I.U.D. user has a double chance of getting this disease. Caution in selecting sexual partners is therefore advised in the weeks before departure on the solo sail.

Bladder infections were discussed in the Infections and Antibiotics section.

Most women sometime or another have been afflicted with vaginitis. It is much more common under the circumstances of a sailing trip. The constant wearing of foul weather pants and the exposure to salt water make that particular area much more prone to irritation, perspiration, and infection.

There are basically three different groups of causative organisms: monilia vaginitis, trichomonas, and non specific vaginitis. Monilia, or yeast, vaginitis is common and is characterized by a cheesy discharge accompanied by intense itching and sometimes a brightly inflamed vaginal mucosa. It is very common after the use of antibiotics, when the "good" germs in the vagina have also been destroyed and the yeast bacillus, having no more adversaries, can quickly multiply.

Monilia vaginitis is easily treated with clotrimazole (Gyne-Lotrimin℞ vaginal tablets or cream). It is such a common and annoying disorder that I recommend that women on an extended crossing take at least fourteen tablets along. If none are on board, the sailor can use Lotrisone cream℞ intravaginally as an alternative. This cream is mentioned on the list of minimal medical supplies (kit #1) in the Medical Provisions section. The chances of needing to take antibiotics on an ocean crossing are increased and this enhances the possibility of a monilia infection. Mycolog is mentioned on the list for minimal medical supplies in the Medical Provisions section.

Trichomonas vaginitis is also very common. It is often associated with a milky profuse discharge. It responds to treatment with Flagyl. If there have been trichomonas infections in the past, it might be worthwhile to take some Flagyl oral tablets along. These Flagyl tablets can also be used for amoebic and a few other infections. It depends a little bit on the pocketbook and the risk factors as to how well-stocked the medicine cabinet should be.

The non-specific vaginites may sometimes also be treated with Flagyl or with other antibiotics, such as tetracycline for chlamydia infections or ampicillin for gardnerella. The more common douches also may be helpful. These vaginal infections will not directly threaten survival, but they may drive the sailor insane, which in itself is a threat to life for the single-handed sailor. So take care!

Speaking about sanity, I will now very hesitantly (being a male) discuss premenstrual syndrome (PMS). There is no subject that is more controversial between the male physician and the female patient than the problem of PMS. I have great sympathy for the woman who, for practical purposes, finds herself still going to a male gynecologist. It is about time that the laws of supply and demand made it a little easier for American women to go to a gynecologist of the same sex! How many of our male physicians would like to go to a female urologist? In Russia most of the primary care physicians are women!

The premenstrual syndrome for the single-handed woman sailor needs to be discussed more extensively. The negative mood of the single sailor can be destructive enough to interfere with the safety of the passage. This is not only true for the single-hander, but also for the female crew member. Getting on each other's nerves, while living for a long time in close quarters, is very common on long ocean voyages. Most sailors who have been on a small boat for a long time know about the tensions that almost any crew has experienced.

I happen to believe there is a male counterpart to PMS. I am suspicious that the human male also goes through a monthly mental cycle, just as the female does. It may not be as easily explained physiologically. Another difficulty with the male is that it seems harder for him to accept a hormonal imbalance and he is usually less able to be introspective about it than is his female counterpart.

It would be interesting to have a group of males describe their outlook on life daily for several months and have them keep a diary. At the same time, a close friend or wife should objectively describe their observations of the men. I am sure that similar, perhaps not so pronounced, monthly waves of mood swings would become apparent! It would be a nice subject for a thesis for a female gynecologist and it might put our conventional male attitude toward this "female" syndrome in a different perspective!

After all these ramblings I dare to continue about the premenstrual syndrome. The causes of premenstrual tension have been a source of several studies, especially in recent years. In all probability the causes are multi-factorial and have to do with the hormonal, metabolic, and electrolyte changes that occur in the second half of the cycle.

The feeling of emotional and physical tension can become so disturbing as to interfere with the common routines of daily life. In its most severe form, it may lead to emotional instability, impaired mental acuity, and depression. Somatic complaints vary and include headaches, breast soreness, abdominal distension, and pelvic pain. The cause and symptomatology of this syndrome differ so much from one individual to another that each patient requires a specific treatment.

Many new different hypotheses have been proposed recently about the etiology of PMS. Rather interesting and promising is the one that correlates the hormonal changes in the second half of the cycle with increased levels and subsequent decreased levels of endogenous opiate peptide (EOP). Many of the symptoms of PMS resemble opium withdrawal symptoms! So there you are, and who told you it was all in your head?

Treatment should be tailored to the specific individual's complaints. It is important to keep a record during a few cycles of the daily changes in mood, sexual desires, energy levels, sleep, weight, appetite, craving for sugar or junk food, caloric intake, and intake of dairy products and sugars. When a diary is made of these changes, it often reveals that in the second half of the cycle many women consume more sugar and dairy products and coffee then during the first half of the cycle. Even though the tendency to do this in itself is probably caused by the hormonal changes, it seems to aggravate the symptoms. Many women get relief from a diet that is relatively high in protein

(15%) and high in vegetable oils. The carbohydrates consumed should be of the complex and slow-releasing kind (i.e., high fiber vegetables and bread, etc.). The simple sugars should be avoided to prevent excessive insulin swings with consequent low blood-sugar levels (i.e., hypoglycemia). Alcohol works in this respect in a similar way and should also be avoided. Many women who have changed their eating habits during the second half of the cycle have reported subjective improvement.

Evaluating the effect of treatment is very difficult because double blind studies are difficult and the results are mostly based on subjective improvement of symptoms. The placebo effect, especially with a sympathetic physician, is also not measurable. The courageousness, intelligence, and physical stamina required for the solo sailor will probably make her a more reliable judge of treatment results than the average woman in this case.

If there is a considerable amount of weight gain not caused by increased caloric intake but by fluid retention (over three pounds), the woman may benefit from the administration of a diuretic like spironolactone (Aldactone℞). If breast tenderness is the main complaint, the administration of bromocryptane mesylate (Parlodel℞) may help if the woman can tolerate the often associated headache and nausea! Your physician should be able to advise. In other cases the cyclic hormone treatment with low-dose (low progesteron) birth control pills alleviates the symptoms. Occasionally the birth control pills aggravate the depression, thus it is essential to continue charting the diary carefully to evaluate the overall effect of this treatment on PMS. Some centers advocate the use of vitamins, especially vitamin B_6 (pyridoxine) in moderate to high dosages (100 mg to 500 mg daily). Magnesium may increase the absorption of this last vitamin. Neurological complications may occur with megadoses of vitamin B_6.

One of the most useful medications for premenstrual anxiety

and depression, if the conservative measures such as diet and vitamins have failed after several months of trial, is the hormone progesteron, often given in suppository form. A suppository of 100 mg is inserted vaginally twice a day during the second half of the cycle, when symptoms start. Medication is stopped at the time of the menses. Again, in certain cases this drug might aggravate the condition.

It should be clear that the cooperation of the patient to help diagnose and evaluate the treatment of this syndrome, more so than with most other illnesses, is of the utmost importance. The female solo sailor should realize that what may be a mild problem in daily life, can become life-threatening when she is alone on the ocean. Here she cannot lie down in a dark room because of the intense headache. What might have been a mild depression on land may develop into a much more severe form. She needs all the mental acuity available and she cannot function to her full capacity if normal anxiety, which most solo sailors experience, becomes exacerbated because of cyclic changes.

MEDICINE IN FOREIGN COUNTRIES

The solo circumnavigator will very likely make landfalls in primitive countries. This chapter will address some of the measures to be taken to minimize the risk of potential medical problems.

The traveler should have a thorough physical examination with appropriate laboratory tests before embarking on his trip.

As will be mentioned later, it may be helpful to have blood serum drawn before leaving and to save it for possible future reference in case difficulties arise with diagnosing some tropical disease. The rising antibodies in the blood will facilitate making a diagnosis after returning home.

It may be helpful to take along a copy of the last blood test results and the last electrocardiogram, especially if they were abnormal. In some cases, having a previous electrocardiogram available for comparison may prevent unnecessarry worry and hospitalization later.

The traveler should start preparing for the trip early. Sometimes six months are necessary to receive all necessary immunizations.

If the patient comes to the office only one week before leaving, the physician will be forced to give some immunizations too close together. Some of them should be given weeks or months apart. The gamma globulin injection for modification of hepatitis A can be given the day before leaving, but this injection may interfere with the effectiveness of the other immunizations.

The doctor should spell out the full month on the health certificate. There still are some doctors who do not realize that of the whole world, the United States is one of the few countries that uses the first number in the date as the month. 12-1-85 may mean December 1 in the United States, but it means January 12 in the rest of the world. Try to explain that to some customs official in South America without some dollar bills in hand! It would be an exercise in futility to Americanize the rest of the world in this respect. Our system seems the less logical of the two, anyway!

It is advisable to know one's status concerning tuberculous infections. A tuberculin converter is someone who has been recently infected by the tuberculosis bacillus for the first time. The T.B. skin test that was previously negative now becomes positive and usually remains positive the rest of one's life. Most of these people do not feel ill even though they have a tuberculous infection. The great majority of people in the United States (especially the younger generation) are tuberculin negative. In a developed country, where there is little chance for exposure to T.B., it is relatively rare for a person to convert his skin test from negative to positive.

The T.B.-negative person has not developed the specific antibodies and therefore has a much greater chance of being infected in a developing country where open T.B. is more common. I therefore strongly advise this traveler to receive at least one more T.B. skin test after returning to the States, to rule out a recent infection.

Most authorities in this country agree that treatment for recent T.B. converters is indicated, even though they usually are not clinically ill and have a normal chest X-ray. Eradicating the infection is relatively harmless and inexpensive. The typical treatment consists of one INH tablet daily, while the liver functions are periodically watched with blood tests. The length of treatment is somewhat controversial and varies from six to twelve months.

The positive tuberculin reactor, i.e., the person who has been infected with tubercle bacilli, may develop clinical tuberculosis later in life. This is more likely to happen after certain treatment modalities that change the resistance of the body's immune system, such as cancer chemotherapy and long-term treatment with cortisone. Tuberculosis skin tests will usually remain positive whether or not the disease is clinically present. To rule out active tuberculosis, one will therefore need a chest X-ray. On the other hand, having developed some immunity, one is less likely to develop active T.B. after re-exposure, in contrast to the negative T.B. reactor.

During the 1950s and 1960s there were great expectations that malaria, like smallpox, would be eradicated before the next decade. The World Health Organization expended world-wide efforts, spraying DDT for rapid control. For a long time, it minimized basic research in the disease itself, thinking that the spraying would be sufficient to wipe out the disease. Although this policy was initially successful, we may now be back to the original prevalence—with the added problem of new and resistant strains emerging. The resurgence of malaria in the 1970s and 1980s has made malaria prophylaxis again one of the most important items to consider for the world traveler.

Worldwide there are over one million deaths every year from malaria. Through the centuries and up until now, malaria has been responsible for more deaths than any other transmissible disease. If the traveler is going to a malarious area, he should take chemoprophylaxis before, during, and for six weeks after the trip. The usual prophylaxis is to take one tablet of chloroquine phosphate (Aralen℞ 500 mg) once a week, starting one week before, and continuing for six weeks after exposure. Many experts prescribe primaquine phosphate during the last two weeks of chloroquine prophylaxis. Primaquine can cause severe anemia in persons with a certain enzyme (G-6-PD) deficiency. Users of this drug should be screened by a blood test for this deficiency.

One of the four types of plasmodia that cause malaria, plasmodium falciparum, has become resistant to chloroquine in some areas. In those areas another drug, Fansidar℞, can be added. Its dosage, like that of chloroquine, is one tablet every week. The drug is quite toxic and should be used only when going to areas with known chloroquine-resistant malaria. Severe side effects of Fansidar have been reported by the FDA (Food and Drug Administration). Fatal reactions have occurred in approximately one out of 22,000 users. Three times as many will get ill. Most of these reactions have occurred in patients receiving multiple doses of Fansidar, usually given for prophylaxis, and are less likely with the common one-dose Fansidar treatment for established malaria. Chloroquine seems to remain the mainstay of preventive malaria treatment. Some authorities recommend that travelers in chloroquine-resistant malaria areas take along a few tablets of Fansidar and use them in case they develop a febrile illness while expert medical care is not immediately available. This certainly seems appropriate for the solo voyager in the tropics or the sailor who might make an unexpected landfall there. They, of course, should have been using chloroquine prophylacticly.

The antibiotic doxycycline (Vibramycin℞) is being evaluated for preventive and therapeutic treatment of malaria. The solo traveler who has been in a malarious area, develops fever, and is unable to make a diagnosis might decide to use Vibramycin to combat both malaria and other infectious diseases, especially when Fansidar is not available.

There are several other drugs on the market outside the United States which may be recommended in a particular area. These are only for prophylaxis and *not* for treatment of malaria. They are not effective in preventing plasmodium falciparum infections resistant to chloroquine. They are: amodiaquine (Basoquine℞, Camoquine℞), related to chloroquine; pyrimethamine (Malocide, available in the United States as Daraprim℞); proguanil (Chlorguanide℞, Paludrine℞).

All these drugs can have serious side effects and should be used only after thorough clinical consultation.

It seems that we have to tailor our medication to the area where we will encounter malaria. If the consulted physician is not an expert, the traveler may have to do the groundwork himself. Call the local or the state health agency, or direct your questions regarding malaria prophylaxis and treatment to the Center for Disease Control, Parasitic Diseases Division, Atlanta, Georgia, 30333. Call (404) 329-3670. For emergencies only, nights and weekends call (404) 329-2888.

The people in the malaria area are often well aware of which drug is most effective for their local malaria strain. However, they have a tendency to minimize the potential risks of these drugs and caution is recommended in using their advice.

With the resurgence of malaria and the many controversial treatment modalities, it becomes again very important to use the old preventive measures, such as using mosquito nets and wearing long-sleeved shirts and trousers. The use of insect repellents is again highly recommended, especially at night. Because of the feeding habits of the Anopheles mosquito, malaria transmission occurs primarily between dusk and dawn. The most effective insect repellents contain diethyl metatoluamide. For spraying the room or tent, sprays containing pyrethrum are recommended.

Different vaccines can be given the same day at different sites of the body, but in general it is preferable to spread the injections over several weeks. Some of the vaccines require multiple doses at intervals of four weeks. Because of their side effects, cholera and typhoid vaccines should preferably not be given at the same time. Immune globulin may diminish the efficacy of vaccines of viral origin. It therefore should not be given three months before or two weeks after a live vaccine is given. It probably does not interfere with yellow fever or oral polio vaccine. If there is a lack of time and a need for multiple vaccinations, the yellow fever and immune globulin can be given at the same time during the last days before departure. The reason for giving the immune globulin last is that, in the usual dose, it is effective only for about two to three months.

There are two different precautions the international traveler has to take. One is to protect against typical tropical diseases, the other is to protect against diseases that were once common in the United States, but which have been mostly wiped out because of hygiene and modern medical care. Formerly common infectious diseases such as polio, measles, and diphtheria are now rare in this country because of widespread immunizations. If our traveler is not immunized and is suddenly exposed to these infectious diseases, he becomes a prime target because he lacks the acquired immunity that the people in the developing countries may have.

If the child or adult is immuno-supressed because of illness or medications, such as cortisone, cancer chemo-therapy, or medications against transplant organ rejection, thorough discussion with the physician should precede any vaccination.

Adult travelers who have had their original oral polio series many years ago should receive one booster dose of trivalent oral polio vaccine. Those never immunized against poliomyelitis should consider the injectable inactivated trivalent polio vaccine (Salk type). Three doses are required. Most children in the United States have been immunized against polio, but it is advisable to make certain you were.

Children who received their measles vaccine before the age of fifteen months should receive another measles vaccine. Any person, child or adult, who has not had a definite diagnosis of the measles confirmed by a physician (and even he might be wrong), and who has not been immunized, should receive the measles vaccine. Measles is still very common in some countries and can have serious consequences. A significant percentage of the reported cases in the United States nowadays are imported, and I wish no one a case of the measles, especially as an adult.

Most children in our country have received diphtheria, tetanus, and whooping cough immunizations. Before traveling, check their records. Because diphtheria is still prevalent in many parts of the world, a booster dose is often indicated for the adult. This is usually given in combination with tetanus (adult Td), which is good for ten years except after major, contaminated trauma. Tetanus is still a deadly disease and the chance for contacting it is increased for the traveler in primitive countries. If the traveler finds himself with contaminated wounds and his tetanus immunization status is outdated, he should be given tetanus immune globulin if available. If not, he should receive tetanus antitoxin after being tested for horse serum sensitivity. All travelers who have not received a tetanus booster for over ten years maximum should therefore receive tetanus toxoid before departure.

The vaccine for yellow fever is an attenuated live virus vaccine. It comes in multi-vial frozen batches which, once opened, must be used in a few hours. For economic reasons it is available only at designated centers and sometimes, depending on the volume of patients, only on certain days of the week. To be internationally acceptable, the manufacturer's number and the batch number must be written on your health certificate. It should have an official stamp from the local health agency.

Yellow Fever vaccine is effective for ten years and is advised for travel into infected areas. The countries at risk vary from month to month. Many doctors receive an update on the list of countries every month. When traveling from one country to another, there may be a requirement for yellow fever vaccination in the second country when coming from the first—even if no certificate was mandatory there. Contact the local or state health authorities for details.

Typhoid fever vaccine is a suspension of killed salmonella

typhi and gives only partial immunity. Two injections are give four weeks apart. It gives pain at the site of injection and sometimes slight fever and headache. It has another drawback. The vaccine, by altering the diagnostic antibodies, may interfere with making the diagnosis of the mild case of typhoid fever that the only partially immunized patient may experience. The treatment for typhoid fever, once the diagnosis is made, is effective. While this vaccine is not routinely recommended it may serve a useful purpose in isolated cases and anticipated heavy exposure.

Paratyphoid vaccinations are even less effective than typhoid vaccinations and are no longer recommended.

Since 1974, smallpox in vivo has been eradicated from this planet and smallpox vaccination is no longer required to visit any country. Up until a few years ago there were sporadic difficulties at some borders of countries where bureaucratic and/or greedy custom officials used the smallpox certificate to enrich their pocketbooks by extracting bribes.

The chance of a careful and somewhat hygienic traveler contacting cholera is small. Outbreaks of cholera are by no means rare and have occurred even in western nations in the last decade ("Cholera on the Texas Gulf Coast," *J.A.M.A* [1982], 247:1598) but do not pose a great threat to the ordinary traveler. Cholera vaccines have limited effectiveness. Some countries at times require a one-dose cholera vaccine within six months of entry.

Plague still occurs, including in the United States, where it has migrated north from Mexico into Arizona. Plague responds very well to antibiotic treatment if the diagnosis is made early. Vaccination is not recommended for the average traveler.

Rabies vaccine is not required for entry into any country. A pre-exposure vaccine is only recommended for people at high risk (veterinarians, animal handlers, etc.) in areas where rabies is a threat. The vaccine consists of three injections of a diploid cell vaccine.

In case of an animal bite and if the animal is caught, the diagnosis should be made quickly by an autopsy of the rabid animal's brain. If the animal is not available for examination, the decision whether or not to treat will have to based on the degree of rabid behavior of the animal and on the prevalence of rabies in the area and in that particular type of animal.

Intensive treatment should begin early. Human rabies immune globulin should be given, if available. If not, equine rabies antiserum can be administered after appropriate testing for horse serum sensitivity. In additon, five injections of the rabies vaccine should be given at intervals over the next four weeks.

For countries with relatively poor hygiene, where the traveler risks contacting hepatitis A, an intramuscular injection of immune globulin is indicated. The dosage is adjusted for the weight of the traveler and the predicted length of stay. The usual amount of two mL for the average traveler will partially protect against hepatitis A for about two to three months. Doubling the dose will prolong, but not double, the duration of protection. As mentioned above, some other immunizations may be made less effective by the simultaneous administration of immune globulin.

The recently developed hepatitis B vaccine is in general not on the priority list for the average traveler. If the traveler is going to areas where hepatitis B is endemic, such as Southeast Asia and sub-Saharan Africa, and he is planning to work in the medical field or be sexually active, it might be prudent for him to receive the expensive shots. Prior immunity can be established through a blood test. The vaccine is more effective if given in the arm instead of the buttocks. A genetically engineered hepatitis B vaccine will be commercially available in the near future. It is unlikely however that the price will be lower than the regular hepatitis B vaccine, which now costs around $100 for the usual three injections to be given in the time span of six months.

Though rare, at times there are outbreaks of meningococcal disease in certain areas of the world. At this writing such an outbreak is taking place in Nepal, and travelers to Nepal are being advised to receive the meningococcal vaccine. The meningococcal vaccine highlights again the importance of being well-informed about the epidemiological situation the traveler may encounter in the different countries at different times.

The pneumococcal vaccine, which protects the patient from many of the pneumococcal strains causing pneumonia, is recommended for the older traveler or the patient with chronic lung disease or other chronic disease.

Vaccinations against other diseases such as mumps, German measles, the flu, etc., may be indicated and should be discussed with the personal physician.

In France, combination vaccines are being used that presumably protect against some of the most common bacterial organisms causing upper respiratory infections (pneumococcus, haemophilus, klebsiella, etc.). They are advocated for people with chronic lung disease and other risk factors. They are often given to professional singers, for whom these infections might interfere with their concert performances.

Extensive research is in progress worldwide to develop vaccines for other infectious diseases such as malaria.

What should the sailor do if he gets sick *after* his sail and he finds himself in a foreign port with some "foreign" disease? The average American (myself included) is pretty well convinced that this country, at least in a technical sense, has the best medicine in the world. Our state of the art treatment of coronaries or other vascular diseases, the early diagnosis and treatment of cancer, and our surgery in general have few equals in the rest of the world. No wonder then that the stranded sick tourist is frantically looking for an American doctor in Zanzibar.

There is also some national chauvinism involved and probably citizens from other countries feel more at ease with *their* doctors. I still have quite a few Dutch patients who come from far away to see a Dutch doctor. One older Dutch lady who was traveling around the world called me from San Francisco to verify my existence so she could be more relaxed knowing that a Dutch doctor was nearby. I suspect that the itinerary of her trip was planned around the proximity of Dutch doctors. I never saw her, though, and assume she was probably very healthy!

Often sick travelers forget that nowadays, in most countries, it will not be that hard to communicate with their own doctor in the home country by phone. Try to figure out the time difference though. It might be the end of a good doctor-patient relationship if you awaken him at 3 a.m. complaining about your sore throat, even if you are in Kenya.

The American physician, except for some rare specialist, is in most cases not familiar with tropical diseases for the simple fact that they still are rare in the United States. This is true even though, with the increased travel of Americans to tropical countries, the incidence of tropical diseases is on the rise.

Years ago I had all the clinical symptoms of malaria, but in my hospital the technicians were unable to confirm the diagnosis. I finally put a bottle of champagne in the laboratory for the technician who would be the first to find the malaria plasmodium in my blood. It was a technician from the Philippines who was the recipient of the champagne and who showed the pathologist the plasmodium on the microscope slide. I am sure that in a hospital in the Philippines the bottle of champagne would not have been necessary to arrive at the same diagnosis. In foreign and especially in developing countries one should trust the local doctor for the local diseases. If I needed major surgery I would, of course, prefer to come home. My advice to the patient in Zanzibar is "do as the Zanzibarans do" and go to the local doctor or pharmacy! It seems that in these countries the local pharmacist is often an experienced diagnostician and it is he who gets the flack if the patient does not get better (money-back guarantee!).

The greatest tropical disease diagnostician I ever met was a pharmacist in Addis Ababa. He had a small pharmacy on the hill in the middle of town where the locals would bring their stool specimens in the morning. Specimen is not the correct word. They would bring "the whole thing" in buckets and would stand in line before opening hours. In the afternoon they would pick up the empty buckets, plus medication. I spent a whole day watching this pharmacist at work. His primary diagnostic tools were his eyes and above all his nose. First he looked at the specimens, contemplating. Then he judged the aroma like a wine connoisseur. That was how he made a diagnosis! For confirmation, and probably for my benefit, he proved his diagnosis with a microscope. Many of my esteemed gastroenterologist colleagues are certainly able to differentiate the bouquet and aroma of a fine Bordeaux wine, but in their profession they have forgotten how to use the olfactory system.

In the United States, we use other methods to make a diagnosis. By culturing the stools, the proficient laboratory is usually able to identify the causative organism. Another method is to use the rising antibodies. During the time of an unknown infection, certain antibodies in the blood will rise. By taking serial blood samples, a rise in antibodies for a particular disease may be evident. Some of these antibodies require sophisticated laboratory methods often not available in a local laboratory. The Center for Disease Control in Atlanta, Georgia will, in many cases free of charge, run a battery of tests on the patient's blood to facilitate making a diagnosis.

I advise my patients who are planning a trip, where exposure to some exotic disease is possible, to have a blood sample drawn before leaving. This blood is stored in the refrigerator.

After returning from the trip, if the patient has contacted some seemingly difficult-to-diagnose disease, another sample is drawn. The "before and after" samples and sometimes later samples can be collected and sent to the Center for Disease Control with some other diagnostic information. However, an earlier diagnosis, made in the area where the disease was contacted, is preferable and probably will result in earlier treatment.

As well trained and well equipped physicians, helping the patient in a developing country, we have to realize that our healing of individual patients may also have an adverse effect on the community at large after we leave the area. During a large American expedition in the Himalayas, the group found a severely burned woman. Money was collected by the Americans and the woman was transferred to Katmandu by helicopter for medical treatment. According to recent information, the woman is grateful to be alive, happy, and productive.* Now that they have seen what can be done, however, I wonder how the people of that village will feel if another major injury occurs and this time, no helicopter is forthcoming.

The opposite kind of culture shock happened in San Francisco where a recent Vietnamese refugee lady tried to board a local bus with a chicken under her arm. "No live animals allowed on the bus," was the stern warning from the bus driver. No problem for our Vietnamese lady, who quickly turned the chicken's neck clockwise a few times and proceeded to board the bus in which several lovely old ladies by now had fainted (Herb Caen, *San Francisco Chronicle*).

The great charm of the people living in the Himalaya mountains is that, because of the particular geography, they have not

---

*Personal communication with Gil Roberts, M.D., who was responsible for the evacuation.

been exposed to some modern amenities. This way they still can be a happy people. Every foreigner who reaches them has to walk for several days. No automobiles or television. The worst they may be exposed to is the polaroid camera or the radio. What a difference from India where, when I was there in 1968, people were starving along the roadside while Cadillacs were passing by them at high speed!

Fortunately, new clinics and hospitals are appearing in the remote areas of Nepal thanks to the coordinated efforts of many Western philanthropic Nepal-lovers (for example the Hillary Foundation) and the Nepalese people. This way the mountain people will also have the advantages of gradually experiencing and learning modern medicine. This time they will have follow-up care and in the future they will be able to take over the management of their hospitals.

When I was on an expedition in the Himalayas in 1968, every morning I faced a crowd of some twenty to thirty people waiting for medical care. Word had gotten around! They were the most stoic people I have ever met. They were suffering mostly from chronic diseases like arthritis and probably many from tuberculosis. This would necessitate long-term care with follow-up which, of course, was impossible. Some had come out of curiosity; others were hoping to receive that magic western medicine "shot."

I felt frustrated realizing that my long and expensive education was not going to help these people, partially because of my inability to speak Nepalese and because I rarely spent more than one day in the same area, making follow-up and continuing care impossible. I certainly contributed less to their welfare than a well-trained Peace Corps worker, who at least would spend some time with these marvelous people. The major help I could provide turned out to be pulling their rotten and painful teeth. I learned quickly and was lucky enough to have had half-an-hour's instruction by my dentist before leaving home. I also learned to explain the effects of local anesthesia beforehand. The first patients, after the local anesthetic took effect, were so happy that they quickly left, thinking that was all there was to it. Unfortunately (?), we had to leave before the anesthetic wore off!

Plans for improvement in medical care in the developing nations must allow for gradual exposure to modern medicine and education, taking into consideration the effects this care may have on the society as a whole. I do not think that a modern hospital ship, equipped with the latest expensive medical equipment and operating rooms to teach the local doctors new techniques, is the ideal way.

In the sixties my wife and I spent some time with a German doctor who was married to an American Peace Corps worker in the highlands in Guatemala. His hospital had around sixty beds, but he had 180 patients, three per bed. He had an old X-ray machine which usually was not working because of lack of electricity. He treated every patient in the hospital for tuberculosis. Most of them were coughing and probably had T.B. The others would get it from their room/bed mates anyway. To make an accurate diagnosis was difficult under the circumstances and the treatment was medication with INH, a relatively harmless drug. That was one medication he had plenty of! I offered to send him some used X-ray and other medical equipment. He had to decline because he could not afford the exorbitant Guatemalan import duties!

On an excursion in the Peruvian Andes, I was called to see a very ill baby who obviously had some form of meningitis. I was able to administer a high dose of penicillin and thought that there was a small chance of saving the child. We went to bed and the following day the mother visited me for another ailment. The baby had been buried already. The family was back working in the field with no outward signs of grief. It was only a *criatura*, a creature. Apparently as defense against the sorrow of losing so many children, they do not talk about "children" until they are older and more viable. Their infant mortality rate must be in the neighborhood of what it was in the American West some 150 years ago.

In some of the most primitive areas in New Guinea I found that almost all children had been immunized against the usual childhood diseases, but I found no evidence of any efforts to teach birth control. The number of children who would greet us when arriving was astounding, and I worry about what is going to happen to them in the near future.

MEDICAL PROVISIONS

The medical provisions for the solo sailor should be tailored to the sailor's individual risk factors and should be made up in consultation with a doctor. Outlined in this section will be some equipment and drugs that will be most helpful for emergencies that anyone might encounter. There are, of course, other variables, such as the longest distance between ports, the climate (extreme hot or cold), and the feasibility of getting help by radio, etc. The sailor should adjust his medicine cabinet accordingly.

Careful shopping may help the financially-strapped sailor diminish the financial burden of buying all these medical supplies. The family doctor might be of help. He may have samples of the medications and some equipment that has better days, but which might suffice in a sailing emergency. Substituting generic for trade name prescriptions may cut down expenses. The relatively small risk in getting generic prescriptions can be minimized by the use of a responsible pharmacist who is aware of the track records of the different pharmaceutical companies.

Outlined are three different kits. The first is the bare minimum, without which no one should venture out onto the ocean. With careful shopping, it should cost less than $60. The second kit is a little bit more sophisticated, and the third kit is the one that is recommended.

Not included in these lists are special medications and equipment for the individual sailor with a high risk for a particular illness such as diabetes (insulin), elderly male sailors (Foley catheter for prostatic obstruction), etc. These sailors should make up their personal medical kits in cooperation with their physicians.

The sailor should be aware of the expiration dates and make sure that the package inserts are available for all medicines so that the side effects will be known and the dosage can be checked for each medication. There will be no one to protect the solo sailor when he gets confused, sleepy, or disoriented. If in doubt, a lower dosage should be taken, to ascertain the particular effects the drug may have on the user.

KIT #1
Absolute Minimum

Sunscreening agent with an SPF of 15 or higher. Avoid PABA, which can cause allergic reactions.

Bacitracin ointment 30 gm tube *or* Polysporin ointment. Avoid ointments containing neomycin such as Neosporin ointment, which often give allergic reactions.

Lotrisone cream℞, 30 gm tube *or* Mycolog II℞ cream, or mix one tube of Micatin ointment with equal amount of Cortaid ointment (See Diseases of the Skin section).

aspirin *and/or* Tylenol

ampicillin℞, 500 mg capsules, #30 (antibiotic). One or two capsules four times daily. Check expiration date and include package insert.

metronidazole (Flagyl℞) 500 mg oral tablets, #30. One tablet three times daily for five to ten days. Antibiotic for abdominal (anaerobic) infections and for trichomonas or amebic infections.

Dramamine or scopolamine patches℞ (Transderm Scop) or ginger or other seasickness remedies, see under "seasickness."

multivitamin pills, 1 daily

band-aids, liberal supply

paper tape

Ace Bandages, 3 or 4 inches wide

Steri-Strips

tincture of benzoin to make tape and Steri-Strips stick

thermometers

tongue blades and *wooden* cotton applicators (Q-Tips)

sterile gauze, 4″ × 4″ #10

the *Merck Manual* medical book

KIT #2
More Elaborate

This kit includes everything in Kit #1, plus:

Gelusil *or* Mylanta *or* Maalox (antacids)

erythromycin℞ 250 mg tablets (antibiotic). One or two tablets four times daily

Silvadene℞ cream, 50 gm jar (for burns)

Garamycin℞ antibiotic eye ointment without cortisone. Eye ointment or drops containing cortisone are not recommended for use by the layman because of the risk of worsening viral eye infections or other ophthalmic diseases.

VoSol otic solution℞ (for external ear infections)

prednisone℞ 5 mg tablets, #50 (a form of cortisone). Usual dose is six tablets first and second days, four tablets third and fourth days, two tablets fifth and sixth days.

Benadryl, 25 mg capsules, #60 (antihistamine). One or two capsules, three or four times daily.

ibuprofen (Advil *or* Nuprin) 200 mg tablets, #40. These are the same as Motrin℞ except for their lower strength. One or two tablets every four hours for pain, headache, joint troubles, menstrual cramps, etc.

disposable enema bag (for constipation). Can also be used to administer medicines rectally in case of vomiting.

Dulcolax suppositories, #20 (for constipation)

Lomotil℞ 2.5 mg tablets, #20. One tablet three or four times daily for diarrhea. See warning in text on "Medical Problems and Antibiotics".

Empirin with codeine℞ 15 mg, #40. One or two tablets every four hours for severe pain.

adhesive bandages, one or two 3" × 10" inch rolls

Bactrim℞ #20 (Sulfa). One tablet twice a day.

KIT #3
Recommended

This kit includes, in addition to everything in Kits #1 and #2, extra antibiotics and diagnostic gadgets, material to suture wounds, injectables, malaria medication and a special section for the female traveler.

chloramphenicol (Chloromycetin℞), 250 mg capsules, #40. Take one or two every six hours. Potent antibiotic. Can cause bone marrow depression. May kill anaerobic bacteria. Might be useful if appendicitis or typhoid fever is suspected.

doxycycline (Vibramycin℞), 100 mg capsules, #20. Usual dosage two tablets the first day, then one capsule daily. Antibiotic, related to tetracycline, especially effective for Montezuma's revenge and some venereal infections. It is being evaluated (with tetracycline) for use in malaria cases.

package of sterile gloves

needle holder, forceps, and hemostat

suture scissors

5-0 silk sutures and 4-0 silk sutures with swedged-on cutting needle. The experienced might prefer nylon sutures. 4-0 absorbable catgut sutures with swedged-on cutting needle for suturing below the skin.

surgical blade handle with two #11 blades (pointed) and two #15 blades (regular knife for cutting)

five 2 mL syringes with 22-gauge and 27-gauge needles

Xylocaine 1% with adrenalin℞, 50 mL (or less) (for local anesthesia)

demerol℞, 50 mg per mL #30 mL bottle. Use 1 mL or 2 mL for injection for severe pain. Not advocated for the single-hander unless extreme circumstances outweigh the risk the sailor losing control of his actions.

Sus-Phrine℞ (epinephrine 1:200) with tuberculine syringes for critical dosage #5 mL vial. 0.1 to 0.3 mL injected subcutaneously for severe, life-threatening, allergic reactions, such as tracheal obstruction, asthma, bee stings, etc. Watch dosage carefully and start with low dose.

dexamethasone (Decadron℞), 4 mg/mL in disposable syringe #4. Injectable cortisone. Give 1 or 2 mL (4 mg or 8 mg) for severe allergic reactions.

Anusol HC℞, rectal suppositories with hydrocortisone #20 (for hemorrhoids)

Uristix, #20 (for diagnosis of urinary tract afflictions). See Infections and Antibiotics.

dental kit, sugarless chewing gum. (See Dental Care in Surgical Injuries section.)

diuretic (water pills) hydrochlorothiazide (Hydrodiuril℞) 50 mg tablets #6. One tablet daily for water retention.

injectable antibiotics. Some are available in disposable syringes but these, when not kept refrigerated, soon become out-dated. For long crossings it is advisable to have the antibiotic in powdered form and to make up the solution at the time of use. This should be discussed with the sailor's physician.

medical signal code. (See Equipment and Supplies section on medical advice via radio communication.)

The Ship's Medicine Chest and Medical Aid at Sea. Extensive book with practical medical advice for the mariner. Includes copy of Medical Signal Code. Regularly updated, loose bound. Order from the Superintendent of Documents, U.S. Government Printing Office, Washington, D.C. 20402.

For the traveler with exposure to malaria:

chloroquine phosphate (Aralen℞), 500 mg, take one tablet weekly, starting one week before and continuing till six weeks after exposure. For malaria prophylaxis.

Fansidar℞ tablets #3. Use 3 tablets in case of having fever caused by malaria which is probably chloroquine resistant and if expert medical care is not immediately available.

Medicines of special interest to the female traveler:

iron tablets (ferrous sulfate tablets U.S.P.) 250 mg. One or two tablets for correction of blood loss or for anemia.

Gyne-Lotrimin vaginal tablets℞ #12. For yeast infections (Monilia). Insert one or two tablets vaginally at night for 3 to 6 days. *Or* mystatin (Mycostatin) vaginal tablets℞, #24. Insert vaginally once daily. *Or* miconazole nitrate (Monistat) 200 mg suppositories℞ Insert one suppository vaginally at bedtime for three days.

adequate supply of birth control pills to regulate heavy or irregular periods.

Bactrim℞ *or* Septra℞ (for bladder infection). Included in kit #2.

disposable douche material

Addendum

to Day 14 of Daybook
Regarding the Musicians Seamounts

After my return to the mainland, I did some research to find the origin of the naming of the Musicians Seamounts. My friend Dr. Robert Drake at the Department of Geology at the University of California, Berkeley, referred me to the Department of Pacific-Arctic Marine Geology in Menlo Park, California.

Tom Chase, Barb Seekins, and Jeanne Wahler of this Department gave me the name of Dr. David K. Rea, who had apparently been involved in the naming of the Musicians Seamounts. They were also nice enough to send me copies of the original seamount charts. These charts (called Physiographic Diagrams of the Ocean's Seafloor) mentioned many more composers than are printed on the regular nautical charts. I was pleased to notice Bach's name on this seafloor chart; he was missing on the nautical chart.

I then contacted Dr. David K. Rea at the Department of Atmospheric and Oceanic Science at the University of Michigan in Ann Arbor. He was kind enough to send me a reprint of his research paper on the subject. (David K. Rea and P. Naugler, "Musicians Seamount Province and Related Structures North of the Hawaiian Ridge," *Marine Geology*, 10 [1971] 89-110)

From this paper I learned that in 1964, H.W. Menard applied the name Musicians Seamounts to the area previously known as the North Hawaiian Seamount Range. When I sailed to Hawaii in 1974 there was no mention yet of seamounts on the nautical chart of the Pacific.

Via personal communication with Dr. Rea I also learned that the Musicians Seamounts had been rather randomly named by him, in cooperation with Fred Naugler, in 1970.

I quote Dr. Rea: "My recollection is that Fred Naugler named those south of the Murray Fracture Zone at Latitude 29° N., and I named those to the north. We were constrained by our knowledge of music, although Fred's was greater than mine. Our supervisor at the time also had something to say about it. Since 1970 other marine geologists have named other seamounts in this group, also somewhat by random choice."

I realize now how wrong I was on day 14 in assuming that the seamounts were named by an Eastern European! Also Bach *was* mentioned on the original seamount chart and Schubert *was* written with the letter "c" in it. These misprints apparently were made later when the musicians' names were transferred to the nautical charts. My apologies to our own American marine geologists are therefore in order. I am grateful for their gracious cooperation in correcting my mistaken assumptions.

to Day 17 of Daybook
Regarding Noon Sight

When discussing the determination of latitude and longitude in my Daybook on day 17, I purposely did not mention some minor corrections that I made so as not to confuse the novice with the smaller details and to more clearly explain the principle of the noon sight. For the sailor who would like to be able to do at least a simple noon sight, I would like to mention a few corrections that have to be explained.

After having studied the noon sight on July 2, 1984, we should look at the nautical almanac. Now everything will start to make sense. It is advisable to have an almanac at hand but some copied pages are included.

We begin studying the daily page and look at the G.M.T. in the left column (page 270). Reading down, October 6, 00 to 24 hours is followed by October 7, 00 to 24 hours, and October 8, all in G.M.T. (Greenwich Mean Time).

Next column is G.H.A. or Greenwich Hour Angle. In our language the G.H.A. indicates, in degrees of longitude, where the local noon is on its daily trip around the world at a given Greenwich time. Remember we started the noon trip at noon in Greenwich? See what happens at twelve noon G.M.T.? The local noon is at about 0°, right at the longitude of Greenwich.

If an almanac is available, we can look at another date at twelve o'clock noon G.M.T. The G.H.A. will be between 355° and 5° or, in other words, between 5° eastern longitude and 5° western longitude.

It is clear that the local noon throughout the year does not always correlate exactly with the twelve o'clock noon Greenwich Mean Time, but it is close enough. For good measurement of longitude though, we obviously need the almanac to take those aberrations into consideration and make our measurement more accurate.

1984 OCTOBER 6, 7, 8 (SAT., SUN., MON.)

G.M.T.	SUN G.H.A.	SUN Dec.	MOON G.H.A.	v	Dec.	d	H.P.
6 00	182 57.4	S 5 06.1	41 30.5	14.4	S16 30.2	10.7	54.3
01	197 57.6	07.1	56 03.9	14.5	16 19.5	10.8	54.3
02	212 57.8	08.0	70 37.4	14.6	16 08.7	10.9	54.3
03	227 58.0 ··	09.0	85 11.0	14.6	15 57.8	10.9	54.3
04	242 58.1	09.9	99 44.6	14.7	15 46.9	10.9	54.3
05	257 58.3	10.9	114 18.3	14.8	15 36.0	11.0	54.3
06	272 58.5	S 5 11.9	128 52.1	14.8	S15 25.0	11.1	54.3
07	287 58.7	12.8	143 25.9	14.9	15 13.9	11.1	54.2
S 08	302 58.9	13.8	157 59.8	14.9	15 02.8	11.2	54.2
A 09	317 59.1 ··	14.7	172 33.7	15.0	14 51.6	11.3	54.2
T 10	332 59.2	15.7	187 07.7	15.0	14 40.3	11.3	54.2
U 11	347 59.4	16.6	201 41.7	15.1	14 29.0	11.3	54.2
R 12	2 59.6	S 5 17.6	216 15.8	15.2	S14 17.7	11.5	54.2
D 13	17 59.8	18.6	230 50.0	15.2	14 06.2	11.4	54.2
A 14	33 00.0	19.5	245 24.2	15.3	13 54.8	11.5	54.2
Y 15	48 00.1 ··	20.5	259 58.5	15.3	13 43.3	11.6	54.2
16	63 00.3	21.4	274 32.8	15.3	13 31.7	11.6	54.2
17	78 00.5	22.4	289 07.1	15.5	13 20.1	11.7	54.1
18	93 00.7	S 5 23.3	303 41.6	15.4	S13 08.4	11.7	54.1
19	108 00.9	24.3	318 16.0	15.5	12 56.7	11.7	54.1
20	123 01.0	25.3	332 50.5	15.6	12 45.0	11.9	54.1
21	138 01.2 ··	26.2	347 25.1	15.6	12 33.1	11.8	54.1
22	153 01.4	27.2	1 59.7	15.7	12 21.3	11.9	54.1
23	168 01.6	28.1	16 34.4	15.7	12 09.4	11.9	54.1
7 00	183 01.8	S 5 29.1	31 09.1	15.8	S11 57.5	12.0	54.1
01	198 02.0	30.1	45 43.9	15.8	11 45.5	12.1	54.1
02	213 02.1	31.0	60 18.7	15.8	11 33.4	12.0	54.1
03	228 02.3 ··	32.0	74 53.5	15.9	11 21.4	12.1	54.1
04	243 02.5	32.9	89 28.4	15.9	11 09.3	12.2	54.1
05	258 02.7	33.9	104 03.3	16.0	10 57.1	12.2	54.1
06	273 02.9	S 5 34.8	118 38.3	16.0	S10 44.9	12.2	54.1
07	288 03.0	35.8	133 13.3	16.1	10 32.7	12.3	54.1
08	303 03.2	36.7	147 48.4	16.1	10 20.4	12.3	54.0
S 09	318 03.4 ··	37.7	162 23.5	16.1	10 08.1	12.3	54.0
U 10	333 03.6	38.7	176 58.6	16.2	9 55.8	12.4	54.0
N 11	348 03.8	39.6	191 33.8	16.2	9 43.4	12.4	54.0
D 12	3 03.9	S 5 40.6	206 09.0	16.2	S 9 31.0	12.5	54.0
A 13	18 04.1	41.5	220 44.2	16.3	9 18.5	12.4	54.0
Y 14	33 04.3	42.5	235 19.5	16.3	9 06.1	12.6	54.0
15	48 04.5 ··	43.4	249 54.8	16.3	8 53.5	12.5	54.0
16	63 04.7	44.4	264 30.1	16.4	8 41.0	12.6	54.0
17	78 04.8	45.3	279 05.5	16.4	8 28.4	12.6	54.0
18	93 05.0	S 5 46.3	293 40.9	16.5	S 8 15.8	12.6	54.0
19	108 05.2	47.3	308 16.4	16.4	8 03.2	12.7	54.0
20	123 05.4	48.2	322 51.8	16.5	7 50.5	12.7	54.0
21	138 05.5 ··	49.2	337 27.3	16.5	7 37.8	12.7	54.0
22	153 05.7	50.1	352 02.8	16.6	7 25.1	12.7	54.0
23	168 05.9	51.1	6 38.4	16.6	7 12.4	12.8	54.0
8 00	183 06.1	S 5 52.0	21 14.0	16.6	S 6 59.6	12.8	54.0
01	198 06.2	53.0	35 49.6	16.6	6 46.8	12.8	54.0
02	213 06.4	53.9	50 25.2	16.7	6 34.0	12.9	54.0
03	228 06.6 ··	54.9	65 00.9	16.6	6 21.1	12.9	54.0
04	243 06.8	55.8	79 36.5	16.7	6 08.2	12.9	54.0
05	258 06.9	56.8	94 12.2	16.7	5 55.3	12.9	54.0
06	273 07.1	S 5 57.7	108 47.9	16.8	S 5 42.4	12.9	54.0
07	288 07.3	58.7	123 23.7	16.7	5 29.5	13.0	54.0
08	303 07.5	5 59.6	137 59.4	16.8	5 16.5	12.9	54.0
M 09	318 07.6	6 00.6	152 35.2	16.8	5 03.6	13.0	54.0
O 10	333 07.8	01.6	167 11.0	16.8	4 50.6	13.0	54.0
N 11	348 08.0	02.5	181 46.8	16.8	4 37.6	13.1	54.0
D 12	3 08.2	S 6 03.5	196 22.6	16.9	S 4 24.5	13.0	54.0
A 13	18 08.3	04.4	210 58.5	16.8	4 11.5	13.1	54.0
Y 14	33 08.5	05.4	225 34.3	16.9	3 58.4	13.1	54.0
15	48 08.7 ··	06.3	240 10.2	16.9	3 45.3	13.0	54.0
16	63 08.9	07.3	254 46.1	16.9	3 32.3	13.1	54.0
17	78 09.0	08.2	269 22.0	16.9	3 19.2	13.2	54.0
18	93 09.2	S 6 09.2	283 57.9	16.9	S 3 06.0	13.1	54.0
19	108 09.4	10.1	298 33.8	16.9	2 52.9	13.1	54.0
20	123 09.6	11.1	313 09.7	16.9	2 39.8	13.2	54.0
21	138 09.7 ··	12.0	327 45.6	17.0	2 26.6	13.1	54.0
22	153 09.9	13.0	342 21.6	16.9	2 13.5	13.2	54.0
23	168 10.1	13.9	356 57.5	16.9	2 00.3	13.2	54.0
	S.D. 16.0 d 1.0		S.D. 14.8		14.7		14.7

Twilight / Moonrise

Lat.	Twilight Naut.	Civil	Sunrise	Moonrise 6	7	8	9
N 72	04 19	05 39	06 47	18 49	18 12	17 44	17 18
N 70	04 27	05 39	06 40	18 26	18 00	17 40	17 20
68	04 34	05 39	06 35	18 08	17 51	17 36	17 22
66	04 39	05 39	06 30	17 53	17 42	17 33	17 24
64	04 44	05 39	06 26	17 41	17 36	17 31	17 26
62	04 47	05 39	06 23	17 30	17 29	17 28	17 27
60	04 50	05 38	06 20	17 21	17 24	17 26	17 28
N 58	04 53	05 38	06 17	17 14	17 20	17 25	17 29
56	04 55	05 38	06 15	17 07	17 15	17 23	17 30
54	04 57	05 38	06 13	17 00	17 12	17 22	17 31
52	04 58	05 37	06 11	16 55	17 08	17 20	17 32
50	05 00	05 37	06 09	16 50	17 05	17 19	17 33
45	05 02	05 36	06 05	16 39	16 58	17 17	17 34
N 40	05 04	05 35	06 02	16 29	16 53	17 14	17 35
35	05 05	05 34	05 59	16 21	16 48	17 12	17 37
30	05 05	05 33	05 57	16 14	16 43	17 11	17 38
20	05 05	05 30	05 52	16 02	16 36	17 08	17 39
N 10	05 05	05 27	05 48	15 52	16 29	17 05	17 41
0	05 00	05 24	05 44	15 42	16 23	17 03	17 43
S 10	04 55	05 19	05 40	15 32	16 17	17 01	17 44
20	04 48	05 14	05 36	15 21	16 10	16 58	17 46
30	04 39	05 07	05 31	15 08	16 02	16 55	17 48
35	04 32	05 03	05 28	15 01	15 58	16 53	17 49
40	04 25	04 57	05 25	14 53	15 53	16 52	17 50
45	04 15	04 51	05 21	14 43	15 47	16 49	17 52
S 50	04 03	04 43	05 16	14 32	15 40	16 47	17 53
52	03 57	04 39	05 14	14 26	15 36	16 45	17 54
54	03 51	04 35	05 11	14 20	15 33	16 44	17 55
56	03 43	04 30	05 09	14 14	15 29	16 43	17 56
58	03 35	04 25	05 06	14 06	15 24	16 41	17 57
S 60	03 24	04 19	05 02	13 57	15 19	16 39	17 58

Sunset / Twilight / Moonset

Lat.	Sunset	Twilight Civil	Naut.	Moonset 6	7	8	9
N 72	16 47	17 54	19 13	25 18	01 18	03 20	05 13
N 70	16 54	17 54	19 05	25 39	01 39	03 30	05 14
68	16 59	17 55	18 59	00 04	01 56	03 37	05 15
66	17 04	17 55	18 54	00 28	02 09	03 44	05 16
64	17 08	17 55	18 50	00 46	02 20	03 49	05 16
62	17 11	17 55	18 47	01 01	02 29	03 54	05 17
60	17 14	17 56	18 44	01 14	02 37	03 58	05 17
N 58	17 17	17 56	18 41	01 24	02 44	04 01	05 18
56	17 19	17 56	18 39	01 34	02 50	04 04	05 18
54	17 21	17 57	18 38	01 42	02 55	04 07	05 18
52	17 23	17 57	18 36	01 49	03 00	04 10	05 19
50	17 25	17 58	18 35	01 56	03 05	04 12	05 19
45	17 29	17 59	18 32	02 10	03 14	04 17	05 19
N 40	17 33	18 00	18 31	02 22	03 22	04 21	05 20
35	17 36	18 01	18 30	02 31	03 29	04 25	05 20
30	17 38	18 02	18 30	02 40	03 35	04 28	05 21
20	17 43	18 05	18 30	02 55	03 45	04 33	05 21
N 10	17 47	18 08	18 32	03 08	03 54	04 38	05 22
0	17 51	18 12	18 36	03 19	04 02	04 42	05 22
S 10	17 55	18 16	18 41	03 31	04 10	04 47	05 22
20	18 00	18 22	18 48	03 44	04 19	04 51	05 23
30	18 05	18 29	18 57	03 58	04 28	04 56	05 23
35	18 08	18 34	19 04	04 06	04 34	04 59	05 24
40	18 12	18 39	19 12	04 16	04 40	05 03	05 24
45	18 16	18 46	19 21	04 27	04 48	05 07	05 24
S 50	18 21	18 54	19 34	04 40	04 56	05 11	05 25
52	18 23	18 58	19 40	04 46	05 01	05 13	05 25
54	18 25	19 02	19 46	04 52	05 05	05 16	05 25
56	18 28	19 07	19 54	05 00	05 10	05 18	05 25
58	18 31	19 12	20 03	05 08	05 15	05 21	05 26
S 60	18 35	19 18	20 13	05 18	05 21	05 24	05 26

Day	SUN Eqn. of Time 00h	12h	Mer. Pass.	MOON Mer. Pass. Upper	Lower	Age	Phase
6	11 49	11 58	11 48	21 52	09 31	11	
7	12 07	12 15	11 48	22 33	10 12	12	◯
8	12 24	12 32	11 47	23 12	10 53	13	

1984 SEPTEMBER 21, 22, 23 (FRI., SAT., SUN.)

G.M.T.	SUN G.H.A.	SUN Dec.	MOON G.H.A.	v	Dec.	d	H.P.
d h	° '	° '	° '	'	° '	'	'
21 00	181 43.2	N 0 43.4	236 05.3	5.5	N24 21.0	6.5	59.1
01	196 43.4	42.4	250 29.8	5.6	24 14.5	6.6	59.1
02	211 43.7	41.4	264 54.4	5.5	24 07.9	6.8	59.1
03	226 43.9	·· 40.4	279 18.9	5.6	24 01.1	6.9	59.2
04	241 44.1	39.5	293 43.5	5.6	23 54.2	7.1	59.2
05	256 44.3	38.5	308 08.1	5.6	23 47.1	7.3	59.2
06	271 44.5	N 0 37.5	322 32.7	5.6	N23 39.8	7.5	59.3
07	286 44.8	36.6	336 57.3	5.6	23 32.3	7.6	59.3
08	301 45.0	35.6	351 21.9	5.7	23 24.7	7.7	59.4
F 09	316 45.2	·· 34.6	5 46.6	5.7	23 17.0	7.9	59.4
R 10	331 45.4	33.6	20 11.3	5.7	23 09.1	8.1	59.4
I 11	346 45.6	32.7	34 36.0	5.7	23 01.0	8.3	59.5
D 12	1 45.9	N 0 31.7	49 00.7	5.8	N22 52.7	8.4	59.5
A 13	16 46.1	30.7	63 25.5	5.8	22 44.3	8.5	59.6
Y 14	31 46.3	29.7	77 50.3	5.8	22 35.8	8.8	59.6
15	46 46.5	·· 28.8	92 15.1	5.8	22 27.0	8.8	59.6
16	61 46.7	27.8	106 39.9	5.9	22 18.2	9.1	59.7
17	76 47.0	26.8	121 04.8	5.9	22 09.1	9.2	59.7
18	91 47.2	N 0 25.9	135 29.7	6.0	N21 59.9	9.3	59.7
19	106 47.4	24.9	149 54.7	6.0	21 50.6	9.5	59.8
20	121 47.6	23.9	164 19.7	6.0	21 41.1	9.7	59.8
21	136 47.8	·· 22.9	178 44.7	6.0	21 31.4	9.8	59.8
22	151 48.1	22.0	193 09.7	6.1	21 21.6	9.9	59.9
23	166 48.3	21.0	207 34.8	6.2	21 11.7	10.1	59.9
22 00	181 48.5	N 0 20.0	222 00.0	6.1	N21 01.6	10.3	59.9
01	196 48.7	19.0	236 25.1	6.2	20 51.3	10.4	60.0
02	211 48.9	18.1	250 50.3	6.3	20 40.9	10.5	60.0
03	226 49.2	·· 17.1	265 15.6	6.3	20 30.4	10.7	60.1
04	241 49.4	16.1	279 40.9	6.3	20 19.7	10.8	60.1
05	256 49.6	15.2	294 06.2	6.4	20 08.9	11.0	60.1
06	271 49.8	N 0 14.2	308 31.6	6.4	N19 57.9	11.1	60.2
07	286 50.0	13.2	322 57.0	6.4	19 46.8	11.3	60.2
S 08	301 50.2	12.2	337 22.4	6.6	19 35.5	11.4	60.2
A 09	316 50.5	·· 11.3	351 48.0	6.5	19 24.1	11.5	60.3
T 10	331 50.7	10.3	6 13.5	6.6	19 12.6	11.7	60.3
U 11	346 50.9	09.3	20 39.1	6.6	19 00.9	11.8	60.3
R 12	1 51.1	N 0 08.3	35 04.7	6.7	N18 49.1	11.9	60.4
D 13	16 51.3	07.4	49 30.4	6.7	18 37.2	12.1	60.4
A 14	31 51.6	06.4	63 56.1	6.8	18 25.1	12.2	60.4
Y 15	46 51.8	·· 05.4	78 21.9	6.8	18 12.9	12.4	60.4
16	61 52.0	04.4	92 47.7	6.9	18 00.5	12.4	60.5
17	76 52.2	03.5	107 13.6	6.9	17 48.1	12.6	60.5
18	91 52.4	N 0 02.5	121 39.5	7.0	N17 35.5	12.7	60.5
19	106 52.7	01.5	136 05.5	7.0	17 22.8	12.9	60.6
20	121 52.9	N 0 00.6	150 31.5	7.1	17 09.9	12.9	60.6
21	136 53.1	S 0 00.4	164 57.6	7.1	16 57.0	13.1	60.6
22	151 53.3	01.4	179 23.7	7.1	16 43.9	13.2	60.6
23	166 53.5	02.4	193 49.8	7.2	16 30.7	13.3	60.7
23 00	181 53.7	S 0 03.3	208 16.0	7.3	N16 17.4	13.5	60.7
01	196 54.0	04.3	222 42.3	7.3	16 03.9	13.5	60.7
02	211 54.2	05.3	237 08.6	7.3	15 50.4	13.7	60.8
03	226 54.4	·· 06.3	251 34.9	7.4	15 36.7	13.8	60.8
04	241 54.6	07.2	266 01.3	7.5	15 23.0	13.9	60.8
05	256 54.8	08.2	280 27.8	7.5	15 09.1	14.0	60.8
06	271 55.0	S 0 09.2	294 54.3	7.5	N14 55.1	14.1	60.9
07	286 55.3	10.2	309 20.8	7.6	14 41.0	14.2	60.9
08	301 55.5	11.1	323 47.4	7.6	14 26.8	14.3	60.9
S 09	316 55.7	·· 12.1	338 14.0	7.7	14 12.5	14.4	60.9
U 10	331 55.9	13.1	352 40.7	7.7	13 58.1	14.5	60.9
N 11	346 56.1	14.1	7 07.4	7.8	13 43.6	14.6	61.0
D 12	1 56.4	S 0 15.0	21 34.2	7.8	N13 29.0	14.7	61.0
A 13	16 56.6	16.0	36 01.0	7.9	13 14.3	14.8	61.0
Y 14	31 56.8	17.0	50 27.9	7.9	12 59.5	14.9	61.0
15	46 57.0	·· 18.0	64 54.8	8.0	12 44.6	14.9	61.1
16	61 57.2	18.9	79 21.8	8.0	12 29.7	15.1	61.1
17	76 57.4	19.9	93 48.8	8.0	12 14.6	15.1	61.1
18	91 57.7	S 0 20.9	108 15.8	8.1	N11 59.5	15.3	61.1
19	106 57.9	21.8	122 42.9	8.1	11 44.2	15.3	61.1
20	121 58.1	22.8	137 10.0	8.2	11 28.9	15.4	61.2
21	136 58.3	·· 23.8	151 37.2	8.2	11 13.5	15.4	61.2
22	151 58.5	24.8	166 04.4	8.3	10 58.1	15.6	61.2
23	166 58.7	25.7	180 31.7	8.3	10 42.5	15.6	61.2
	S.D. 16.0 d 1.0		S.D. 16.2		16.4		16.6

Lat.	Twilight Naut.	Twilight Civil	Sunrise	Moonrise 21	Moonrise 22	Moonrise 23	Moonrise 24
°	h m	h m	h m	h m	h m	h m	h m
N 72	02 59	04 30	05 39	▢	23 55	27 03	03 03
N 70	03 19	04 39	05 40	▢	▢	00 41	03 19
68	03 35	04 45	05 41	22 15	25 11	01 11	03 32
66	03 47	04 51	05 42	23 12	25 33	01 33	03 42
64	03 57	04 55	05 43	23 45	25 50	01 50	03 50
62	04 05	04 59	05 44	24 10	00 10	02 05	03 58
60	04 12	05 03	05 44	24 29	00 29	02 16	04 04
N 58	04 18	05 06	05 45	24 45	00 45	02 27	04 09
56	04 24	05 08	05 45	24 58	00 58	02 36	04 14
54	04 28	05 10	05 46	25 10	01 10	02 43	04 18
52	04 32	05 12	05 46	25 20	01 20	02 51	04 22
50	04 36	05 14	05 46	00 07	01 29	02 57	04 26
45	04 43	05 18	05 47	00 31	01 48	03 10	04 34
N 40	04 49	05 20	05 48	00 50	02 04	03 21	04 40
35	04 53	05 23	05 48	01 06	02 17	03 31	04 45
30	04 57	05 24	05 48	01 19	02 28	03 39	04 50
20	05 01	05 27	05 49	01 43	02 48	03 53	04 58
N 10	05 04	05 28	05 49	02 03	03 05	04 06	05 05
0	05 05	05 29	05 49	02 22	03 20	04 17	05 12
S 10	05 05	05 28	05 49	02 41	03 36	04 29	05 19
20	05 02	05 28	05 49	03 01	03 53	04 41	05 26
30	04 58	05 26	05 49	03 24	04 12	04 55	05 34
35	04 55	05 24	05 49	03 38	04 23	05 03	05 39
40	04 51	05 22	05 49	03 53	04 36	05 12	05 44
45	04 45	05 20	05 49	04 12	04 51	05 22	05 50
S 50	04 39	05 16	05 49	04 35	05 09	05 35	05 57
52	04 35	05 15	05 49	04 46	05 17	05 41	06 00
54	04 31	05 13	05 48	04 58	05 27	05 48	06 04
56	04 27	05 11	05 48	05 12	05 37	05 55	06 08
58	04 22	05 09	05 48	05 29	05 50	06 03	06 12
S 60	04 16	05 06	05 48	05 49	06 04	06 12	06 17

Lat.	Sunset	Twilight Civil	Twilight Naut.	Moonset 21	Moonset 22	Moonset 23	Moonset 24
°	h m	h m	h m	h m	h m	h m	h m
N 72	18 04	19 12	20 42	▢	20 35	19 24	18 45
N 70	18 03	19 04	20 22	▢	19 47	19 06	18 38
68	18 02	18 58	20 07	20 11	19 15	18 51	18 33
66	18 01	18 52	19 56	19 13	18 52	18 39	18 28
64	18 00	18 48	19 46	18 39	18 33	18 28	18 23
62	18 00	18 44	19 38	18 14	18 18	18 19	18 20
60	17 59	18 41	19 31	17 54	18 05	18 12	18 17
N 58	17 59	18 38	19 25	17 37	17 54	18 05	18 14
56	17 59	18 36	19 20	17 23	17 44	17 59	18 11
54	17 58	18 34	19 15	17 11	17 35	17 54	18 09
52	17 58	18 32	19 12	17 00	17 27	17 49	18 07
50	17 58	18 30	19 08	16 50	17 20	17 44	18 05
45	17 57	18 27	19 01	16 30	17 05	17 34	18 00
N 40	17 57	18 24	18 56	16 13	16 52	17 26	17 57
35	17 57	18 22	18 51	15 59	16 42	17 19	17 54
30	17 56	18 20	18 48	15 47	16 32	17 13	17 51
20	17 56	18 18	18 44	15 26	16 16	17 02	17 46
N 10	17 56	18 17	18 41	15 07	16 01	16 53	17 42
0	17 56	18 17	18 41	14 50	15 48	16 43	17 37
S 10	17 56	18 17	18 44	14 32	15 34	16 34	17 33
20	17 56	18 18	18 44	14 14	15 19	16 24	17 29
30	17 56	18 20	18 48	13 52	15 02	16 13	17 23
35	17 56	18 22	18 51	13 39	14 52	16 06	17 20
40	17 57	18 24	18 55	13 24	14 40	15 59	17 17
45	17 57	18 26	19 01	13 06	14 27	15 50	17 13
S 50	17 57	18 30	19 08	12 44	14 10	15 39	17 08
52	17 58	18 31	19 11	12 34	14 02	15 34	17 06
54	17 58	18 33	19 15	12 22	13 53	15 28	17 03
56	17 58	18 35	19 20	12 08	13 43	15 22	17 00
58	17 59	18 38	19 25	11 52	13 32	15 15	16 57
S 60	17 59	18 41	19 31	11 32	13 19	15 07	16 54

	SUN			MOON			
Day	Eqn. of Time 00h	Eqn. of Time 12h	Mer. Pass.	Mer. Pass. Upper	Mer. Pass. Lower	Age	Phase
	m s	m s	h m	h m	h m	d	
21	06 52	07 03	11 53	08 36	21 05	26	
22	07 14	07 24	11 53	09 34	22 03	27	
23	07 35	07 45	11 52	10 30	22 58	28	◖

A2 ALTITUDE CORRECTION TABLES 10°-90°—SUN, STARS, PLANETS

OCT.—MAR. SUN APR.—SEPT.

App. Alt.	Lower Limb	Upper Limb	App. Alt.	Lower Limb	Upper Limb
9 34	+10.8	−21.5	9 39	+10.6	−21.2
9 45	+10.9	−21.4	9 51	+10.7	−21.1
9 56	+11.0	−21.3	10 03	+10.8	−21.0
10 08	+11.1	−21.2	10 15	+10.9	−20.9
10 21	+11.2	−21.1	10 27	+11.0	−20.8
10 34	+11.3	−21.0	10 40	+11.1	−20.7
10 47	+11.4	−20.9	10 54	+11.2	−20.6
11 01	+11.5	−20.8	11 08	+11.3	−20.5
11 15	+11.6	−20.7	11 23	+11.4	−20.4
11 30	+11.7	−20.6	11 38	+11.5	−20.3
11 46	+11.8	−20.5	11 54	+11.6	−20.2
12 02	+11.9	−20.4	12 10	+11.7	−20.1
12 19	+12.0	−20.3	12 28	+11.8	−20.0
12 37	+12.1	−20.2	12 46	+11.9	−19.9
12 55	+12.2	−20.1	13 05	+12.0	−19.8
13 14	+12.3	−20.0	13 24	+12.1	−19.7
13 35	+12.4	−19.9	13 45	+12.2	−19.6
13 56	+12.5	−19.8	14 07	+12.3	−19.5
14 18	+12.6	−19.7	14 30	+12.4	−19.4
14 42	+12.7	−19.6	14 54	+12.5	−19.3
15 06	+12.8	−19.5	15 19	+12.6	−19.2
15 32	+12.9	−19.4	15 46	+12.7	−19.1
15 59	+13.0	−19.3	16 14	+12.8	−19.0
16 28	+13.1	−19.2	16 44	+12.9	−18.9
16 59	+13.2	−19.1	17 15	+13.0	−18.8
17 32	+13.3	−19.0	17 48	+13.1	−18.7
18 06	+13.4	−18.9	18 24	+13.2	−18.6
18 42	+13.5	−18.8	19 01	+13.3	−18.5
19 21	+13.6	−18.7	19 42	+13.4	−18.4
20 03	+13.7	−18.6	20 25	+13.5	−18.3
20 48	+13.8	−18.5	21 11	+13.6	−18.2
21 35	+13.9	−18.4	22 00	+13.7	−18.1
22 26	+14.0	−18.3	22 54	+13.8	−18.0
23 22	+14.1	−18.2	23 51	+13.9	−17.9
24 21	+14.2	−18.1	24 53	+14.0	−17.8
25 26	+14.3	−18.0	26 00	+14.1	−17.7
26 36	+14.4	−17.9	27 13	+14.2	−17.6
27 52	+14.5	−17.8	28 33	+14.3	−17.5
29 15	+14.6	−17.7	30 00	+14.4	−17.4
30 46	+14.7	−17.6	31 35	+14.5	−17.3
32 26	+14.8	−17.5	33 20	+14.6	−17.2
34 17	+14.9	−17.4	35 17	+14.7	−17.1
36 20	+15.0	−17.3	37 26	+14.8	−17.0
38 36	+15.1	−17.2	39 50	+14.9	−16.9
41 08	+15.2	−17.1	42 31	+15.0	−16.8
43 59	+15.3	−17.0	45 31	+15.1	−16.7
47 10	+15.4	−16.9	48 55	+15.2	−16.6
50 46	+15.5	−16.8	52 44	+15.3	−16.5
54 49	+15.6	−16.7	57 02	+15.4	−16.4
59 23	+15.7	−16.6	61 51	+15.5	−16.3
64 30	+15.8	−16.5	67 17	+15.6	−16.2
70 12	+15.9	−16.4	73 16	+15.7	−16.1
76 26	+16.0	−16.3	79 43	+15.8	−16.0
83 05	+16.1	−16.2	86 32	+15.9	−15.9
90 00			90 00		

STARS AND PLANETS

App. Alt.	Corrⁿ	App. Alt.	Additional Corrⁿ
9 56	−5.3		**1984**
10 08	−5.2		**VENUS**
10 20	−5.1		Jan. 1-Dec. 12
10 33	−5.0		°
10 46	−4.9		60 +0.1
11 00	−4.8		Dec. 13-Dec. 31
11 14	−4.7		°
11 29	−4.6		41 +0.2
11 45	−4.5		76 +0.1
12 01	−4.4		
12 18	−4.3		
12 35	−4.2		
12 54	−4.1		
13 13	−4.0		**MARS**
13 33	−3.9		Jan. 1-Mar. 4
13 54	−3.8		°
14 16	−3.7		60 +0.1
14 40	−3.6		Mar. 5-Apr. 24
15 04	−3.5		°
15 30	−3.4		41 +0.2
15 57	−3.3		76 +0.1
16 26	−3.2		Apr. 25-June 15
16 56	−3.1		°
17 28	−3.0		34 +0.3
18 02	−2.9		60 +0.2
18 38	−2.8		80 +0.1
19 17	−2.7		June 16-Aug. 27
19 58	−2.6		°
20 42	−2.5		41 +0.2
21 28	−2.4		76 +0.1
22 19	−2.3		Aug. 28-Dec. 31
23 13	−2.2		°
24 11	−2.1		60 +0.1
25 14	−2.0		
26 22	−1.9		
27 36	−1.8		
28 56	−1.7		
30 24	−1.6		
32 00	−1.5		
33 45	−1.4		
35 40	−1.3		
37 48	−1.2		
40 08	−1.1		
42 44	−1.0		
45 36	−0.9		
48 47	−0.8		
52 18	−0.7		
56 11	−0.6		
60 28	−0.5		
65 08	−0.4		
70 11	−0.3		
75 34	−0.2		
81 13	−0.1		
87 03	0.0		
90 00			

DIP

Ht. of Eye (m)	Corrⁿ	Ht. of Eye (ft.)	Ht. of Eye	Corrⁿ
2.4	−2.8	8.0	1.0 −	1.8
2.6	−2.9	8.6	1.5 −	2.2
2.8	−3.0	9.2	2.0 −	2.5
3.0	−3.1	9.8	2.5 −	2.8
3.2	−3.2	10.5	3.0 −	3.0
3.4	−3.3	11.2	See table	
3.6	−3.4	11.9	←	
3.8	−3.5	12.6	m	
4.0	−3.6	13.3	20 −	7.9
4.3	−3.7	14.1	22 −	8.3
4.5	−3.8	14.9	24 −	8.6
4.7	−3.9	15.7	26 −	9.0
5.0	−4.0	16.5	28 −	9.3
5.2	−4.1	17.4		
5.5	−4.2	18.3	30 −	9.6
5.8	−4.3	19.1	32 −	10.0
6.1	−4.4	20.1	34 −	10.3
6.3	−4.5	21.0	36 −	10.6
6.6	−4.6	22.0	38 −	10.8
6.9	−4.7	22.9		
7.2	−4.8	23.9	40 −	11.1
7.5	−4.9	24.9	42 −	11.4
7.9	−5.0	26.0	44 −	11.7
8.2	−5.1	27.1	46 −	11.9
8.5	−5.2	28.1	48 −	12.2
8.8	−5.3	29.2	ft.	
9.2	−5.4	30.4	2 −	1.4
9.5	−5.5	31.5	4 −	1.9
9.9	−5.6	32.7	6 −	2.4
10.3	−5.7	33.9	8 −	2.7
10.6	−5.8	35.1	10 −	3.1
11.0	−5.9	36.3	See table	
11.4	−6.0	37.6	←	
11.8	−6.1	38.9	ft.	
12.2	−6.2	40.1	70	8.1
12.6	−6.3	41.5	75	8.4
13.0	−6.4	42.8	80 −	8.7
13.4	−6.5	44.2	85 −	8.9
13.8	−6.6	45.5	90 −	9.2
14.2	−6.7	46.9	95 −	9.5
14.7	−6.8	48.4	100 −	9.7
15.1	−6.9	49.8	105 −	9.9
15.5	−7.0	51.3	110 −	10.2
16.0	−7.1	52.8	115 −	10.4
16.5	−7.2	54.3	120 −	10.6
16.9	−7.3	55.8	125 −	10.8
17.4	−7.4	57.4	130 −	11.1
17.9	−7.5	58.9	135 −	11.3
18.4	−7.6	60.5	140 −	11.5
18.8	−7.6	62.1	145 −	11.7
19.3	−7.7	63.8	150	11.9
19.8	−7.8	65.4	155 −	12.1
20.4	−7.9	67.1		
20.9	−8.0	68.8		
21.4	−8.1	70.5		

App. Alt. = Apparent altitude = Sextant altitude corrected for index error and dip.

30ᵐ   INCREMENTS AND CORRECTIONS   **31ᵐ**

30ᵐ	SUN PLANETS	ARIES	MOON	v or Corrⁿ d	v or Corrⁿ d	v or Corrⁿ d	31ᵐ	SUN PLANETS	ARIES	MOON	v or Corrⁿ d	v or Corrⁿ d	v or Corrⁿ d
s	° ′	° ′	° ′	′ ′	′ ′	′ ′	s	° ′	° ′	° ′	′ ′	′ ′	′ ′
00	7 30·0	7 31·2	7 09·5	0·0 0·0	6·0 3·1	12·0 6·1	00	7 45·0	7 46·3	7 23·8	0·0 0·0	6·0 3·2	12·0 6·3
01	7 30·3	7 31·5	7 09·7	0·1 0·1	6·1 3·1	12·1 6·2	01	7 45·3	7 46·5	7 24·1	0·1 0·1	6·1 3·2	12·1 6·4
02	7 30·5	7 31·7	7 10·0	0·2 0·1	6·2 3·2	12·2 6·2	02	7 45·5	7 46·8	7 24·3	0·2 0·1	6·2 3·3	12·2 6·4
03	7 30·8	7 32·0	7 10·2	0·3 0·2	6·3 3·2	12·3 6·3	03	7 45·8	7 47·0	7 24·5	0·3 0·2	6·3 3·3	12·3 6·5
04	7 31·0	7 32·2	7 10·5	0·4 0·2	6·4 3·3	12·4 6·3	04	7 46·0	7 47·3	7 24·8	0·4 0·2	6·4 3·4	12·4 6·5
05	7 31·3	7 32·5	7 10·7	0·5 0·3	6·5 3·3	12·5 6·4	05	7 46·3	7 47·5	7 25·0	0·5 0·3	6·5 3·4	12·5 6·6
06	7 31·5	7 32·7	7 10·9	0·6 0·3	6·6 3·4	12·6 6·4	06	7 46·5	7 47·8	7 25·2	0·6 0·3	6·6 3·5	12·6 6·6
07	7 31·8	7 33·0	7 11·2	0·7 0·4	6·7 3·4	12·7 6·5	07	7 46·8	7 48·0	7 25·5	0·7 0·4	6·7 3·5	12·7 6·7
08	7 32·0	7 33·2	7 11·4	0·8 0·4	6·8 3·5	12·8 6·5	08	7 47·0	7 48·3	7 25·7	0·8 0·4	6·8 3·6	12·8 6·7
09	7 32·3	7 33·5	7 11·6	0·9 0·5	6·9 3·5	12·9 6·6	09	7 47·3	7 48·5	7 26·0	0·9 0·5	6·9 3·6	12·9 6·8
10	7 32·5	7 33·7	7 11·9	1·0 0·5	7·0 3·6	13·0 6·6	10	7 47·5	7 48·8	7 26·2	1·0 0·5	7·0 3·7	13·0 6·8
11	7 32·8	7 34·0	7 12·1	1·1 0·6	7·1 3·6	13·1 6·7	11	7 47·8	7 49·0	7 26·4	1·1 0·6	7·1 3·7	13·1 6·9
12	7 33·0	7 34·2	7 12·4	1·2 0·6	7·2 3·7	13·2 6·7	12	7 48·0	7 49·3	7 26·7	1·2 0·6	7·2 3·8	13·2 6·9
13	7 33·3	7 34·5	7 12·6	1·3 0·7	7·3 3·7	13·3 6·8	13	7 48·3	7 49·5	7 26·9	1·3 0·7	7·3 3·8	13·3 7·0
14	7 33·5	7 34·7	7 12·8	1·4 0·7	7·4 3·8	13·4 6·8	14	7 48·5	7 49·8	7 27·2	1·4 0·7	7·4 3·9	13·4 7·0
15	7 33·8	7 35·0	7 13·1	1·5 0·8	7·5 3·8	13·5 6·9	15	7 48·8	7 50·0	7 27·4	1·5 0·8	7·5 3·9	13·5 7·1
16	7 34·0	7 35·2	7 13·3	1·6 0·8	7·6 3·9	13·6 6·9	16	7 49·0	7 50·3	7 27·6	1·6 0·8	7·6 4·0	13·6 7·1
17	7 34·3	7 35·5	7 13·6	1·7 0·9	7·7 3·9	13·7 7·0	17	7 49·3	7 50·5	7 27·9	1·7 0·9	7·7 4·0	13·7 7·2
18	7 34·5	7 35·7	7 13·8	1·8 0·9	7·8 4·0	13·8 7·0	18	7 49·5	7 50·8	7 28·1	1·8 0·9	7·8 4·1	13·8 7·2
19	7 34·8	7 36·0	7 14·0	1·9 1·0	7·9 4·0	13·9 7·1	19	7 49·8	7 51·0	7 28·4	1·9 1·0	7·9 4·1	13·9 7·3
20	7 35·0	7 36·2	7 14·3	2·0 1·0	8·0 4·1	14·0 7·1	20	7 50·0	7 51·3	7 28·6	2·0 1·1	8·0 4·2	14·0 7·4
21	7 35·3	7 36·5	7 14·5	2·1 1·1	8·1 4·1	14·1 7·2	21	7 50·3	7 51·5	7 28·8	2·1 1·1	8·1 4·3	14·1 7·4
22	7 35·5	7 36·7	7 14·7	2·2 1·1	8·2 4·2	14·2 7·2	22	7 50·5	7 51·8	7 29·1	2·2 1·2	8·2 4·3	14·2 7·5
23	7 35·8	7 37·0	7 15·0	2·3 1·2	8·3 4·2	14·3 7·3	23	7 50·8	7 52·0	7 29·3	2·3 1·2	8·3 4·4	14·3 7·5
24	7 36·0	7 37·2	7 15·2	2·4 1·2	8·4 4·3	14·4 7·3	24	7 51·0	7 52·3	7 29·5	2·4 1·3	8·4 4·4	14·4 7·6
25	7 36·3	7 37·5	7 15·5	2·5 1·3	8·5 4·3	14·5 7·4	25	7 51·3	7 52·5	7 29·8	2·5 1·3	8·5 4·5	14·5 7·6
26	7 36·5	7 37·7	7 15·7	2·6 1·3	8·6 4·4	14·6 7·4	26	7 51·5	7 52·8	7 30·0	2·6 1·4	8·6 4·5	14·6 7·7
27	7 36·8	7 38·0	7 15·9	2·7 1·4	8·7 4·4	14·7 7·5	27	7 51·8	7 53·0	7 30·3	2·7 1·4	8·7 4·6	14·7 7·7
28	7 37·0	7 38·2	7 16·2	2·8 1·4	8·8 4·5	14·8 7·5	28	7 52·0	7 53·3	7 30·5	2·8 1·5	8·8 4·6	14·8 7·8
29	7 37·3	7 38·5	7 16·4	2·9 1·5	8·9 4·5	14·9 7·6	29	7 52·3	7 53·5	7 30·7	2·9 1·5	8·9 4·7	14·9 7·8
30	7 37·5	7 38·8	7 16·7	3·0 1·5	9·0 4·6	15·0 7·6	30	7 52·5	7 53·8	7 31·0	3·0 1·6	9·0 4·7	15·0 7·9
31	7 37·8	7 39·0	7 16·9	3·1 1·6	9·1 4·6	15·1 7·7	31	7 52·8	7 54·0	7 31·2	3·1 1·6	9·1 4·8	15·1 7·9
32	7 38·0	7 39·3	7 17·1	3·2 1·6	9·2 4·7	15·2 7·7	32	7 53·0	7 54·3	7 31·5	3·2 1·7	9·2 4·8	15·2 8·0
33	7 38·3	7 39·5	7 17·4	3·3 1·7	9·3 4·7	15·3 7·8	33	7 53·3	7 54·5	7 31·7	3·3 1·7	9·3 4·9	15·3 8·0
34	7 38·5	7 39·8	7 17·6	3·4 1·7	9·4 4·8	15·4 7·8	34	7 53·5	7 54·8	7 31·9	3·4 1·8	9·4 4·9	15·4 8·1
35	7 38·8	7 40·0	7 17·9	3·5 1·8	9·5 4·8	15·5 7·9	35	7 53·8	7 55·0	7 32·2	3·5 1·8	9·5 5·0	15·5 8·1
36	7 39·0	7 40·3	7 18·1	3·6 1·8	9·6 4·9	15·6 7·9	36	7 54·0	7 55·3	7 32·4	3·6 1·9	9·6 5·0	15·6 8·2
37	7 39·3	7 40·5	7 18·3	3·7 1·9	9·7 4·9	15·7 8·0	37	7 54·3	7 55·5	7 32·6	3·7 1·9	9·7 5·1	15·7 8·2
38	7 39·5	7 40·8	7 18·6	3·8 1·9	9·8 5·0	15·8 8·0	38	7 54·5	7 55·8	7 32·9	3·8 2·0	9·8 5·1	15·8 8·3
39	7 39·8	7 41·0	7 18·8	3·9 2·0	9·9 5·0	15·9 8·1	39	7 54·8	7 56·0	7 33·1	3·9 2·0	9·9 5·2	15·9 8·3
40	7 40·0	7 41·3	7 19·0	4·0 2·0	10·0 5·1	16·0 8·1	40	7 55·0	7 56·3	7 33·4	4·0 2·1	10·0 5·3	16·0 8·4
41	7 40·3	7 41·5	7 19·3	4·1 2·1	10·1 5·1	16·1 8·2	41	7 55·3	7 56·6	7 33·6	4·1 2·2	10·1 5·3	16·1 8·5
42	7 40·5	7 41·8	7 19·5	4·2 2·1	10·2 5·2	16·2 8·2	42	7 55·5	7 56·8	7 33·8	4·2 2·2	10·2 5·4	16·2 8·5
43	7 40·8	7 42·0	7 19·8	4·3 2·2	10·3 5·2	16·3 8·3	43	7 55·8	7 57·1	7 34·1	4·3 2·3	10·3 5·4	16·3 8·6
44	7 41·0	7 42·3	7 20·0	4·4 2·2	10·4 5·3	16·4 8·3	44	7 56·0	7 57·3	7 34·3	4·4 2·3	10·4 5·5	16·4 8·6
45	7 41·3	7 42·5	7 20·2	4·5 2·3	10·5 5·3	16·5 8·4	45	7 56·3	7 57·6	7 34·6	4·5 2·4	10·5 5·5	16·5 8·7
46	7 41·5	7 42·8	7 20·5	4·6 2·3	10·6 5·4	16·6 8·4	46	7 56·5	7 57·8	7 34·8	4·6 2·4	10·6 5·6	16·6 8·7
47	7 41·8	7 43·0	7 20·7	4·7 2·4	10·7 5·4	16·7 8·5	47	7 56·8	7 58·1	7 35·0	4·7 2·5	10·7 5·6	16·7 8·8
48	7 42·0	7 43·3	7 21·0	4·8 2·4	10·8 5·5	16·8 8·5	48	7 57·0	7 58·3	7 35·3	4·8 2·5	10·8 5·7	16·8 8·8
49	7 42·3	7 43·5	7 21·2	4·9 2·5	10·9 5·5	16·9 8·6	49	7 57·3	7 58·6	7 35·5	4·9 2·6	10·9 5·7	16·9 8·9
50	7 42·5	7 43·8	7 21·4	5·0 2·5	11·0 5·6	17·0 8·6	50	7 57·5	7 58·8	7 35·7	5·0 2·6	11·0 5·8	17·0 8·9
51	7 42·8	7 44·0	7 21·7	5·1 2·6	11·1 5·6	17·1 8·7	51	7 57·8	7 59·1	7 36·0	5·1 2·7	11·1 5·8	17·1 9·0
52	7 43·0	7 44·3	7 21·9	5·2 2·6	11·2 5·7	17·2 8·7	52	7 58·0	7 59·3	7 36·2	5·2 2·7	11·2 5·9	17·2 9·0
53	7 43·3	7 44·5	7 22·1	5·3 2·7	11·3 5·7	17·3 8·8	53	7 58·3	7 59·6	7 36·5	5·3 2·8	11·3 5·9	17·3 9·1
54	7 43·5	7 44·8	7 22·4	5·4 2·7	11·4 5·8	17·4 8·8	54	7 58·5	7 59·8	7 36·7	5·4 2·8	11·4 6·0	17·4 9·1
55	7 43·8	7 45·0	7 22·6	5·5 2·8	11·5 5·8	17·5 8·9	55	7 58·8	8 00·1	7 36·9	5·5 2·9	11·5 6·0	17·5 9·2
56	7 44·0	7 45·3	7 22·9	5·6 2·8	11·6 5·9	17·6 8·9	56	7 59·0	8 00·3	7 37·2	5·6 2·9	11·6 6·1	17·6 9·2
57	7 44·3	7 45·5	7 23·1	5·7 2·9	11·7 5·9	17·7 9·0	57	7 59·3	8 00·6	7 37·4	5·7 3·0	11·7 6·1	17·7 9·3
58	7 44·5	7 45·8	7 23·3	5·8 2·9	11·8 6·0	17·8 9·0	58	7 59·5	8 00·8	7 37·7	5·8 3·0	11·8 6·2	17·8 9·3
59	7 44·8	7 46·0	7 23·6	5·9 3·0	11·9 6·0	17·9 9·1	59	7 59·8	8 01·1	7 37·9	5·9 3·1	11·9 6·2	17·9 9·4
60	7 45·0	7 46·3	7 23·8	6·0 3·1	12·0 6·1	18·0 9·2	60	8 00·0	8 01·3	7 38·1	6·0 3·2	12·0 6·3	18·0 9·5

1984 JULY 2, 3, 4 (MON., TUES., WED.)

G.M.T.	SUN G.H.A.	Dec	MOON G.H.A.	v	Dec.	d	H.P.
2 00	179 01.0	N23 02.6	137 53.3	6.8	N20 02.5	10.5	59.6
01	194 00.9	02.4	152 19.1	6.9	19 52.0	10.6	59.6
02	209 00.8	02.2	166 45.0	7.0	19 41.4	10.8	59.6
03	224 00.6 ··	02.0	181 11.0	7.1	19 30.6	10.8	59.6
04	239 00.5	01.8	195 37.1	7.1	19 19.8	11.0	59.7
05	254 00.4	01.7	210 03.2	7.2	19 08.8	11.1	59.7
06	269 00.3	N23 01.5	224 29.4	7.3	N18 57.7	11.2	59.7
07	284 00.2	01.3	238 55.7	7.4	18 46.5	11.4	59.7
08	299 00.0	01.1	253 22.1	7.4	18 35.1	11.4	59.7
09	313 59.9 ··	00.9	267 48.5	7.5	18 23.7	11.6	59.7
10	328 59.8	00.7	282 15.0	7.6	18 12.1	11.7	59.7
11	343 59.7	00.5	296 41.6	7.7	18 00.4	11.8	59.7
12	358 59.6	N23 00.3	311 08.3	7.8	N17 48.6	11.9	59.7
13	13 59.5	23 00.1	325 35.1	7.8	17 36.7	12.0	59.7
14	28 59.3	22 59.9	340 01.9	7.9	17 24.7	12.1	59.7
15	43 59.2 ··	59.7	354 28.8	8.0	17 12.6	12.2	59.7
16	58 59.1	59.6	8 55.8	8.1	17 00.4	12.3	59.7
17	73 59.0	59.4	23 22.9	8.2	16 48.1	12.4	59.7
18	88 58.9	N22 59.2	37 50.1	8.2	N16 35.7	12.5	59.7
19	103 58.8	59.0	52 17.3	8.3	16 23.2	12.6	59.7
20	118 58.6	58.8	66 44.6	8.4	16 10.6	12.8	59.7
21	133 58.5 ··	58.6	81 12.0	8.4	15 57.8	12.8	59.7
22	148 58.4	58.4	95 39.4	8.6	15 45.0	12.9	59.7
23	163 58.3	58.2	110 07.0	8.6	15 32.1	12.9	59.7
3 00	178 58.2	N22 58.0	124 34.6	8.7	N15 19.2	13.1	59.7
01	193 58.1	57.8	139 02.3	8.7	15 06.1	13.2	59.7
02	208 57.9	57.6	153 30.0	8.9	14 52.9	13.2	59.7
03	223 57.8 ··	57.4	167 57.9	8.9	14 39.7	13.4	59.7
04	238 57.7	57.2	182 25.8	8.9	14 26.3	13.4	59.7
05	253 57.6	57.0	196 53.7	9.1	14 12.9	13.5	59.7
06	268 57.5	N22 56.8	211 21.8	9.1	N13 59.4	13.5	59.7
07	283 57.4	56.5	225 49.9	9.2	13 45.9	13.7	59.7
08	298 57.2	56.3	240 18.1	9.3	13 32.2	13.7	59.7
09	313 57.1 ··	56.1	254 46.4	9.3	13 18.5	13.8	59.7
10	328 57.0	55.9	269 14.7	9.4	13 04.7	13.9	59.7
11	343 56.9	55.7	283 43.1	9.5	12 50.8	13.9	59.7
12	358 56.8	N22 55.5	298 11.6	9.6	N12 36.9	14.0	59.7
13	13 56.7	55.3	312 40.2	9.6	12 22.9	14.1	59.7
14	28 56.6	55.1	327 08.8	9.6	12 08.8	14.2	59.7
15	43 56.4 ··	54.9	341 37.4	9.8	11 54.6	14.2	59.7
16	58 56.3	54.7	356 06.2	9.8	11 40.4	14.3	59.7
17	73 56.2	54.5	10 35.0	9.9	11 26.1	14.3	59.7
18	88 56.1	N22 54.2	25 03.9	9.9	N11 11.8	14.4	59.7
19	103 56.0	54.0	39 32.8	10.0	10 57.4	14.4	59.6
20	118 55.9	53.8	54 01.8	10.0	10 43.0	14.5	59.6
21	133 55.8 ··	53.6	68 30.8	10.1	10 28.5	14.6	59.6
22	148 55.6	53.4	82 59.9	10.2	10 13.9	14.6	59.6
23	163 55.5	53.2	97 29.1	10.3	9 59.3	14.7	59.6
4 00	178 55.4	N22 52.9	111 58.4	10.2	N 9 44.6	14.7	59.6
01	193 55.3	52.7	126 27.6	10.4	9 29.9	14.8	59.6
02	208 55.2	52.5	140 57.0	10.4	9 15.1	14.8	59.6
03	223 55.1 ··	52.3	155 26.4	10.5	9 00.3	14.8	59.6
04	238 55.0	52.1	169 55.9	10.5	8 45.5	14.9	59.6
05	253 54.9	51.9	184 25.4	10.5	8 30.6	15.0	59.6
06	268 54.7	N22 51.6	198 54.9	10.6	N 8 15.6	15.0	59.6
07	283 54.6	51.4	213 24.5	10.7	8 00.6	15.0	59.6
08	298 54.5	51.2	227 54.2	10.7	7 45.6	15.0	59.6
09	313 54.4 ··	51.0	242 23.9	10.8	7 30.6	15.1	59.6
10	328 54.3	50.7	256 53.7	10.8	7 15.5	15.2	59.6
11	343 54.2	50.5	271 23.5	10.8	7 00.3	15.1	59.5
12	358 54.1	N22 50.3	285 53.3	10.9	N 6 45.2	15.2	59.5
13	13 54.0	50.1	300 23.2	11.0	6 30.0	15.2	59.5
14	28 53.9	49.8	314 53.2	10.9	6 14.8	15.3	59.5
15	43 53.7 ··	49.6	329 23.1	11.1	5 59.5	15.3	59.5
16	58 53.6	49.4	343 53.2	11.0	5 44.2	15.3	59.5
17	73 53.5	49.1	358 23.2	11.1	5 28.9	15.3	59.5
18	88 53.4	N22 48.9	12 53.3	11.2	N 5 13.6	15.4	59.5
19	103 53.3	48.7	27 23.5	11.2	4 58.2	15.3	59.5
20	118 53.2	48.5	41 53.7	11.2	4 42.9	15.4	59.5
21	133 53.1 ··	48.2	56 23.9	11.2	4 27.5	15.4	59.5
22	148 53.0	48.0	70 54.1	11.3	4 12.1	15.4	59.4
23	163 52.9	47.8	85 24.4	11.3	3 56.7	15.5	59.4
	S.D. 15.8	d 0.2	S.D. 16.3		16.3		16.2

(MONDAY = 2nd, TUESDAY = 3rd, WEDNESDAY = 4th)

Lat.	Twilight Naut.	Civil	Sunrise	Moonrise 2	3	4	5
N 72	□	□	□	□	06 42	09 19	11 37
N 70	□	□	□	04 08	07 11	09 30	11 37
68	□	□	□	05 07	07 32	09 39	11 38
66	////	////	00 36	05 41	07 49	09 47	11 39
64	////	////	01 45	06 05	08 02	09 53	11 39
62	////	////	02 20	06 25	08 14	09 58	11 40
60	////	01 08	02 44	06 40	08 23	10 03	11 40
N 58	////	01 52	03 04	06 54	08 31	10 07	11 40
56	////	02 19	03 20	07 05	08 39	10 11	11 40
54	01 03	02 40	03 34	07 15	08 45	10 14	11 41
52	01 43	02 58	03 46	07 24	08 51	10 17	11 41
50	02 09	03 12	03 56	07 32	08 56	10 20	11 41
45	02 52	03 41	04 18	07 48	09 08	10 25	11 42
N 40	03 22	04 03	04 36	08 02	09 17	10 30	11 42
35	03 45	04 21	04 51	08 14	09 25	10 34	11 43
30	04 03	04 36	05 03	08 24	09 32	10 38	11 43
20	04 31	05 00	05 25	08 41	09 44	10 44	11 43
N 10	04 53	05 20	05 43	08 56	09 54	10 50	11 44
0	05 12	05 38	06 01	09 10	10 04	10 55	11 44
S 10	05 29	05 55	06 18	09 24	10 14	11 00	11 45
20	05 44	06 12	06 36	09 39	10 24	11 06	11 45
30	06 00	06 30	06 56	09 55	10 36	11 12	11 46
35	06 09	06 40	07 09	10 05	10 42	11 15	11 46
40	06 18	06 52	07 22	10 16	10 50	11 19	11 46
45	06 28	07 05	07 39	10 29	10 59	11 24	11 47
S 50	06 39	07 21	07 59	10 45	11 09	11 29	11 48
52	06 45	07 28	08 08	10 53	11 14	11 32	11 48
54	06 50	07 36	08 19	11 01	11 20	11 35	11 48
56	06 56	07 45	08 31	11 10	11 26	11 38	11 48
58	07 02	07 55	08 46	11 20	11 32	11 41	11 49
S 60	07 10	08 06	09 02	11 32	11 40	11 45	11 49

Lat.	Sunset	Twilight Civil	Naut.	Moonset 2	3	4	5
N 72	□	□	□	□	01 24	00 36	
N 70	□	□	□	02 01	00 53	{00 22 / 23 59}	23 38
68	□	□	□	01 00	00 30	{00 11 / 23 55}	23 41
66	23 27	////	////	00 25	00 11	{00 01 / 23 52}	23 44
64	22 22	////	////	{00 00 / 23 57}	23 53	23 49	23 46
62	21 48	////	////	23 44	23 46	23 47	23 47
60	21 23	22 58	////	23 33	23 40	23 45	23 49
N 58	21 04	22 16	////	23 24	23 35	23 43	23 50
56	20 48	21 48	////	23 16	23 30	23 41	23 51
54	20 34	21 27	23 03	23 08	23 25	23 39	23 53
52	20 22	21 10	22 25	23 02	23 21	23 38	23 54
50	20 12	20 56	21 59	22 56	23 18	23 37	23 54
45	19 50	20 27	21 16	22 43	23 10	23 34	23 57
N 40	19 32	20 05	20 46	22 32	23 03	23 31	23 58
35	19 18	19 47	20 24	22 23	22 58	23 29	24 00
30	19 05	19 32	20 05	22 14	22 52	23 27	24 01
20	18 44	19 08	19 37	22 00	22 44	23 24	24 03
N 10	18 25	18 48	19 15	21 48	22 36	23 21	24 05
0	18 08	18 30	18 56	21 36	22 28	23 18	24 07
S 10	17 51	18 14	18 40	21 24	22 21	23 16	24 09
20	17 33	17 57	18 24	21 11	22 13	23 12	24 11
30	17 12	17 38	18 08	20 56	22 03	23 09	24 13
35	17 00	17 28	18 00	20 48	21 58	23 07	24 14
40	16 46	17 17	17 51	20 38	21 52	23 05	24 16
45	16 30	17 03	17 41	20 26	21 45	23 02	24 17
S 50	16 10	16 48	17 29	20 12	21 36	22 58	24 19
52	16 00	16 41	17 24	20 05	21 32	22 57	24 20
54	15 49	16 33	17 19	19 58	21 27	22 55	24 21
56	15 37	16 24	17 13	19 49	21 22	22 53	24 23
58	15 23	16 14	17 06	19 40	21 17	22 51	24 24
S 60	15 06	16 03	16 59	19 29	21 11	22 49	24 25

Day	SUN Eqn. of Time 00h	12h	Mer. Pass.	MOON Mer. Pass. Upper	Lower	Age	Phase
2	03 56	04 01	12 04	15 23	02 55	03	
3	04 07	04 13	12 04	16 16	03 50	04	◗
4	04 18	04 23	12 04	17 07	04 42	05	

Now let us look at the next vertical column for the sun and we see the Dec or Declination for 0 hours until 24 hours on September 21 (page 271).

Declination represents the latitude of the sun. We can see how slowly the sun goes farther south.

On September 22 (1984) between 20 and 21 hours G.M.T., the declination turns from north to south. It is one of those magic dates when the sun crosses the equator. Notice again how slowly the declination changes every day in contrast to the G.H.A., which goes around approximately 360 degrees daily. Check the figures on some different days and things will become clearer.

We will have to look in the almanac at some other information besides the daily pages. The first page of the almanac gives the Altitude Correction Tables and is copied on page 272 of this book. First, the left column for the sun. This is a combination of three corrections that have been calculated for us and which mainly have to do with refraction and parallax. This is not the place to go into details. Let us thank the genius who has calculated all those corrections into one.

All one has to do, after the sextant observation has been made, is to add the minutes to the sight, abbreviated (Hs), taking into consideration the month of the year as indicated.

Example: On October 10 the lower limb of the sun is measured to be at 15°52.2′ (15 degrees and 52.2 minutes) above the horizon (Hs). We look in the column and find we have to add 12.9′. Corrected altitude is 16°5.1′. This correction is always positive for the lower limb of the sun.

We find one more correction on the same page on the right side. This one corrects the error made by the altitude of the observer. It is called the dip correction. On a yacht you estimate the height of your eye and add the height of the deck above the waterline in meters or feet. This correction is always a few minutes negative and is subtracted. Hs, the sextant reading, will become Ho after these two corrections have been added or subtracted.

One more adjustment! When we looked at the daily pages, the G.M.T. was only given in full hours but, of course, our time of observation will be measured in minutes and seconds.

In the back of the almanac are the increments for every minute and down the page for every second. On page 273 the increments are given for 30 minutes and up to 60 seconds.

If an almanac is available, look at the last page and look under 59 minutes and 60 seconds. One hour's increment is fifteen degrees. In one hour the sun moves fifteen degrees or, in twenty-four hours, it moves 360 degrees (24 × 15 = 360). Makes sense, doesn't it?

To recapitulate: The G.H.A. (Greenwich Hour Angle) gives the location of the local noon in 0° to 360° longitude at Greenwich time, following the sun on its daily trip around the world. The declination gives the northern or southern latitude of the sun on its yearly pass between the Tropics.

I hope we do have a sextant and a horizon? If the navigator is not near the ocean or a big lake or big river, he can buy an artificial horizon, which uses an air bubble in water, for a few dollars. These are used by airplane navigators. Even for the really destitute navigator without a sextant there is a solution.

All we are interested in is measuring the angle of the sun ("a" on drawing on next page) with the horizon or something horizontal. One can put a perpendicular stick in the ground and measure the length of the shadow (see figure). Remember Pythagoras? A is the length of the stick and B the length of the shade. Tangent a is A divided by B. I have never done this and I hope to hear from somebody how well this works in practice in comparison to a sextant.

We do need Greenwich Mean Time. California time is eight hours behind G.M.T., the East Coast five hours behind G.M.T. During Daylight Saving time deduct one hour. Put your watch

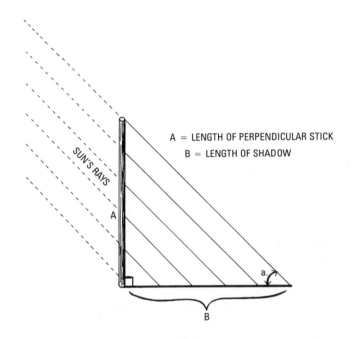

A = LENGTH OF PERPENDICULAR STICK
B = LENGTH OF SHADOW

on this time and remember that, at the end of your day they may have entered the next day in Greenwich. Make sure, when looking in the almanac, to use the right day.

Now what time do we begin? You do know (I hope) your approximate longitude.

Look up the G.H.A. of the particular day that corresponds to your longitude. The G.M.T. will tell what time the local noon is. Start about an hour earlier so there will be plenty of time to set everything up.

Start measuring the angle of the sun as often possible and write down the time in minutes. The sun will get higher and higher, then will hang there for a few minutes, and then will come down. Keep on measuring the angle of the sun on its way down for another half hour. Make a nice curve, plotting the rise of the sun against the time. Now relax, do something else, and when ready, start the calculations.

From the time and the angles measured, you should be able

to determine: 1) the highest *angle* of the sun, and 2) the *time* that the sun was highest in the sky. The angle will give the latitude and the time a rough estimation of the longitude.

The longitude can basically be read off the G.H.A. in the almanac for that day using the time of local noon. Remember, add the minutes and seconds of time, using the increments and corrections of the almanac.

Two more definitions: Zenith is the point in the heavens immediately above the observer. In order not to have to write too many details, I have included a drawing (See day 17 of Daybook, page 144) to explain zenith and zenith distance and to explain why the Ho (the adjusted sextant angle) will have to be subtracted from ninety degrees in order to obtain the zenith distance. Zenith distance is the angle between the observer's zenith and the zenith (in this case) of the sun.

The angle obtained by our sight (Hs) has to be adjusted first.

Study carefully the drawing made to explain our noonshot on day 17 of the Daybook. When every line and number makes sense to the reader, he will understand the determination of latitude with the help of the sun.

Let us say on that Sunday, October 7, 1984, we observed the sun to be at its highest at 19 hours, 30 minutes, and 15 seconds G.M.T., the angle (Hs) being 40° and 15.5′. We used the sextant at an height of nine feet above water level (we are on a small sailboat, about three feet above the waterline and are six feet tall). Dip correction is −2.9 minutes (page 270, right column).

Altitude correction between October and April for 40° is +15.1 minutes (page 272, left column).

We presume that we know we are in the northern hemisphere.

    40°15.5′ N. Hs

     − 2.9′

     + 15.1′

  = 40°27.7′ N. Ho

Declination is 5°47.3′ S. from almanac (page 270).

We did not discuss the adjustment for the extra minutes and seconds for the declination. The declination changes so slowly as compared to the G.H.A. that we can ignore the seconds. At the bottom of the daily pages under the declination is a "d" (delta) with a number behind it. In this case it is 1.0. This number is used on the increments for the minutes. Look again at the increments and corrections (page 273). Next to the columns for Sun, Aries, and Moon there are three columns for the "d" correction for that particular minute.

The declination was 5°47.3' S. "d" is 1.0'. For 30 minutes the increment is 0.5'. For 30 minutes it is only half a minute (half a nautical mile)! It now becomes clear how accurate our latitude is going to be, provided that our sextant reading is accurate.

Adjusted declination is 5°47.3' + 0.5' = 5°47.8'.

To find the zenith distance from the sun we subtract the Ho from 90 degrees = 89°60.0'

$$-40°27.7'$$

and we get   49°32.3', the zenith distance.

49°32.3' = 48°92.3'

Now subtract (south) the declination 5°47.8'

48°92.3'

−5°47.8'

= 43°44.5' latitude

If zenith distance and declination are both south or both north, one has to add to find the latitude. If zenith distance and declination are different in this respect, you subtract, as in our example.

In short: find the angle of the sun (Hs) at local noon, adjust for height of eye and A2 correction (page 2 almanac) to calculate Ho.

Deduct Ho from 90 to find zenith distance. Add or subtract declination and there is the latitude.

If, for some reason, you hit the jackpot and were doing the noonshot on March 20 or September 22, 1984, things would even be simpler. Look in the almanac on those dates again. The sun is right above the Equator. Therefore the declination is around 0°. You would get the latitude just by subtracting Ho from 90°. Even if local noon would not correspond with the the G.M.T. of the change in declination from south to north (equinox), the "fix" would still be accurate within ten to twenty miles on those dates. Looking at the declinations for the different G.M.T.s of these days it will be obvious that they all are 0°, with only up or down to 20 minutes (miles). This again gives us some idea how accurate the latitude is going to be provided that our sight is reliable and that the time of local noon is taken into consideration.

Now the longitude. The sun was the highest in the sky (local noon) at 19 hours, 30 minutes, and 15 seconds G.M.T.

On October 7 at 19:00 hours, the G.H.A. in the almanac is 108°05.2' (page 270). To adjust for the extra 30 minutes and 15 seconds, look at "Increments and Corrections" in the back of the almanac (page 273 in this book). The answer should be 7°33.8'. Add those two numbers and we find our longitude to be 115°39.0'. I think we are somewhere in Idaho.

To recapitulate: To find the longitude, use the full hour of local noon (time in G.M.T. when sun was highest) to find the G.H.A. on the daily page and use the "Increments and Corrections" for the minutes and seconds. The adjusted G.H.A. is the longitude.

This noon shot is rather cumbersome. It takes at least an hour and it can only be done when the sun is out at local noon. The advantage is that it is mathematically simple. The latitude obtained is rather reliable, more so then the longitude. The main advantage, though, is that a real position or fix is obtained.

At other times of the day than local noon, one is only able to find a line of position (L.O.P.). All we know with a line of position is that we are somewhere on that line, but to find our exact position it is necessary to do another sight at another time and/or of another heavenly body to find a second line of position. Our "fix" will be where those two lines intersect. Also, unless a small navigational computer is available, one has to learn to use the sight reduction tables.

The only tools necessary for a noon shot are the sextant, a watch, and the nautical almanac. No need for the complicated sight reduction tables (H.O.249). Lots of people have sailed to Hawaii from California, relying only on dead reckoning and periodic noonsights.

Provided he has the above-mentioned tools, the shipwrecked sailor in a lifeboat should be able to roughly determine his position.

If our reader has gotten a taste for celestial navigation after reading this and wants to expand his skills, he will have to study further and learn more about the Line of Position. Usually one tries to get two sights at the same time, like sun and moon or two planets at twilight. I personally like the last because at twilight the planets are readily visible while the stars are not yet.

If there is a long timespan between the determination of two L.O.P.s, adjustments for the change in position with dead-reckoning will have to be made. By meticulously measuring speed (knotmeter), and taking into consideration compass heading, current, and drift, one should be able to determine the change in position. On a sailboat this is not too hard because of the relatively low speed.

In their book *Sailing*, Henry Beard and Roy McKie aptly describe sailing as "the fine art of getting wet and becoming ill while going nowhere at great expense." (N.Y.: Workman Publishing Co., 1981)

For land-lubbers: a knot is a nautical mile per hour. The use of "knot per hour" is a reason to be keelhauled. The word "knot" comes from the fact that in the fifteenth century, when the nautical mile began to be used, speed at sea was measured with a line with knots, spaced uniformly, dragged behind the boat in the water. The line would be thrown overboard, the knots would be counted when they went in the water and compared with the running of sand in a log-glass. By counting the knots and using the timepiece the speed could be calculated in "knots." By careful dead reckoning, Columbus therefore could determine his longitude while sailing east or west at the same latitude.

One may think, now that the satellite navigator and the Loran are relatively inexpensive, that there is no need to know the art of celestial navigation. The chances of running out of electricity or other mechanical or electrical failures on a bouncing, wet boat, however, are great enough to make it irresponsible to go out any distance on the ocean without having some ability to locate the position in some other manner. Some people claim to have sailed to Hawaii following the jet planes! If one does not mind sailing the Great Circle route, which is certainly not the preferred route for a sailing vessel, or taking the risk of ending up in Japan (wrong plane!), it might be just the thing to do.

Celestial navigation is fun and I encourage the reader to try it out. Next time you go to the beach, take along an inexpensive plastic sextant and try to find out not only *where* but also *who* you really are!

General Index
SEE ALSO MEDICAL INDEX

Medical Index
SEE ALSO GENERAL INDEX